The Black Man Comes to the City

THE BLACK MAN COMES TO THE CITY

A DOCUMENTARY ACCOUNT
FROM THE GREAT MIGRATION TO THE
GREAT DEPRESSION

1915 to 1930

Robert B. Grant

Professional/Technical Series

Nelson-Hall Company Chicago

ISBN 0-911012-45-1

Library of Congress Catalog Card No. 72-83821

Copyright © 1972 by Robert B. Grant

Nelson-Hall Company, Publishers, 325 W. Jackson Blvd., Chicago, Ill. 60606

Manufactured in the United States of America

To my father
Albert L. Grant
1895-1958

Contents

Tables

Preface

The documents that make up the bulk of this study contain much of the story of what happened to the black migrants who left the South and moved to the cities of the North during the years between the First World War and the Great Depression. They sought economic opportunity and with it fuller participation in the mainstream of American life. The documents include personal letters, official testimony, newspaper accounts, excerpts from novels and poems, contemporary magazine pieces, and reports from investigative agencies. Considerable effort has been made to include material relating to ordinary people as well as the manifestoes and constitutions of well-known organizations.

From the point of view of historical study, the documents in this collection may be used to illustrate historical reality, to provide opportunity for evaluation of various kinds of primary evidence, and to stir up controversy over historical propositions. Take testimony before a government committee, for example. Is it fair to conclude from testimony that stresses discrimination in employment that such discrimination was widely practiced? If, to such testimony, we add official union constitutions, reports from employment surveys, and the personal story of a black worker, can we draw firmer conclusions?

By using a wide variety of documentary sources, some with the strong intrinsic interest of first-person accounts, students will have an opportunity to develop skill in the examination of evidence. They may be, and should be, skeptical about forming an opinion on the basis of a single newspaper account. Examination of a variety of sources hopefully will. yield to these students some understanding of the value of source materials: the objective view of a statistical report, the novelist's symbolic grasp, the human factors of a case history. Students will have an opportunity to gain understanding of the history of black people. In so doing they will necessarily gain perspective on the present, for the race problem of today has roots which go far back into the past, roots which are clearly visible in the years between the Great Migration and the Great Depression.

It is appropriate here to say a few words of thanks to the many people who offered help and encouragement in the preparation of this book. The staffs of several libraries were more than kind, particularly the staff at the Schomburg Collection of the New York Public Library. I thank all of the people whose suggestions and comments were of assistance. In particular, I want to express my gratitude to Professor Harvey A. Levenstein of McMaster University, Ontario, whose suggestions helped get the book under way, and to Professor Raymond A. Ducharme, Jr., of Smith College, friend, critic, and colleague, who read nearly every word of the manuscript and offered valuable criticism. Of course, the flaws that remain are mine alone.

Acknowledgments

The author wishes to express his gratitude for permission to reprint material from the following sources:

The Afro-American Newspapers for the selections on pp. 164-68, from "Kelly Miller Says," Baltimore *Afro-American*, Aug. 8, 1924 and Aug. 14, 1926. Arno Press Inc. for the selection on pp. 213-17, from *The Walls of Jericho* by Rudolph Fisher, Arno Press Edition, 1969. Beloit *News* for the selection on pp. 40-41, Editorial, Beloit *News*, Aug. 25, 1916. *Chicago Daily Defender* for the selections on pp. 31-32, 43, 45-48, *Chicago Defender*, Aug. 12 and 19, 1916, Sept. 2 and 9, 1916, Feb. 10, 1917, March 24, 1917, May 19, 1917, June 30, 1917, July 7, 1917, Aug. 11, 1917, Aug. 22, 1917 and Dec. 1, 1917.

The Chicago Tribune Company for the selections on pp. 148-51, "The New Negro Psychology" and "Criticism from the South," *Chicago Daily Tribune*, May 9, 1919 and Aug. 6, 1919. *The Christian Century* for the selection on pp. 93-95, from "From Job to Job" by George S. Schuyler, *The World Tomorrow*, May 1923. Columbia University Press for the selections on pp. 38-40, from *Sea Island to City* by Clyde Vernon Kiser, Columbia University Press, 1932. Crisis Publishing Company for the selection on pp. 178-80, "The N.A.A.C.P. Battle Front," *Crisis*, Feb. 1928.

The Detroit Free Press for the selection on pp. 78-81, *Detroit Free Press*, Nov. 19, 1925. Shirley Graham DuBois for the selection on pp. 211-13, from *Darkwater* by W.E.B. DuBois, Austin Jenkins Co., 1920. Mrs. James Weldon Johnson for the selection on pp. 199-202, from *Black Manhattan* by James Weldon Johnson, Alfred

A. Knopf, 1930. Alfred A. Knopf, Inc., for the selection on pp. 48-49, "Bound No'th Blues," from *Selected Poems* by Langston Hughes, Copyright 1927 by Alfred A. Knopf, Inc., renewed 1955 by Langston Hughes. The Estate of Claude McKay for the selection on pp. 109-12, from *Home to Harlem* by Claude McKay, Harper and Brothers, 1929. Memphis Publishing Company for the selection on pp. 43-44, Editorial, *Commercial Appeal*, Oct. 5, 1916. The Methodist Churchman for the selection on pp. 152-53, from "New Outlook in Race Relationships," *Zion's Herald*, Nov. 1, 1922. Metro-Goldwyn-Mayer Inc. for the selection on pp. 141-42, from "HALLELUJAH," Screen play, © 1929 by Metro-Goldwyn-Mayer Distributing Corporation, Copyright renewed 1957 by Loew's Incorporated.

National Tuberculosis Association for the selection on pp. 59-61, from *Health Conditions in North Harlem, 1923-1927* by Winfred B. Nathan, National Tuberculosis Association, 1932. The National Urban League, Inc., for the material on pp. 52-56, from "Where Negroes Live in Philadelphia" by A. L. Manly, *Opportunity*, May 1923. Also for the selection on pp. 180-82, from "The National Urban League" by Eugene Kinckle Jones, *Opportunity*, January 1925. Also for the selection on pp. 86-92, from "Industrial Problems in Cities," *Opportunity*, February 1926. Also for the selection on pp. 209-10, "No Images" by Waring Cuney, *Opportunity*, June 1926. Also for the selection on pp. 193-96, from "The Garvey Movement" by E. Franklin Frazier, *Opportunity*, October 1927. Also for the selection on p. 209, "To a Dark Girl" by Gwendolyn B. Bennett, *Opportunity*, October 1927. Also for the selection on pp. 202-8, from "Chicago: A Cross-Section of Negro Life" by E. Franklin Frazier, *Opportunity*, March 1929.

New York *Amsterdam News* for the selection on pp. 158-60, from "Oswald Garrison Villard Issues 20th Anniversary NAACP Call," March 27, 1929. Harold Ober Associates Inc. for the selections on pp. 123-24, 210-11, "Brass Spittoons" and "Laughers" by Langston Hughes, *Fine Clothes to the Jew*, Alfred A. Knopf, Inc., 1927, Copyright 1927 by Langston Hughes. Princeton University Press for the selection on pp. 127-29, from *A Study of American Intelligence* by Carl C. Brigham, Princeton University Press, 1923, Copyright 1922 by Carl C. Brigham. Twayne Publishers, Inc., for the selection on p. 221, "If We Must Die," from *Selected Poems of Claude McKay*, Copyright © 1953 by Bookman Associates.

For further acknowledgments, see the Notes, page 229.

The Black Man Comes to the City

Introduction

"They found themselves expected to settle down into the humdrum routine of American life as if nothing had happened. . . ," wrote Frederick Lewis Allen of the generation that had returned from the Great War of 1914-18. "They couldn't do it, and they very disrespectfully said so."[1] This was the era of prohibition, bathtub gin, and flappers. This was the time of a booming economy, rising stock prices, and unbounded optimism. The Roaring Twenties. Yet, one group of Americans, while participants in all this, remained separate, apart, different. The members of this group were Negro, or black, or colored, or Afro-American. The very absence of a clear, agreed-upon term of designation is indicative of the uncertainty of their position in the nation and suggestive of the frustration often involved in occupying that position.

During the American colonial period, and early in the national period of the United States, the terms "Negro" (or "negro" or "negra") and "black" were commonly used.[2] Also in common usage was the term "African," as in the African Union Society, which was a benevolent society formed in 1780 in Newport, Rhode Island, to provide mutual assistance

1

and burial benefits for its members.³ The Free African Society, a mutual-benefit, religious organization, was formed in 1787 by Richard Allen and Absalom Jones; Allen subsequently became the first bishop of the African Methodist Episcopal Church.

The emphasis on the word "African" tended to fade out after 1831, when James Forten called the first National Convention of Colored Men held in the United States. The movement away from the designation "African" may perhaps be explained partly by an increase in the number of mulattoes in the United States, many of them refugees from the disorders accompanying the Haitian revolutions. But more important, there was widespread rejection by free Negroes of the American Colonization Society, and of the colonization movement generally on the ground that it sought merely to rid the country of its free black population.⁴ This rejection led to a counteremphasis on the necessity of ending slavery and discrimination which were injuring *American* people of color here in this country.⁵

All of the terms of racial designation so far mentioned continued in use, if only in titles such as the still-named A.M.E. Church. What is significant is the symbolic importance and emotional charge of such words. Because, for so many generations, black Americans have been treated as inferior beings, *any* label has become suspect as, in itself, constituting a badge of inferiority. For this reason black people themselves have been unable to agree on an acceptable term of racial designation. W. E. B. DuBois, for example, a founder of the Niagara Movement and of the National Association for the Advancement of Colored People, wrote of his grandfather, "He was not a 'Negro'; he was a man!"⁶ Yet, DuBois came to use the word "Negro" as a matter of course, although he had formerly used "colored,"⁷ and in 1963 he explained, "It was a *short* word; it was a *strong* word; I knew that it had been debased, but I thought it could be resuscitated, and given dignity."⁸ To Robert S. Abbott, publisher of the Negro newspaper *Chicago Defender*, the word was completely objectionable, and such circumlocutions as "race man" or "member of the race" were commonly employed.[9]

The United States Census Bureau, interestingly enough, did not use the word "Negro" as a description of that portion of the population until 1880. In 1860 the racial designations were "white," "free colored," and "slaves"; and in 1870 the word "colored" was used. Since that time, controversy over proper usage has raged. "Colored" has remained in fairly common usage and is still used in the title of the NAACP. "Afro-American" became the title of a Baltimore newspaper in the 1890s, and even "Aframerican" was used to some extent.[10]

It is the word "Negro" that has had the widest currency in the twentieth century, however. In addition to the support given this term by DuBois, it was the designation preferred by such eminent race leaders as Booker T. Washington and Marcus Garvey. Garvey went so far as to say that he published his newspaper, *The Negro World*, "to preserve the term Negro to the race."[11] Because of the widespread use of the word "Negro," energetic efforts were made to get white newspapers to spell it with a capital "N." Even the *Chicago Defender*, despite its dislike for the word, asked at least for the dignity of capitalization,[12] but this effort met with little success until the *New York Times*, in an editorial on March 7, 1930, announced its decision to use a capital.[13] That such effort should be spent on a symbol is indicative of the emotional investment placed in that symbol.

The word "black" has been infrequently used in polite conversation from the beginning until well past the middle of this century. There have been notable exceptions to this generalization, of course, as in DuBois' brilliant *The Souls of Black Folk* (1903) or St. Clair Drake's fine study of Chicago, *Black Metropolis* (1945). Generally, however, the word has been one of derogation. Langston Hughes reported in 1940, for instance, being denounced by a minister whom he had described as "black." Most Negroes, Hughes believed at that time, "prefer to be referred to as *brownskin*, or at the most as dark *brownskin*—no matter how dark they really are."[14] Since mid-century, and especially since 1960, "black" has become a respectable and even a preferred designation. A new sense of race pride, encouraged by events both at home and in Africa, has led to increased use of "black" because, according to one scholar, "it was not designated by white people."[15] And it is not uncommon at present to find "Black" capitalized. Nevertheless, the word "Negro" retains its importance. According to one college senior, "It is probably the most precise and intellectually satisfying term describing us."[16] In this study the words "Negro" and "black" are used in the commentary and notes. They are respectable words and appropriate parallels to "Caucasian" and "white."

Whether "black" or "Negro" or "Afro-American," the people so called have evidenced an extraordinary ability to resist the indignities and terrors directed against them, and to make a constant effort to pursue recognition of their rights as men and women. In the first decade of the twentieth century there were 846 lynchings in the United States, and of these 754 were of blacks.[17] Also at that time the Jim Crow principle was being vigorously applied, particularly in the South. Development of Jim Crow received considerable impetus as a result of the "separate but equal" decision of the Supreme Court in *Plessy* v. *Ferguson* in 1896,[18] and after the turn of the century nearly all southern states required that segregation be maintained not only on railroad trains and in waiting rooms but also in city streetcars, state penal and welfare institutions, and even in some instances in factories. Attempts by such municipalities as Baltimore, New Orleans, Louisville, Atlanta, and Richmond to require residential segregation were declared unconstitutional by the Supreme Court in 1917.[19] Although the Supreme Court held that Negroes had the right to sit on juries,[20] black faces were rarely seen in the jury box. Discrimination in the administration of justice was observable in the operation of the convict lease system and subsequently in the chain-gang system. In both cases the profit-making possibilities in hiring out convicts led to abuses that fell most heavily on blacks.[21]

The South was not alone in oppressing black Americans. Although civil rights laws existed in many northern states, instances of discrimination became increasingly common in the North, with hotels, stores, restaurants, theaters, and even churches drawing the color line.[22] Northern blacks had never been well established in the skilled trades, and after 1900 even their strong position in domestic, hotel, and restaurant work was being undermined.[23] In addition, trade unions were growing increasingly hostile to black workers, often excluding them, if not by union rule then by a pretext of one kind or another.[24] The status of blacks throughout the nation was reflected in the policies of the national administration in Washington. Among the government's policies during President Wilson's administration was the expansion of segregation in federal buildings in the capital. In 1916, for example, male employees in the State, War, and Navy Department Building were assigned to separate rest rooms, a change from previous policy.[25]

To account for these anti-Negro manifestations, one must recognize the pervasiveness of racism in the United States. This is not to say that racism is uniquely American and that it does not exist in Europe, Asia, and Africa. It is to say, however, that a belief in the innate inferiority of one or more races or ethnic stocks was and is widespread in this country. In the early twentieth century such a belief received strong support from scientists, historians, and religious leaders. No other group felt the impact of this belief so forcefully as did blacks. Henry Fairfield Osborn, a well-known and well-respected naturalist, for example, argued that Negro intelligence rarely exceeded "that of the eleven-year-old youth of the species *Homo sapiens*,"[26] implicitly accepting the extreme view that blacks constituted a separate biological species.

The idea of Negro inferiority was accepted by a number of distinguished scholars including sociologist Edward A. Ross, psychologist G. Stanley Hall, and economist John R. Commons,[27] men who were not by any means popular agitators in the cause of racism. To the support of such a distinguished group of scientists and social scientists must be added that of an equally distinguished corps of historians, men to whom the inferiority of the black man was self-evident in the history of the nation. Either explicitly or implicitly, such scholars as James Ford Rhodes, John W. Burgess, Walter L. Fleming, and Ulrich B. Phillips agreed with William A. Dunning about the "fact of racial inequality."[28] These men were not conscious advocates of scientific theories of racial inferiority and probably did not view themselves as bigots. Nevertheless, the racist character of their historical scholarship was both a reflection of and an ingredient in the racist climate of thought in America.

Still another ingredient in that climate of thought was supplied by proponents of racism that drew upon religion. Churchmen such as Charles B. Galloway, Theodore DuBose Bratton, and William Montgomery Brown argued that racial inequality is the work of God, who created the separate races each with its distinctive qualities and capacities. Biblical authority coincided with common sense in assigning to black people a subordinate role in the Divine Plan that encompassed those distinctive qualities and capacities.[29] Since religion is a living force in the lives of men, such arguments made their mark, and even if their literal followers were concentrated in the South, Protestant churches throughout the land gave ample evidence of being somewhat affected by these arguments to the degree that the churches made blacks unwelcome and unwanted.[30]

Writers of pseudoscientific and popular books, and editors of newspapers and magazines, found strong support for racial antipathy from scientific and religious authorities that attested to the inherent inferiority of black people. Since historians of the twentieth century have tended to write primarily for other historians, the popularization of historical racism fell to such literary figures as Thomas Nelson Page and Thomas Dixon. Both men contributed to building the romantic myth of the Old South, peopled largely by courtly gentlemen and vivacious and charming ladies, who ruled over an underclass of incompetent Negroes. In such works as

The Negro: The Southerner's Problem,[31] a collection of essays, and in short stories such as "Old Jake's Marital Experiments" and "Mam' Lyddy's Recognition,"[32] Page drew a picture of the black man as being docile, more or less stupid, and contented with his lot as servant and subordinate. Dixon, on the other hand, in his novel *The Clansman*,[33] told the story of Reconstruction in the South, with carpetbaggers and Negroes sharing the role of villain. While the carpetbaggers were evil and scheming, the Negroes were vicious and depraved — they were beasts who gave free rein to their animal passions when not subject to white guardianship. Dixon's interpretation of Reconstruction received further dissemination when his novel was used as the basis of David W. Griffith's famous film, *Birth of a Nation* (1915).

The view of black men as docile and contented on the one hand and animalistic and depraved on the other is likewise to be found in newspaper reportage, the inherent contradiction conveniently ignored. Northern newspapers used such terms as "nigger," "niggah," and "darky," although less and less frequently as the century wore on. Even so, the Cincinnati *Enquirer* reported in a 1918 headline "Yah Suh! — Black Boys Are Happy," referring to Negro troops in France, and in 1913 the *New York Times* published this prayer by a black preacher:

Gibe dis pore brudder de eye of de eagle, dat he spy out sin afar off. Glue his hands to de gospel plow. Tie his tongue to de line of truf. Nail his years to de gospel pole. Bow his head way down between his knees, Oh Lord, and fix his knees way down in some lonely, dark, and narrow valley, where prayer is much wanted to be made. 'Noint him with de ile of salvation and set him afire.[34]

At the same time, the Cincinnati *Enquirer* tended to support mob action in lynchings on the incorrect assumption that lynchings were most often retaliations against "the unspeakable crime," rape. The San Francisco *Examiner* likewise condoned lynching, although such important newspapers as the *Chicago Tribune* and the Boston *Evening Transcript* expressed disapproval.[35] The degree to which crime was emphasized in news about black Americans, and the frequency with which crimes of brutality involving blacks were played up by the newspapers, point up the truly schizophrenic conception of black people often held by whites.[36] On the one hand blacks were simple souls, content with second place. On the other hand, they were beasts. In either case, they were inferior.

Faced by a hostile public opinion, confronted by overt discrimination, and burdened by a heritage of slavery, black Americans sought to deal with their situation. In the early years of the twentieth century two major movements developed. The first, led by Booker T. Washington, tended to follow a policy of accommodation. Based in the South at Tuskegee Institute, Alabama, Washington urged a policy of individualist economic enterprise, founded on the assumption that when Negroes had demonstrated their ability to strive and succeed, white America would be forced to revise its conception of black America. To this end, Washington advocated a policy of industrial education and of training in the virtues of cleanliness, thrift, and hard work. He eschewed, at least publicly, agitation for political and social equality, adopting the position that "when your head is in the lion's mouth, use your hand to pet him." Washington soon won a reputation among Caucasians as *the* Negro spokesman. He came to wield considerable influence both in the distribution of money offered by white philanthropists to improve the status of Negroes and in the distribution of those governmental posts open to black men.[37]

Partly in reaction to this accumulation of power in Washington's hands and partly in protest against Washington's accommodationist policy, opposition developed that centered around W. E. Burghardt DuBois. DuBois, a northern Negro and holder of a Harvard doctoral degree, refused to yield on the question of education, urging the cultivation of scholarly ability in the "talented tenth" of the black population. He likewise insisted upon all the rights of citizenship for black Americans.[38] In 1905 a group of black men meeting under DuBois' leadership in Niagara Falls, Canada, drew up a manifesto that demanded, among other things, freedom of speech, manhood suffrage, the abolition of all distinctions based upon race, and recognition of the principle of human brotherhood. [39]

Within a few years the Niagara Movement was absorbed into a new organization devoted to achieving the same "radical" goals but more broadly based and more powerful. In 1909 a mixed group of liberal and radical white reformers, such as Oswald Garrison Villard (grandson of abolitionist William Lloyd Garrison), William English Walling, and Mary White Ovington, arranged for a National Negro Conference to be held in New York. The members of the Niagara Movement were invited to attend and most of them accepted. Plans were made at the conference for the creation of a permanent organization which came to be the National Association for the Advancement of Colored People. Its program called for abolition of segregation, equal education for black and white children, manhood suffrage, and enforcement of the Fourteenth and Fifteenth Amendments. With the exception of DuBois, who served as an officer of the Association and editor of its influential journal, *The Crisis*, leadership was in the hands of whites. Nevertheless, the organization adopted a vigorous "radical" program pressing for industrial opportunities for blacks and for protection against lynching and lawlessness in the South.

Although the NAACP was concerned with industrial opportunity for Negroes, more and more of its energies were devoted to eradicating lynching and segregation and to securing the right of blacks to vote. Organized effort in the economic sphere fell largely to such groups as the National Negro Business League and the National Urban League. The former organization was founded in 1900 by Booker T. Washington and concentrated on the development of black capitalism. The latter group, known as the National League on Urban Conditions Among Negroes, was created in 1911 by a merger of three earlier organizations concerned with the problems of urban Negroes. [40] The League tended to be more conservative in its racial philosophy than was the NAACP, reflecting the views of such sponsors as Booker T. Washington, Kelly Miller, and Robert R. Moton, all important black southern educational leaders.

By the end of the first decade of this century, the problem of aiding urban blacks was growing significantly, for the migration of southern blacks searching for better conditions was increasing. This migration was not a new phenomenon. Black farmers had been moving to better lands for years — to Florida, to the Yazoo Delta, to parts of Arkansas and Texas. At times this slow movement took on dramatic proportions, as in the case of the Kansas Exodus of 1879.

Negro movement to urban centers, particularly in the South, had also been going on for years. Black farmers left the land for the same economic reasons that motivated the whites. Between 1890 and 1910 the proportion of Negroes classified as urban by the United States Census rose from about twenty percent to twenty-seven percent. A dozen cities, eight of them in the South, had over forty thousand black citizens in 1910, and Washington and New York had more than ninety thousand. [41] All this movement was a mere trickle, however, when compared to the migration of Negroes bound for the cities during World War I and after. Although black people had suffered injustice and oppression, had been required to conform to the humiliating rules of race etiquette, and had seen their brothers lynched and their sisters prostituted, they were not defeated. Many, it is true, had themselves come to accept the widespread assumptions about black inferiority. [42] Nevertheless, when the economic boom that was created by World War I provided unprecedented opportunity in the North, tens of thousands of black citizens flocked northward to take advantage of it. Often they were greeted with hostility — sometimes quietly oppressive, sometimes of the sort that characterized the race riots that took place in 1917-19. But the blacks survived, they made a place for themselves, and they and their descendants are to this day striving for equality of treatment and for an end to all forms of racial oppression.

The reaction of northern whites to the arrival of southern blacks was heavily dependent on racist preconceptions.

These preconceptions, it often seemed to the whites, were amply supported by the behavior of the undereducated, unhealthy black masses flocking to the cities, for the migrants generally lacked both industrial skills and preparation for urban life. Whereas these deficiencies were often charac- teristic of white immigrant groups and of city in-migrants generally, Negroes felt the disapproval of Caucasians with special force. Founded on the assumption of racial inferiority this disapproval was manifest in the North at the very least in discrimination in employment, in housing, and in the use of those facilities such as parks and places of entertainment that added to the quality of urban living. At its worst, race prejudice led to violence and even murder.

Although many Caucasians bore no personal hostility toward Negroes, the color line in the North was strong enough to institutionalize the maintenance of social distance between the races. For blacks this meant learning the dimen- sions of their "place," far less well defined than in the South, but real nonetheless. That most blacks were not content with second-class citizenship is axiomatic. Empirical evidence, if any is needed, lies in the numbers of instances of in- dividual effort to cross the color line in employment and housing, in the tendency to use black churches as a social refuge from the larger society, and in the enormous appeal of Marcus Garvey, who offered the black masses race pride and hope for the future. What happened to the black migrants that went North to the larger cities during the Great Migra- tion and the subsequent decade is set forth in the pages that follow.

1

Migration

Mobility has been an aspect of American life since the founding of the nation—and for more than a century and a half before that. Almost all of us are immigrants or the descendents of immigrants, and migration within our nation's borders has been an important characteristic of our national behavior. Indeed, some historians point to migratory behavior as an essential key to understanding American national character. "Migration has been a force of greatest moment in American civilization," [1] writes Everett Lee, and George W. Pierson, has discussed the "M-Factor," the migration factor, as a basic component in the creation of the American character. [2]

Do historians mean to include black Americans in their generalizations about migration? Before the Civil War, most blacks had no control over changes of residence. They did not migrate; they were *shipped*. During the half century or so following the ratification of the Thirteenth Amendment, the migrations of blacks were generally short-distance moves either within the South or to states immediately adjacent. [3] Of the total black population of the United States in 1830, 92.8 percent resided in the South. In 1910, the figure was still 89 percent.[4] Although there was fairly general agreement that the North afforded greater personal liberty, no more than a .small stream of black migrants went there. Employers in northern industry tended to prefer white labor, and European immigrant laborers filled the needs of the industrial North. As late as 1910, 52.3 percent of the blacks who did leave the South went west across the Mississippi.[5]

About the time of World War I, dramatic changes occurred in the pattern of black migration. Such earlier movement into the North as had taken place had been mostly from border states, such as Maryland, Virginia, and Kentucky. Now, however, there were frequent long-distance moves from Florida and Georgia straight through to Pennsylvania and New York, from Alabama, Mississippi, and Louisiana to Illinois and Michigan.[6]

For the black Southerner, in addition to the infamy of Jim Crow, inferior schools, legal injustice, and lynching, a series of natural calamities made life more difficult than ever. During 1915 and 1916, a series of floods and storms battered portions of Louisiana, Mississippi, Georgia, the Carolinas, and Virginia, resulting in loss of life and millions of dollars in property damage.[7] Cotton agriculture suffered from the ravages of the boll weevil, a pest that had entered the United States from Mexico and moved slowly east from Texas. Department of Agriculture reports on the cotton crop were glum.[8]

Most important of all, however, in stimulating black people to migrate, was the opening of job opportunities in the North. Northern employers, prior to 1915, had come to depend for much of their labor supply upon the great numbers of European immigrants arriving in the United States. Except during strikes, employers had generally drawn the color line. The war changed this situation. Immigration fell from an all-time high in 1914 of 1,218,480 to 326,700 in 1915 and 110,618 in 1918.[9] At the same time, production demands leaped ahead. The production of steel ingots and castings, for example, jumped more than ten million long tons in 1916 from the 1915 production level of 32,151,036 long tons.[10] The color line grew less restrictive as employers were forced to draw on the domestic labor supply.

Negro publications, particularly the *Chicago Defender* with its large readership outside Chicago, spread the news of job opportunities in the North. Labor agents representing northern railroads and industrial concerns traveled south to recruit workers. A "Northern fever" swept the black South, not unlike the "America fever" that had brought many Europeans across the Atlantic. A significant feature of the "great migration" north was the degree to which it tended to concentrate in urban centers. Like Caucasians, Negroes had for many years shown a rising proportion of urban dwellers as compared to rural. The sudden increase in the number of urban blacks during and after World War I was marked.

STATISTICS OF THE MIGRATION

Statistical data compiled by the Bureau of the Census document the northward urban movement of black Americans during the first three decades of this century. It must be noted, however, that census data are often unreliable for the South and especially for Negroes. The 1920 census in particular has been criticized for errors in enumerating the black population.[11] Nevertheless, the general dimensions of the movement of blacks north to the cities emerge clearly.

Population Distribution

The tables that follow show black and white population distribution in the United States between 1910 and 1930 by political subdivision as well as by urban-rural distribution. Urban population, as the term is used here, is that population residing in cities or other incorporated places having twenty-five hundred or more inhabitants. The data in the tables on pages 16 through 30 reveal, in absolute figures and in percentages, the extraordinary attraction of the cities and the sweep of the northward movement.

TABLE 1: BLACK AND WHITE POPULATION, BY SECTIONS, DIVISIONS, AND STATES 1910 to 1930

SECTION, DIVISION, AND STATE	1910 Total	1910 Black	1910 White[a]	1910 Other Races[a]	1920 Total	1920 Black	1920 White[a]	1920 Other Races[a]	1930 Total	1930 Black	1930 White[a]	1930 Other Races[a]
United States	91,972,266	9,827,763	81,364,447	780,056	105,710,620	10,463,131	94,120,374	1,127,115	122,775,046	11,891,143	108,864,207	2,019,696
The North	55,757,115	1,027,674	54,627,598	101,843	63,681,845	1,472,309	62,085,612	123,924	73,021,191	2,409,219	70,388,367	223,605
The South	29,389,330	8,749,427	20,316,253	323,650	33,125,803	8,912,231	23,731,899	481,673	37,857,633	9,361,577	27,673,879	822,177
The West	6,825,821	50,662	6,420,596	354,563	8,902,972	78,591	8,302,863	521,518	11,896,222	120,327	10,801,961	973,914
GEOGRAPHIC DIVISIONS												
New England	6,552,681	66,306	6,480,468	5,907	7,400,909	79,051	7,315,995	5,863	8,166,341	94,086	8,065,113	7,142
Middle Atlantic	19,315,892	417,870	18,879,881	18,141	22,261,144	600,183	21,638,625	22,336	26,260,750	1,052,899	25,172,104	35,747
East North Central	18,250,621	300,836	17,926,513	23,272	21,475,543	514,554	20,931,279	29,710	25,297,185	930,450	24,277,663	89,072
West North Central	11,637,921	242,662	11,340,736	54,523	12,544,249	278,521	12,199,713	66,016	13,296,915	331,784	12,873,487	91,644
South Atlantic	12,194,895	4,112,488	8,071,473	10,934	13,990,272	4,325,120	9,648,556	16,596	15,793,589	4,421,388	11,349,284	22,917
East South Central	8,409,901	2,652,513	5,754,154	3,234	8,893,307	2,523,532	6,367,166	2,609	9,887,214	2,658,238	7,224,614	4,362
West South Central	8,784,534	1,984,426	6,490,626	309,482	10,242,224	2,063,579	7,716,177	462,468	12,176,830	2,281,951	9,099,981	794,898
Mountain	2,633,517	21,467	2,445,515	166,535	3,336,101	30,801	3,071,405	233,895	3,701,789	30,225	3,303,586	367,978
Pacific	4,192,304	29,195	3,975,081	188,028	5,566,871	47,790	5,231,458	287,623	8,194,433	90,122	7,498,375	605,936
NEW ENGLAND												
Maine	742,371	1,363	739,991	1,017	768,014	1,310	765,693	1,011	797,423	1,096	795,183	1,183
New Hampshire	430,572	564	429,906	102	443,083	621	442,330	132	465,293	790	464,350	153
Vermont	355,956	1,621	354,298	37	352,428	572	351,816	40	359,611	568	358,965	78
Massachusetts	3,366,416	38,055	3,324,897	3,464	3,852,356	45,466	3,803,467	3,423	4,249,614	52,365	4,192,926	4,323
Rhode Island	542,610	9,529	532,488	593	604,397	10,036	593,976	385	687,497	9,913	677,016	568
Connecticut	1,114,756	15,174	1,098,888	694	1,380,631	21,046	1,358,713	872	1,606,903	29,354	1,576,673	876
MIDDLE ATLANTIC												
New York	9,113,614	134,191	8,966,525	12,898	10,385,227	198,483	10,170,548	16,196	12,588,066	412,814	12,150,293	24,959
New Jersey	2,537,167	89,760	2,445,820	1,587	3,155,900	117,132	3,036,832	1,936	4,041,334	208,828	3,829,209	3,297
Pennsylvania	7,665,111	193,919	7,467,536	3,656	8,720,017	284,568	8,431,245	4,204	9,631,350	431,257	9,192,602	7,491
EAST NORTH CENTRAL												
Ohio	4,767,121	111,452	4,654,758	911	5,759,394	186,187	5,570,951	2,256	6,646,697	309,304	6,331,136	6,257
Indiana	2,700,876	60,320	2,639,876	680	2,930,390	80,810	2,848,346	1,234	3,238,503	111,982	3,116,136	10,385
Illinois	5,638,591	109,049	5,526,241	3,301	6,485,280	182,274	6,294,999	8,007	7,630,654	328,972	7,266,361	35,321
Michigan	2,810,173	17,115	2,785,135	7,923	3,668,412	60,082	3,600,283	8,047	4,842,325	169,453	4,650,171	22,701
Wisconsin	2,333,860	2,900	2,320,503	10,457	2,632,067	5,201	2,616,700	10,166	2,939,006	10,739	2,913,859	14,408

TABLE 1: BLACK AND WHITE POPULATION, BY SECTIONS, DIVISIONS, AND STATES   1910 to 1930   (Continued)

SECTION, DIVISION, AND STATE	1910				1920				1930			
	Total	Black	White*	Other Races*	Total	Black	White*	Other Races*	Total	Black	White*	Other Races*
WEST NORTH CENTRAL												
Minnesota	2,075,708	7,084	2,059,143	9,481	2,387,125	8,809	2,368,586	9,730	2,563,953	9,445	2,538,973	15,535
Iowa	2,224,771	14,973	2,208,682	1,116	2,404,021	19,005	2,381,293	3,723	2,470,939	17,380	2,448,382	5,177
Missouri	3,293,335	157,452	3,133,570	2,313	3,404,055	178,241	3,221,661	4,153	3,629,367	223,840	3,398,887	6,640
North Dakota	577,056	617	569,845	6,594	646,872	467	639,912	6,493	680,845	377	671,243	9,225
South Dakota	583,888	817	563,747	19,324	636,547	832	619,052	16,663	692,849	646	669,453	22,750
Nebraska	1,192,214	7,689	1,179,994	1,531	1,296,372	13,242	1,276,473	6,657	1,377,963	13,752	1,353,702	10,509
Kansas	1,690,949	54,030	1,625,755	11,164	1,769,257	57,925	1,692,736	18,596	1,880,999	66,344	1,792,847	21,808
SOUTH ATLANTIC												
Delaware	202,322	31,181	171,100	41	223,003	30,335	192,585	83	238,380	32,602	205,694	84
Maryland	1,295,346	232,250	1,062,627	469	1,449,661	244,479	1,204,690	492	1,631,526	276,379	1,354,170	977
District of Columbia	331,069	94,446	236,113	510	437,571	109,966	326,825	780	486,869	132,068	353,914	887
Virginia	2,061,612	671,096	1,389,802	714	2,309,187	690,017	1,617,871	1,299	2,421,851	650,165	1,770,405	1,281
West Virginia	1,221,119	64,173	1,156,811	135	1,463,701	86,345	1,377,180	176	1,729,205	114,893	1,613,934	378
North Carolina	2,206,287	697,843	1,500,508	7,936	2,559,123	763,407	1,783,769	11,947	3,170,276	918,647	2,234,948	16,681
South Carolina	1,515,400	835,843	679,159	398	1,683,724	864,719	818,532	473	1,738,765	793,681	944,040	1,044
Georgia	2,609,121	1,176,987	1,431,786	348	2,895,832	1,206,365	1,689,070	397	2,908,506	1,071,125	1,836,974	407
Florida	652,619	308,669	443,567	383	968,470	329,487	638,034	949	1,468,211	431,828	1,035,205	1,178
EAST SOUTH CENTRAL												
Kentucky	2,289,905	261,656	2,027,926	323	2,416,630	235,938	2,180,462	230	2,614,589	226,040	2,388,364	185
Tennessee	2,184,789	473,088	1,711,417	284	2,337,885	451,758	1,885,939	188	2,616,556	477,646	2,138,619	291
Alabama	2,138,093	908,282	1,228,789	1,022	2,348,174	900,652	1,446,958	564	2,646,248	944,834	1,700,775	639
Mississippi	1,797,114	1,009,487	786,022	1,605	1,790,618	935,184	853,807	1,627	2,009,821	1,009,718	996,856	3,247
WEST SOUTH CENTRAL												
Arkansas	1,574,449	442,891	1,130,878	680	1,752,204	472,220	1,279,479	505	1,854,482	478,463	1,374,906	1,113
Louisiana	1,656,388	713,874	939,789	2,725	1,798,509	700,257	1,093,991	4,261	2,101,593	776,326	1,318,160	7,107
Oklahoma	1,657,155	137,612	1,441,577	77,966	2,028,283	149,408	1,813,217	65,658	2,396,040	172,198	2,123,424	100,418
Texas	3,896,542	690,049	2,978,382	228,111	4,663,228	741,694	3,529,490	392,044	5,824,715	854,964	4,283,491	686,260
MOUNTAIN												
Montana	376,053	1,834	360,491	13,728	548,889	1,658	533,991	13,240	537,606	1,256	517,327	19,023
Idaho	325,594	651	319,074	5,869	431,866	920	424,540	6,406	445,032	668	437,562	6,802
Wyoming	145,965	2,235	139,990	3,740	194,402	1,375	188,146	4,881	225,565	1,250	214,067	10,248
Colorado	799,024	11,453	780,146	7,425	939,629	11,318	909,763	18,948	1,035,791	11,828	961,117	62,846
New Mexico	327,301	1,628	283,574	42,099	360,350	5,733	301,879	52,738	423,317	2,850	331,755	88,712

TABLE 1: BLACK AND WHITE POPULATION, BY SECTIONS, DIVISIONS, AND STATES 1910 to 1930 (Continued)

SECTION, DIVISION, AND STATE	1910				1920				1930			
	Total	Black	White[a]	Other Races[a]	Total	Black	White[a]	Other Races[a]	Total	Black	White[a]	Other Races[a]
MOUNTAIN (Con.)												
Arizona	204,354	2,009	122,360	79,985	334,162	8,005	202,985	123,172	435,573	10,749	264,378	160,446
Utah	373,351	1,144	366,425	5,782	449,396	1,446	440,699	7,251	507,847	1,108	495,955	10,784
Nevada	81,875	513	73,455	7,907	77,407	346	69,402	7,659	91,058	516	81,425	9,117
PACIFIC												
Washington	1,141,990	6,058	1,108,967	26,965	1,356,621	6,883	1,319,393	30,345	1,563,396	6,840	1,521,099	35,457
Oregon	672,765	1,492	654,833	16,440	783,389	2,144	768,530	12,715	953,786	2,234	937,029	14,523
California	2,377,549	21,645	2,211,281	144,623	3,426,861	38,763	3,143,535	244,563	5,677,251	81,048	5,040,247	555,956

a. In 1930 Mexicans were classified with "Other Races." Figures for white population in 1910 and 1920 are adjusted by deducting the estimated Mexicans and adding to "Other Races."

Source: Based on U.S., Department of Commerce, Bureau of the Census, Negro Population 1790-1915 (Washington, D.C.: Government Printing Office, 1918), p. 43, Table 13; and U.S., Department of Commerce, Bureau of the Census, Negroes in the United States, 1920-32 (Washington, D.C.: Government Printing Office, 1935), p. 9, Table 12.

TABLE 2: BLACK POPULATION, URBAN AND RURAL, BY SECTIONS, DIVISIONS, AND STATES   1910, 1920, and 1930

SECTION, DIVISION, AND STATE	URBAN			RURAL			PERCENT Urban			PERCENT Rural			BLACK PERCENTAGE OF TOTAL Urban			BLACK PERCENTAGE OF TOTAL Rural		
	1910	1920	1930	1910	1920	1930	1910	1920	1930	1910	1920	1930	1910	1920	1930	1910	1920	1930
United States	2,684,797	3,559,473	5,193,913	7,142,966	6,903,658	6,637,230	27.3	34.0	43.7	72.7	66.0	56.3	6.4	6.6	7.5	14.3	13.4	12.4
The North	790,534	1,250,312	2,128,329	237,140	221,997	280,890	76.9	84.9	88.3	23.1	15.1	11.7	2.5	3.1	4.3	1.0	1.0	1.2
The South	1,854,455	2,250,969	2,966,325	6,849,972	6,661,262	6,395,252	21.3	25.3	31.7	78.8	74.7	68.2	28.0	24.2	23.0	30.3	28.0	25.6
The West	39,808	58,192	99,259	10,854	20,399	21,088	78.6	74.0	82.5	21.4	26.0	17.5	1.2	1.2	1.4	.3	.5	.4
GEOGRAPHIC DIVISIONS																		
New England	56,445	71,416	81,443	9,861	7,635	12,643	85.1	90.3	86.6	14.9	9.7	13.4	1.1	1.2	1.3	0.6	0.5	0.7
Middle Atlantic	339,346	517,432	939,064	78,624	82,751	113,835	81.2	86.2	89.2	18.8	13.8	10.8	2.5	3.1	4.6	1.4	1.5	1.9
East North Central	230,542	448,873	848,627	70,294	65,681	81,823	76.6	87.2	91.2	23.4	12.8	8.8	2.4	3.4	5.1	.8	.8	1.0
West North Central	164,301	212,591	259,195	78,361	65,930	72,589	67.7	76.3	78.1	32.3	23.7	21.9	4.2	4.5	4.7	.8	.8	.9
South Atlantic	909,520	1,144,371	1,462,904	3,202,968	3,180,749	2,958,484	22.1	26.5	33.1	77.9	73.5	66.9	29.4	26.4	25.7	35.2	33.0	29.3
East South Central	509,097	571,316	759,166	2,143,416	1,952,216	1,899,072	19.2	22.6	28.6	80.8	77.4	71.4	32.3	28.6	27.3	31.4	28.3	26.7
West South Central	435,838	535,282	744,255	1,548,588	1,528,297	1,537,696	22.0	25.9	32.6	78.0	74.1	67.4	22.3	18.0	16.8	22.7	21.0	19.8
Mountain	15,446	16,678	21,032	6,021	14,123	9,193	72.0	54.1	69.6	28.0	45.9	30.4	1.0	1.4	1.4	.4	.7	.4
Pacific	24,362	41,514	78,227	4,833	6,276	11,895	83.4	86.9	86.8	16.6	13.1	13.2	1.0	1.2	1.4	.3	.3	.4
NEW ENGLAND																		
Maine	792	766	703	571	544	393	58.1	58.5	64.1	41.9	41.5	35.9	0.3	0.3	0.2	0.1	0.1	0.1
New Hampshire	356	441	594	208	180	196	63.1	71.0	75.2	36.9	29.0	24.8	.1	.2	.2	.1	.1	.1
Vermont	326	220	213	1,295	352	355	20.1	38.5	37.5	79.9	61.5	62.5	.3	.2	.2	.5	.9	.1
Massachusetts	35,243	43,624	46,323	2,812	1,842	6,042	92.6	95.9	88.5	7.4	4.1	11.5	1.2	1.2	1.2	.9	.9	1.4
Rhode Island	9,055	9,710	9,079	474	326	834	95.0	96.8	91.6	5.0	3.2	8.4	1.7	1.6	1.4	2.6	2.1	1.6
Connecticut	10,673	16,655	24,531	4,501	4,391	4,823	70.3	79.1	83.6	29.7	20.9	16.4	1.5	1.8	2.2	1.2	1.0	1.0
MIDDLE ATLANTIC																		
New York	117,486	185,212	390,499	16,705	13,271	22,315	87.6	93.3	94.6	12.4	6.7	5.4	1.6	2.2	3.7	.9	.7	1.1
New Jersey	65,427	92,328	174,985	24,333	24,804	33,843	72.9	78.8	83.8	27.1	21.2	16.2	3.4	3.7	5.2	3.9	3.6	4.8
Pennsylvania	156,333	239,892	373,580	37,586	44,676	57,677	80.6	84.3	86.6	19.4	15.7	13.4	3.4	4.3	5.7	1.2	1.4	1.9
EAST NORTH CENTRAL																		
Ohio	82,282	155,975	271,972	29,170	30,212	37,332	73.8	83.8	87.9	26.2	16.2	12.1	3.1	4.2	6.0	1.4	1.5	1.7
Indiana	48,427	71,813	103,042	11,895	8,997	8,940	80.3	88.9	92.0	19.7	11.1	8.0	4.2	4.8	5.7	.8	.8	.6
Illinois	85,538	161,728	304,036	23,511	20,546	24,936	78.4	88.7	92.4	21.6	11.3	7.6	2.5	3.7	5.4	1.1	1.0	1.2
Michigan	12,156	55,006	159,704	4,959	5,076	9,749	71.0	91.6	94.2	29.0	8.4	5.8	.9	2.5	4.8	.3	.4	.6
Wisconsin	2,141	4,351	9,873	759	850	866	73.8	83.7	91.9	26.2	16.3	8.1	.2	.3	.6	.1	.1	.1

TABLE 2: BLACK POPULATION, URBAN AND RURAL, BY SECTIONS, DIVISIONS, AND STATES 1910, 1920, and 1930 (Continued)

SECTION, DIVISION, AND STATE	URBAN			RURAL			PERCENT						BLACK PERCENTAGE OF TOTAL					
							Urban			Rural			Urban			Rural		
	1910	1920	1930	1910	1920	1930	1910	1920	1930	1910	1920	1930	1910	1920	1930	1910	1920	1930
WEST NORTH CENTRAL																		
Minnesota	6,518	8,250	9,110	566	559	335	92.0	93.7	96.5	8.0	6.3	3.5	.8	.8	.7	(a)	(a)	(a)
Iowa	9,786	15,345	15,185	5,187	3,660	2,195	65.4	80.7	87.4	34.6	19.3	12.6	1.4	1.8	1.6	.2	.3	.1
Missouri	104,461	134,167	169,954	52,990	44,074	53,886	66.3	75.3	75.9	33.7	24.7	24.1	7.5	8.5	9.1	2.8	2.4	3.0
North Dakota	306	272	216	311	195	161	49.6	58.2	57.3	50.4	41.8	42.7	.5	.3	.2	(a)	.1	.1
South Dakota	412	340	337	405	492	309	50.4	40.9	52.2	49.6	59.1	47.8	.5	.3	.3	.1	.1	.1
Nebraska	6,621	12,121	13,112	1,068	1,121	640	86.1	91.5	95.3	13.9	8.5	4.7	2.1	3.0	2.7	.1	.1	.1
Kansas	36,196	42,096	51,281	17,834	15,829	15,063	67.0	72.7	77.3	33.0	27.3	22.7	7.3	6.8	7.0	1.5	1.4	1.3
SOUTH ATLANTIC																		
Delaware	11,157	12,992	15,037	20,024	17,343	17,565	35.8	42.8	46.1	64.2	57.2	53.9	11.5	10.8	12.2	19.0	17.0	15.2
Maryland	99,230	124,509	159,654	133,020	119,970	116,725	42.7	50.9	57.8	57.3	49.1	42.2	15.1	14.3	16.4	20.9	20.7	17.8
District of Columbia	94,446	109,966	132,068	—	—	—	100.0	100.0	100.0	—	—	—	28.5	25.1	27.1	—	—	—
Virginia	158,218	209,134	213,401	512,878	480,883	436,764	23.6	30.3	32.8	76.4	69.7	67.2	33.2	31.0	27.2	32.4	29.4	26.7
West Virginia	15,380	22,484	31,224	48,793	63,861	83,669	24.0	26.0	27.2	76.0	74.0	72.8	6.7	6.1	6.4	4.9	5.8	6.8
North Carolina	115,975	115,165	246,237	581,868	608,242	672,410	16.6	16.0	26.8	83.4	84.0	73.2	36.4	31.6	30.4	30.8	29.4	28.5
South Carolina	101,702	116,489	138,354	734,141	748,230	655,327	12.2	13.5	17.4	87.8	86.5	82.6	45.2	39.6	37.3	56.9	53.8	47.9
Georgia	224,826	273,036	316,637	952,161	933,329	754,488	19.1	22.6	29.6	80.9	77.4	70.4	41.7	37.4	35.4	46.0	46.0	37.5
Florida	88,586	120,596	210,292	220,083	208,891	221,536	28.7	36.6	48.7	71.3	63.4	51.3	40.4	33.9	27.7	41.2	34.1	31.3
EAST SOUTH CENTRAL																		
Kentucky	106,631	105,393	116,561	115,025	130,545	109,479	40.8	44.7	51.6	59.2	55.3	48.4	19.2	16.6	14.6	8.9	7.3	6.0
Tennessee	150,506	170,464	240,168	322,582	281,294	237,478	31.8	37.7	50.3	68.2	62.3	49.7	34.1	27.9	26.8	18.5	16.3	13.8
Alabama	156,603	196,833	268,450	751,679	703,819	676,384	17.2	21.9	28.4	82.8	78.1	71.6	42.3	38.6	36.1	42.5	38.3	35.6
Mississippi	95,337	98,626	133,987	914,130	836,558	875,731	9.4	10.5	13.3	90.6	89.5	86.7	46.0	41.1	39.5	57.5	54.0	52.4
WEST SOUTH CENTRAL																		
Arkansas	59,147	73,592	89,162	383,744	398,623	389,301	13.4	15.6	18.6	86.6	84.4	81.4	29.2	25.3	23.3	28.0	27.3	26.5
Louisiana	160,845	190,413	257,463	553,029	509,844	518,863	22.5	27.2	33.2	77.5	72.8	66.8	32.4	30.3	30.9	47.7	43.6	40.9
Oklahoma	36,982	47,904	67,801	100,630	101,504	104,397	26.9	32.1	39.4	73.1	67.9	60.6	11.6	8.3	8.3	7.5	6.8	6.6
Texas	178,864	223,373	329,829	511,185	518,321	525,135	25.9	30.1	38.6	74.1	69.9	61.4	19.1	14.8	13.8	17.3	16.5	15.3
MOUNTAIN																		
Montana	1,455	1,270	1,027	379	388	229	79.3	76.6	81.8	20.7	23.4	18.2	1.1	.7	.6	.2	.1	.1
Idaho	426	645	502	225	275	166	65.4	70.1	75.1	34.6	29.9	24.9	.6	.5	.5	.1	.1	.1
Wyoming	1,041	833	859	1,194	542	391	46.6	60.6	68.7	53.4	39.4	31.3	2.4	1.5	1.2	1.2	.4	.3
Colorado	9,359	9,364	10,471	2,094	1,954	1,357	81.7	82.7	88.5	18.3	17.3	11.5	2.3	2.1	2.0	.5	.4	.3
New Mexico	795	861	1,718	833	1,872	1,132	48.8	15.0	60.3	51.2	85.0	39.9	1.7	1.3	1.6	.3	1.6	.4

TABLE 2: BLACK POPULATION, URBAN AND RURAL, BY SECTIONS, DIVISIONS, AND STATES   1910, 1920, and 1930   (Continued)

SECTION, DIVISION, AND STATE	URBAN			RURAL			PERCENT						BLACK PERCENTAGE OF TOTAL					
							Urban			Rural			Urban			Rural		
	1910	1920	1930	1910	1920	1930	1910	1920	1930	1910	1920	1930	1910	1920	1930	1910	1920	1930
MOUNTAIN (Con.)																		
Arizona	1,310	2,631	5,147	699	5,374	5,602	65.2	32.9	47.9	34.8	67.1	52.1	2.1	2.2	3.4	.5	2.5	2.0
Utah	959	1,006	944	185	440	164	83.8	69.6	85.2	16.2	30.4	14.8	.6	.5	.4	.1	.2	.1
Nevada	101	68	364	412	278	152	19.7	19.7	70.5	80.3	80.3	29.5	.8	.4	1.1	.6	.4	.3
PACIFIC																		
Washington	4,699	5,782	5,818	1,359	1,101	1,022	77.6	84.0	85.1	22.4	16.0	14.9	.8	.8	.7	.3	.2	.2
Oregon	1,264	1,844	1,890	228	300	344	84.7	86.0	84.6	15.3	14.0	15.4	.5	.5	.4	.1	.1	.1
California	18,399	33,888	70,519	3,246	4,875	10,529	84.0	87.4	87.0	15.0	12.6	13.0	1.3	1.5	1.7	.4	.4	.7

a. Less than one-tenth of 1 percent.

Source: U.S., Department of Commerce, Bureau of the Census, Negroes in the United States, 1920–32 (Washington, D.C.: Government Printing Office, 1935), p. 53, Table 8.

TABLE 3: BLACK AND WHITE POPULATION, URBAN (BY CLASSES OF CITIES AND OTHER URBAN PLACES) AND RURAL, FOR THE UNITED STATES 1910, 1920, and 1930

AREA	POPULATION								
	All Classes[a]			Black			White[b]		
	1910	1920	1930	1910	1920	1930	1910	1920	1930
	NUMBER								
UNITED STATES	91,972,266	105,710,620	122,775,046	9,827,763	10,463,131	11,891,143	81,731,957	94,820,915	108,864,207
Urban Territory	42,623,383	54,304,603	68,954,823	2,689,229	3,559,473	5,193,913	39,831,913	50,620,084	62,836,605
Places of 2,500 to 10,000	8,470,359	9,591,747	10,614,746	655,266	667,848	726,574	7,798,201	8,903,499	9,692,504
Places of 10,000 to 25,000	5,609,208	6,942,742	9,097,200	408,362	480,778	627,851	5,186,578	6,450,414	8,383,915
Places of 25,000 to 100,000	8,241,678	10,340,788	12,917,141	602,040	726,271	957,698	7,626,923	9,594,234	11,781,664
Places of 100,000 to 500,000	8,790,297	11,060,025	15,497,194	626,946	958,378	1,533,613	8,117,117	10,073,615	13,719,573
Places of 500,000 and over	11,511,941	16,369,301	20,828,542	396,615	726,198	1,348,177	11,103,094	15,598,322	19,258,949
Rural Territory	49,348,883	51,406,017	53,820,223	7,138,534	6,903,658	6,697,230	41,900,044	44,200,831	46,027,602
	PERCENT DISTRIBUTION BY AREA								
UNITED STATES	100.0	100.0	100.0	100.0	100.0	100.0	100.0	100.0	100.0
Urban Territory	46.3	51.4	56.2	27.4	34.0	43.7	48.7	53.4	57.7
Places of 2,500 to 10,000	9.2	9.1	8.6	6.7	6.4	6.1	9.5	9.4	8.9
Places of 10,000 to 25,000	6.1	6.6	7.4	4.2	4.6	5.3	6.3	6.8	7.7
Places of 25,000 to 100,000	9.0	9.8	10.5	6.1	6.9	8.1	9.3	10.1	10.8
Places of 100,000 to 500,000	9.6	10.5	12.6	6.4	9.2	12.9	9.9	10.6	12.6
Places of 500,000 and over	12.5	15.5	17.0	4.0	6.9	11.3	13.6	16.5	17.7
Rural Territory	53.7	48.6	43.8	72.6	66.0	56.3	51.3	46.6	42.3

TABLE 3: BLACK AND WHITE POPULATION, URBAN (BY CLASSES OF CITIES AND OTHER URBAN PLACES) AND RURAL, FOR THE UNITED STATES 1910, 1920, and 1930 (Continued)

POPULATION

PERCENT DISTRIBUTION BY RACIAL CLASS

AREA	All Classes[a]			Black			White[b]		
	1910	1920	1930	1910	1920	1930	1910	1920	1930
UNITED STATES	100.0	100.0	100.0	10.7	9.9	9.7	88.9	89.7	88.7
Urban Territory	100.0	100.0	100.0	6.3	6.6	7.5	93.5	93.2	91.1
Places of 2,500 to 10,000	100.0	100.0	100.0	7.7	7.0	6.8	92.1	92.8	91.3
Places of 10,000 to 25,000	100.0	100.0	100.0	7.3	6.9	6.9	92.5	92.9	92.2
Places of 25,000 to 100,000	100.0	100.0	100.0	7.3	7.0	7.4	92.5	92.8	91.2
Places of 100,000 to 500,000	100.0	100.0	100.0	7.1	8.7	9.9	92.3	92.1	88.5
Places of 500,000 and over	100.0	100.0	100.0	3.4	4.4	6.5	96.4	95.3	92.5
Rural Territory	100.0	100.0	100.0	14.5	13.4	12.4	84.9	86.0	85.5

a. Includes "Other Races."

b. The white population in 1910 and 1920 included 367,510 and 700,541 persons (estimated), respectively, who would have been classified as Mexicans in 1930.

Source: U.S., Department of Commerce, Bureau of the Census, Negro Population 1790-1915 (Washington, D.C.: Government Printing Office,1918), p.88,Table 1; and U.S., Department of Commerce, Bureau of the Census, Negroes in the United States, 1920-32 (Washington, D.C.: Government Printing Office, 1935), p.49, Table 1.

TABLE 4: INCREASES IN THE BLACK AND WHITE POPULATION, BY SECTIONS, DIVISIONS, AND STATES 1900-1930

A minus sign (−) denotes decrease.

SECTION, DIVISION, AND STATE	1900-1910 BLACK Number	Percent	1900-1910 WHITE Number	Percent	1910-1920 BLACK Number	Percent*	1910-1920 WHITE Number	Percent*	1920-1930 BLACK Number	Percent	1920-1930 WHITE Number	Percent
United States	993,769	11.2	14,922,761	22.3	635,368	6.4	12,755,927	15.7	1,428,012	13.6	14,743,833	15.7
The North	146,903[a]	16.7[a]	8,226,451[a]	17.7[a]	444,635	43.3	7,548,014	13.8	936,910	63.6	8,302,755	13.4
The South	826,458[a]	10.4[a]	4,025,450[a]	24.4[a]	162,804	1.9	3,415,646	16.8	499,346	5.0	3,941,980	16.6
The West	20,408[a]	13.1[a]	2,670,860[a]	68.9[a]	27,929	55.1	1,882,267	29.3	41,756	53.1	2,499,098	30.1
GEOGRAPHIC DIVISIONS												
New England	7,207	12.2	953,488	17.3	12,745	19.2	835,527	12.9	15,035	19.0	749,118	10.2
Middle Atlantic	91,949	28.2	3,769,590	24.9	182,313	43.6	2,758,744	14.6	452,716	75.4	3,533,479	16.3
East North Central	42,994	16.7	3,217,569	14.1	213,718	71.0	3,004,766	16.8	415,896	80.8	3,946,384	16.0
West North Central	4,753	2.0	1,285,804	12.8	35,859	14.8	858,977	7.6	53,263	19.1	673,774	5.5
South Atlantic	383,471	10.3	1,365,945	20.4	212,632	5.2	1,577,083	19.5	96,268	2.2	1,700,728	12.6
East South Central	152,627	6.1	709,479	14.1	−128,981	− 4.9	613,012	10.7	134,706	5.3	857,448	13.5
West South Central	290,360	17.1	1,950,426	40.9	79,153	4.0	1,225,551	18.9	218,372	10.6	1,383,804	17.9
Mountain	5,877	37.7	940,600	59.5	9,334	43.5	625,890	25.6	576	1.9	232,181	7.6
Pacific	14,531	99.1	1,730,260	75.4	18,595	63.7	1,256,377	31.6	42,332	88.6	2,266,917	43.3
NEW ENGLAND												
Maine	44	3.3	47,769	6.9	−53	− 3.9	25,702	3.5	214	16.3	29,490	3.9
New Hampshire	−98	− 14.8	19,115	4.7	57	10.1	12,424	2.9	169	27.2	22,020	5.0
Vermont	795	96.2	11,527	3.4	−1,049	− 64.7	2,482	− .7	4	0.7	7,149	2.0
Massachusetts	6,081	19.0	555,162	20.0	7,411	19.5	478,570	14.4	6,899	15.2	389,459	10.2
Rhode Island	437	4.8	113,442	27.1	507	5.3	61,488	11.4	123	1.2	83,040	14.0
Connecticut	−52	− 0.3	206,473	23.1	5,872	38.7	259,825	23.6	8,308	39.5	217,960	16.0
MIDDLE ATLANTIC												
New York	34,959	35.2	1,809,964	25.3	64,292	47.9	1,204,023	13.4	214,331	108.0	1,979,745	19.5
New Jersey	19,916	28.5	633,577	35.0	27,372	30.5	591,012	24.2	91,696	78.3	792,377	26.1
Pennsylvania	37,074	23.6	1,326,049	21.6	90,649	46.7	963,709	12.9	146,689	51.5	761,357	9.0

TABLE 4: INCREASES IN THE BLACK AND WHITE POPULATION, BY SECTIONS, DIVISIONS, AND STATES 1900-1930 (Continued)

A minus sign (−) denotes decrease.

	1900-1910				1910-1920				1920-1930			
	BLACK		WHITE		BLACK		WHITE		BLACK		WHITE	
SECTION, DIVISION, AND STATE	Number	Percent	Number	Percent	Number	Percent*	Number	Percent*	Number	Percent	Number	Percent
EAST NORTH CENTRAL												
Ohio	14,551	15.0	594,693	14.6	74,735	67.1	916,193	19.7	123,172	66.1	760,185	13.6
Indiana	2,815	4.9	181,459	7.4	20,490	34.0	208,470	7.9	31,172	38.6	267,790	9.4
Illinois	23,971	28.2	792,089	16.7	73,225	67.1	768,758	13.9	146,698	80.5	971,362	15.4
Michigan	1,299	8.2	386,684	16.1	42,967	251.0	815,148	29.3	109,371	182.0	1,049,888	29.2
Wisconsin	358	14.1	262,644	12.8	2,301	79.3	296,197	12.8	5,538	106.5	297,159	11.4
WEST NORTH CENTRAL												
Minnesota	2,125	42.9	322,191	18.5	1,725	24.4	309,443	15.0	636	7.2	170,387	7.2
Iowa	2,280	18.0	9,476	0.4	4,032	26.9	172,611	7.8	1,625	8.6	67,089	2.8
Missouri	− 3,782	− 2.3	190,089	6.5	20,789	13.2	88,091	2.8	45,599	25.6	177,226	5.5
North Dakota	331	115.7	258,143	82.8	150	− 24.3	70,067	12.3	− 90	− 19.3	31,331	4.0
South Dakota	352	75.7	183,057	48.1	15	1.8	55,305	9.8	186	22.4	50,401	8.1
Nebraska	1,420	22.7	123,767	11.7	5,553	72.2	96,479	8.2	510	3.9	77,229	6.1
Kansas	2,027	3.9	218,033	15.4	3,895	7.2	66,981	4.1	8,419	14.5	100,111	5.9
SOUTH ATLANTIC												
Delaware	484	1.6	17,125	11.1	− 846	− 2.7	21,485	12.6	2,267	7.5	13,109	6.8
Maryland	− 2,814	− 1.2	110,215	11.6	12,229	5.3	142,063	13.4	31,900	13.0	149,480	12.4
District of Columbia	7,744	8.9	44,596	23.3	15,520	16.4	90,712	38.4	28,102	20.1	27,089	8.3
Virginia	10,374	1.6	196,954	16.5	18,921	2.8	228,069	16.4	− 39,852	− 5.8	152,594	9.4
West Virginia	20,674	47.5	241,584	26.4	22,172	34.6	220,369	18.9	28,548	33.1	236,754	17.2
North Carolina	73,374	11.7	236,908	18.7	65,564	9.4	283,261	18.0	155,240	20.3	451,179	25.3
South Carolina	53,522	6.8	121,354	21.8	28,876	3.5	139,373	20.5	71,038	8.2	125,508	15.3
Georgia	142,174	13.7	250,508	21.2	29,378	2.5	257,294	18.0	− 135,240	− 11.2	147,904	8.8
Florida	77,939	33.8	146,301	49.2	20,818	6.7	194,467	43.8	102,341	31.1	397,171	62.2
EAST SOUTH CENTRAL												
Kentucky	− 23,050	− 8.1	165,642	8.9	− 25,718	− 9.8	152,536	7.5	− 9,898	− 4.2	207,902	9.5
Tennessee	− 7,155	− 1.5	171,246	11.1	− 21,330	− 4.5	174,522	10.2	25,888	5.7	252,680	13.4
Alabama	80,975	9.8	227,680	22.7	− 7,630	− 0.8	218,169	17.8	44,182	4.9	253,817	12.5
Mississippi	101,857	11.2	144,911	22.6	− 74,303	− 7.4	67,785	8.6	74,534	8.0	143,049	16.8

TABLE 4: INCREASES IN THE BLACK AND WHITE POPULATION, BY SECTIONS, DIVISIONS, AND STATES 1900-1930 (Continued)

A minus sign (−) denotes decrease.

SECTION, DIVISION, AND STATE	1900-1910 BLACK Number	Percent	1900-1910 WHITE Number	Percent	1910-1920 BLACK Number	Percent[a]	1910-1920 WHITE Number	Percent[a]	1920-1930 BLACK Number	Percent	1920-1930 WHITE Number	Percent
WEST SOUTH CENTRAL												
Arkansas	76,035	20.7	186,446	19.7	29,329	6.6	148,601	13.1	6,243	1.3	95,427	7.5
Louisiana	63,070	9.7	211,474	29.0	− 13,617	− 1.9	154,202	16.4	76,069	10.9	224,169	20.5
Oklahoma	81,928	147.1	774,327	115.5	11,796	8.6	371,640	25.8	22,790	15.3	310,207	17.1
Texas	69,327	11.2	778,179	32.1	51,645	7.5	551,108	18.5	113,270	15.3	754,001	21.4
MOUNTAIN												
Montana	311	20.4	134,297	59.3	− 176	− 9.6	173,500	48.1	− 402	− 24.2	16,664	3.1
Idaho	358	122.2	164,726	106.6	269	41.3	105,466	33.0	− 252	− 27.4	13,022	3.1
Wyoming	1,295	137.8	51,267	57.6	860	− 38.5	48,156	34.4	125	9.1	25,921	13.8
Colorado	2,883	33.6	254,369	48.1	135	− 1.2	129,617	16.6	510	4.5	51,354	5.6
New Mexico	18	1.1	124,387	69.0	4,105	252.1	18,305	6.5	2,883	50.3	29,876	9.9
Arizona	161	8.7	78,565	84.6	5,996	298.5	80,625	65.9	2,744	34.3	61,393	30.2
Utah	472	70.2	94,118	34.5	302	26.4	74,274	20.3	338	− 23.4	55,256	12.5
Nevada	379	282.8	38,871	109.8	− 167	− 32.6	− 4,053	− 5.5	170	49.1	12,023	17.3
PACIFIC												
Washington	3,544	141.0	612,807	123.5	825	13.6	210,426	19.0	43	− 0.6	201,706	15.3
Oregon	387	35.0	260,508	66.0	652	43.7	113,697	17.4	90	4.2	168,499	21.9
California	10,600	96.0	856,945	61.1	17,118	79.1	932,294	42.1	42,285	109.1	1,896,712	60.3

a. Figures calculated from those provided by the census.

Source: U.S., Department of Commerce, Bureau of the Census, Negroes in the United States, 1920-32 (Washington, D.C.: U.S. Government Printing Office, 1935), p. 12, Table 13; and U.S., Department of Commerce, Bureau of the Census, Negro Population 1790-1915 (Washington, D.C.: U.S. Government Printing Office, 1918), p. 37, Table 7.

TABLE 5: INCREASE BY TWENTY YEAR PERIODS FOR BLACK AND WHITE POPULATION, BY SECTIONS 1890 to 1930

INCREASE OF POPULATION

PERIOD	UNITED STATES		THE SOUTH		THE NORTH		THE WEST	
	Black	White	Black	White	Black	White	Black	White
NUMBER								
1890-1910	2,339,087	26,263,189	1,988,850	7,122,800	326,656	15,591,800	23,581	3,548,589
1910-1930	2,063,380	27,499,760	612,150	7,357,626	1,381,545	15,760,769	69,685	4,381,365
PERCENT								
1890-1910	31.2	47.7	29.4	54.0	46.6	39.9	87.1	123.6
1910-1930	21.0	33.8	7.0	36.2	134.4	28.9	137.5	68.2

Source: U.S., Department of Commerce, Bureau of the Census, Negroes in the United States, 1920–32 (Washington, D.C.: Government Printing Office, 1935), p. 4, Table 1.

TABLE 6: CITIES HAVING A BLACK POPULATION OF 10,000 OR MORE IN 1930, WITH COMPARATIVE FIGURES FOR 1910 and 1920, AND PERCENT INCREASE IN WHITE POPULATION 1910 to 1930

| CITY | BLACK POPULATION | | | Increase or Decrease (−) | | | | Percent of Total Population | | | Percent Increase or Decrease (−) in White Population | |
| | 1910 | 1920 | 1930 | 1910 to 1920 | | 1920 to 1930 | | 1910 | 1920 | 1930 | 1910-1920 | 1920-1930 |
				Number	Percent	Number	Percent					
New York, N.Y.	91,709	152,467	327,706	60,758	66.3	175,239	114.9	1.9	2.7	4.7	16.9	20.7
Chicago, Ill.	44,103	109,458	233,903	65,355	148.2	124,445	113.7	2.0	4.1	6.9	21.0	20.5
Philadelphia, Pa.	84,459	134,229	219,599	49,770	58.9	85,370	63.6	5.5	7.4	11.3	15.4	2.4
Baltimore, Md.	84,749	108,322	142,106	23,573	27.8	33,784	31.2	15.2	14.8	17.7	32.1	5.9
Washington, D.C.	94,446	109,966	132,068	15,520	16.4	22,102	20.1	28.5	25.1	27.1	38.4	8.3
New Orleans, La.	89,262	100,930	129,632	11,668	13.1	28,702	28.4	26.3	26.1	28.3	14.6	14.9
Detroit, Mich.	5,741	40,838	120,066	35,097	611.3	79,228	194.0	1.2	4.1	7.7	107.0	51.4
Birmingham, Ala.	52,305	70,230	99,077	17,925	34.3	28,847	41.1	39.4	39.3	38.2	35.1	47.9
Memphis, Tenn.	52,441	61,181	96,550	8,740	16.7	35,369	57.8	40.0	37.7	38.1	28.7	54.8
St. Louis, Mo.	43,960	69,854	93,580	25,894	58.9	23,726	34.0	6.4	9.0	11.4	9.4	3.5
Atlanta, Ga.	51,902	62,796	90,075	10,894	21.0	27,279	43.4	33.5	31.3	33.3	34.0	30.8
Cleveland, Ohio	8,448	34,451	71,899	26,003	307.8	37,448	108.7	1.5	4.3	8.0	38.1	8.6
Houston, Texas	23,929	33,960	63,337	10,031	41.9	29,377	86.5	30.4	24.6	21.7	90.2	116.6
Pittsburgh, Pa.	25,623	37,725	54,983	12,102	47.2	17,258	45.7	4.8	6.4	8.2	8.3	11.6
Richmond, Va.	46,733	54,041	52,988	7,308	15.6	− 1,053	1.9	36.6	31.5	29.0	45.4	10.5
Jacksonville, Fla.	29,293	41,520	48,196	12,227	41.7	6,676	16.1	50.8	45.3	37.2	76.4	62.7
Cincinnati, Ohio	19,639	30,079	47,818	10,440	53.2	17,739	59.0	5.4	7.5	10.6	7.9	8.6
Louisville, Ky.	40,522	40,087	47,354	− 435	1.1	7,267	18.1	18.1	17.1	15.4	6.2	33.7
Indianapolis, Ind.	21,816	34,678	43,967	12,862	59.0	9,289	26.8	9.3	11.0	12.1	31.9	14.5
Norfolk, Va.	25,039	43,392	43,942	18,353	73.3	550	1.3	37.1	37.5	33.9	70.5	18.4
Nashville, Tenn.	36,523	35,633	42,836	− 890	2.4	7,203	20.2	33.1	30.1	27.8	12.0	34.2
Savannah, Ga.	33,246	39,179	38,896	5,933	17.8	− 283	.7	51.1	47.1	45.7	38.5	4.6
Los Angeles, Calif.	7,599	15,579	38,894	7,980	105.0	23,315	149.7	2.4	2.7	3.1	79.1	107.6
Newark, N.J.	9,475	16,977	38,880	7,502	79.2	21,903	129.0	2.7	4.1	8.8	17.6	1.4
Dallas, Texas	18,024	24,023	38,742	5,999	33.3	14,719	61.3	19.6	15.1	14.9	82.2	63.4
Kansas City, Mo.	23,566	30,719	38,574	7,153	30.4	7,855	25.6	9.5	9.5	9.6	30.6	22.7
Chattanooga, Tenn.	17,942	18,889	33,289	947	5.3	14,400	76.2	40.2	32.6	27.8	46.3	121.8
Columbus, Ohio	12,739	22,181	32,774	9,442	74.1	10,593	47.8	7.0	9.4	11.3	27.3	20.0
Winston-Salem, N.C.	9,087	20,735	32,566	11,648	128.2	11,831	57.1	40.0	42.8	43.3	103.2	54.5
Montgomery, Ala.	19,322	19,827	29,970	505	2.6	10,143	51.2	50.7	45.6	45.4	25.7	52.8

TABLE 6: CITIES HAVING A BLACK POPULATION OF 10,000 OR MORE IN 1930, WITH COMPARATIVE FIGURES FOR 1910 and 1920,
AND PERCENT INCREASE IN WHITE POPULATION   1910 to 1930   (Continued)

CITY	BLACK POPULATION			Increase or Decrease (−)				Percent of Total Population			Percent Increase or Decrease (−) in White Population	
	1910	1920	1930	1910 to 1920		1920 to 1930		1910	1920	1930	1910-1920	1920-1930
				Number	Percent	Number	Percent					
Charleston, S.C.	33,056	32,326	28,062	1,270	4.1	− 4,264	13.2	52.8	47.6	45.1	28.2	− 4.0
Shreveport, La.	13,896	17,485	27,219	3,589	25.8	9,734	55.7	49.6	39.9	35.5	87.0	86.9
Charlotte, N.C.	11,752	14,641	25,163	2,889	24.6	10,522	71.9	34.6	31.6	30.4	42.4	81.4
Miami, Fla.	2,258	9,270	25,116	7,012	310.5	15,846	170.9	41.3	31.3	22.7	531.6	321.6
Mobile, Ala.	22,763	23,906	24,514	1,143	5.0	608	2.5	44.2	39.3	35.9	28.2	18.3
Augusta, Ga.	18,344	22,582	24,190	4,238	23.1	1,608	7.1	44.7	43.0	40.1	32.0	20.4
Macon, Ga.	18,150	23,093	23,158	4,943	27.2	65	.3	44.6	43.6	43.0	32.8	2.6
Fort Worth, Texas	13,280	15,896	22,234	2,616	19.7	6,338	39.9	18.1	14.9	13.6	50.9	59.5
Tampa, Fla.	8,951	11,531	21,172	2,580	28.8	9,641	83.6	23.7	22.3	20.9	39.1	99.5
Boston, Mass.	13,564	16,350	20,574	2,786	20.5	4,224	25.8	2.0	2.2	2.6	11.4	3.9
Kansas City, Kans.	9,286	14,405	19,872	5,119	55.1	5,467	38.0	11.3	14.2	16.3	18.8	17.6
Little Rock, Ark.	14,539	17,477	19,698	2,938	20.2	2,221	12.7	31.6	26.8	24.1	51.8	30.0
Columbia, S.C.	11,546	14,455	19,519	2,909	25.2	5,064	35.0	43.9	38.5	37.8	56.2	38.9
Jackson, Miss.	10,554	9,936	19,423	− 618	5.9	9,487	95.5	49.6	43.5	40.2	20.3	124.0
Portsmouth, Va.	11,617	23,245	18,849	11,628	100.1	− 4,396	18.9	35.0	42.7	41.2	44.2	− 13.9
Durham, N.C.	6,869	7,654	18,717	785	11.4	11,063	144.5	37.7	35.2	36.0	23.6	136.9
Beaumont, Texas	6,896	13,210	18,551	6,314	91.6	5,341	40.4	33.4	32.7	32.1	98.0	41.6
San Antonio, Texas	10,716	14,341	17,978	3,625	33.8	3,637	25.4	11.1	11.0	7.8	71.1	24.1
Gary, Ind.	383	5,299	17,922	4,916	1,283.6	12,623	238.2	2.3	9.6	17.8	205.1	58.4
Knoxville, Tenn.	7,638	11,302	17,093	3,664	48.0	5,791	51.2	21.0	14.5	16.2	131.7	33.4
Dayton, Ohio	4,842	9,025	17,077	4,183	86.4	8,055	89.2	4.2	5.9	8.5	28.5	28.1
Atlantic City, N.J.	9,834	10,946	15,611	1,112	11.3	4,665	42.6	21.3	21.6	23.6	9.5	27.3
Tulsa, Okla.	1,959	8,878	15,203	6,919	353.2	6,325	71.2	10.8	12.3	10.8	292.7	97.6
Oklahoma City, Okla.	6,546	8,241	14,662	1,695	25.9	6,421	77.9	10.2	9.0	7.9	44.1	106.1
Youngstown, Ohio	1,936	6,662	14,552	4,726	244.1	7,890	118.4	2.4	5.0	8.6	62.9	23.6
Asheville, N.C.	5,359	7,145	14,255	1,786	33.3	7,110	99.5	28.6	25.1	28.4	59.3	68.3
Columbus, Ga.	7,644	9,093	14,157	1,449	19.0	5,064	55.7	37.2	29.2	32.8	70.7	31.5
Greensboro, N.C.	5,710	5,973	14,050	263	4.6	8,077	135.2	35.9	30.1	26.2	36.4	184.6
Buffalo, N.Y.	1,773	4,511	13,563	2,738	154.4	9,052	200.7	.4	.9	2.4	19.0	11.3
Newport News, Va.	7,259	14,077	13,281	6,818	93.9	− 796	5.7	35.9	39.5	38.6	66.0	− 1.6

TABLE 6: CITIES HAVING A BLACK POPULATION OF 10,000 OR MORE IN 1930, WITH COMPARATIVE FIGURES FOR 1910 AND 1920, AND PERCENT INCREASE IN WHITE POPULATION 1910 to 1930 (Continued)

CITY	BLACK POPULATION			Increase or Decrease (−)				Percent of Total Population			Percent Increase or Decrease (−) in White Population	
	1910	1920	1930	1910 to 1920		1920-1930		1910	1920	1930	1910- 1920	1920- 1930
				Number	Percent	Number	Percent					
Toledo, Ohio	1,877	5,691	13,260	3,814	203.2	7,569	133.0	1.1	2.3	4.6	42.5	16.7
Galveston, Texas	8,036	9,888	13,226	1,852	23.0	3,338	33.8	12.7	22.3	25.0	18.8	8.0
Wilmington, N.C.	12,107	13,461	13,106	1,354	11.2	− 355	− 2.6	47.0	40.3	40.6	46.0	3.7
Lexington, Ky.	11,011	12,450	12,759	1,439	13.1	309	2.5	31.4	30.0	27.9	20.8	13.4
Petersburg, Va.	11,014	13,608	12,600	2,594	23.6	−1,008	− 7.4	45.7	43.9	44.1	32.7	8.2
Jersey City, N.J.	5,960	8,000	12,575	2,040	34.2	4,575	57.2	2.2	2.7	4.0	10.8	4.8
Raleigh, N.C.	7,372	8,544	12,575	1,172	15.9	4,031	47.2	38.4	35.0	33.6	34.0	56.2
Roanoke, Va.	7,924	9,331	12,368	1,407	17.8	3,037	32.5	22.7	18.4	17.9	54.0	37.0
Wilmington, Del.	9,081	10,746	12,080	1,665	18.3	1,334	12.4	10.4	9.8	11.3	26.9	−26.9
Vicksburg, Miss.	12,053	9,148	11,915	−2,905	− 24.1	2,767	30.2	57.9	50.6	51.9	1.9	23.5
Bessemer, Ala.	6,210	10,561	11,691	4,351	70.1	1,130	10.7	57.2	56.6	56.4	74.5	11.3
East St. Louis, Ill.	5,882	7,437	11,536	1,555	26.4	4,099	55.1	10.0	11.1	15.5	12.6	5.8
Meridian, Miss.	9,321	8,343	11,352	− 978	− 10.5	3,009	36.1	40.0	35.7	35.5	7.8	36.9
Camden, N.J.	6,076	8,500	11,340	2,424	39.9	2,840	33.4	6.4	7.3	9.6	21.9	− 0.4
Omaha, Nebr.	5,143	10,315	11,123	5,172	100.6	808	7.8	3.4	5.4	5.2	24.9	11.8
Akron, Ohio	657	5,580	11,080	4,923	749.3	5,500	98.6	1.0	2.7	4.3	196.4	20.2
Greenville, S.C.	6,319	8,184	10,871	1,865	29.5	2,687	32.8	40.1	35.4	37.3	58.6	22.3
Baton Rouge, La.	7,899	8,560	10,675	661	8.4	2,115	24.7	53.0	43.7	34.7	89.2	51.7
Monroe, La.	5,320	5,540	10,112	220	4.1	4,572	82.5	52.1	43.7	38.9	46.0	122.2
Port Arthur, Texas	1,493	3,910	10,003	2,417	161.9	6,093	155.8	19.5	17.6	19.7	197.2	112.7

a. The figures for the white population in 1920 for cities having 100,000 or more inhabitants and 100 or more Mexicans in 1930 were adjusted (for comparison with 1930 only) by deducting the estimated 700,545 persons who would have been classified as Mexicans under the 1930 classification.

Source: U.S., Department of Commerce, Bureau of the Census, Negroes in the United States, 1920–32 (Washington, D.C.: Government Printing Office, 1935), p. 55, Table 10.

STIMULUS TO MIGRATION

Job Opportunities Available

The *Chicago Defender* first appeared in 1905. By September, 1917, the weekly claimed a circulation of one hundred thousand. Its distribution in the South, its advocacy of advancement for the race, and its news of opportunity in the North made it a significant force in stimulating migration. "In Gulfport, Mississippi, it was stated, a man was regarded as 'intelligent' if he read the *Defender*, and in Laurel, Mississippi, it was said that old men who had never known how to read, bought the paper simply because it was regarded as precious." [12] In its news columns, its help wanted ads such as those that follow, and its editorial page, the *Chicago Defender* urged migration to the North.

Wanted — Men for laborers and semi-skilled occupations. Address or apply to the employment department, Westinghouse Electric & Manufacturing Co., East Pittsburgh, Pa. [13]

Wanted — Men and Women — architects, mechanics, cement masons, carpenters, painters and decorators; cement workers, electricians, plumbers, steamfitters, bookkeepers, steno-typewriters. All must be qualified to take charge of their positions. Apply by letter only, with self-addressed stamped envelope to International Ideal Home and Investment Bankers. Charles D. Basse, 183 N. Wabash Avenue. [14]

Girls wanted on power machines to make aprons and house dresses; girls that are willing to work steady should apply. Steinberg & Sopkin Bros., 831 W. Adams Street, Chicago. [15]

Moulders Wanted — No Fee charged — Good Pay, Good Working Conditions. Firms Supply Cottages for Married Men. Apply T.L. Jefferson, 3439 State Street. [16]

Reliable Steady Laborers Wanted — To unload coal cars; trim lake coal steamers and for general labor work. Hours, 7 to 6. Wages, $3.30 to $3.52. Take a No. 5 car to 93d st. and Commercial ave.; transfer to 112th st. and Torrence ave. car. Apply at Gate House of

Coke Plant at end of line. If you mean business, we will give you steady employment.[17]

Men!! If you are seeking employment, come to Milwaukee, Wisconsin. Wages $2.50 to $6.00 per day. Board and lodging reasonable. For further information call on or address The Booker T. Washington Social and Industrial Center, 318 Cherry Street, Milwaukee, Wisconsin.[18]

Rochester, New York, February 10. The State Employment Bureau hopes to effect a partial amelioration of the domestic problem by cooperating with Rev. L. B. Brown, pastor of Olive Baptist church, to bring about 75 here from the south to take places in households, which it has been found next to impossible to fill. Seventy-five women are wanted here from 18 to 30 years old. Part of their fare will be paid. Women workers are in great demand. Such places are open: shirt makers, bindery workers, laundry workers, weavers, pastry cooks, children's nurses and laundresses. Those who wish information about transportation may write State Public Employment Bureau, 120 St. Paul Street, Rochester, N.Y.[19]

The *Defender* invites all to come north. Plenty of room for the good, sober, industrious man. Plenty of work. For those who will not work, the jails will take care of you. When you have served your 90 days at hard labor you will then have learned how to work. Anywhere in God's country is far better than the Southland. Henson was with Perry [*sic*] (white) at the north pole.[20] No pneumonia there. He stills enjoys life in Brooklyn, N.Y. Don't let the crackers fool you. Come join the ranks of the free. Cast the yoke from around your neck. See the light. When you have crossed the Ohio river, breathe the fresh air and say, "Why didn't I come before?"[21]

Letters of Inquiry from the South

Letters from the South indicated that the *Defender's* appeals reached its readers. In addition to inquiries, some letters complained of conditions in the South, some spoke of numbers of men and women eager to begin their journey, and some spoke of wider opportunities, not only in employment but in such matters as education. Although numbers of those who went North left home precipitously, many planned as carefully as possible before taking such a momentous step. The letters below have been selected from those preserved in the Carter G. Woodson Papers, Library of Congress.

May 5, 1917
Port Arthur, Texas

Dear Sir: Permitt me in inform you that I have had the pleasure of reading the Defender for the first time in my life as I never dreamed that there was such a race paper published and I must say that its some paper.

However I can unhesitatingly say that it is extraordinarily interesting and had I know that there was such a paper in my town or such being handled in my vicinity I would have been a subscriber years ago.

Nevertheless I read every space of the paper dated April 28th which is my first and only paper at present. Although I am greatfully anticipating the pleasure of receiving my next Defender as I now consider myself a full fledged defender fan and I have also requested the representative of said paper to deliver my Defender weekly.

In reading the Defenders want ad I notice that there is lots of work to be had and if I havent miscomprehended I think I also understand that the transportation is advanced to able bodied working men who is out of work and desire work. Am I not right? with the understanding that those who have been advanced transportation same will be deducted from their salary after they have begun work. Now then if this is they proposition I have about 10 or 15 good working men who is out of work and are dying to leave the south and I assure you that they are working men and will be too glad to come north east or west, any where but the south.

Now then if this is the proposition kindly let me know by return mail. However I assure you that it shall be my pleasure to furnish you with further or all information that you may undertake to ask or all information necessary concerning this communication.

Thanking you in advance for the courtesy of a prompt reply with much interest, I am . . . .

April 25, 1917
Pensacola, Florida

Dear Sir: Having read in the "Chicago Defender" are helping the negroes of the South to secure employment I am writing you this note asking you to please put me & my friend in touch with some firm that are employing men.

Please do what you can for us.

April 21, 1917
Mobile, Alabama

Dear Sirs: We have a club of 108 good men wants work we are willing to go north or west but we are not able to pay rail road fare now if you can help us get work and get to it please answer at once. Hope to hear from you.

May 11, 1917
Mobile, Alabama

Dear sir and brother: on last Sunday I addressed you a letter asking you for information and I have received no answer. but we would like to know could 300 or 500 men and women get employment? and will the company or thoes that needs help send them a ticket or a pass and let them pay it back in weekly payments? We have men and women here in all lines of work we have organized a association to help them through you.

We are anxiously awaiting your reply.

January 17, 1917
Fayette, Georgia

Dear Sir: I have learned of the splendid work which you are doing in placing colored men in touch with industrial opportunities. I therefore write you to ask if you have an opening anywhere for me. I am a college graduate and understand Bookkeeping. But I am not above doing hard labor in a foundry or other industrial establishment. Please let me know if you can place me.

April 20, 1917
Daphne, Alabama

Sir: I am writing you to let you know that there is 15 or 20 familys wants to come up there at once but cant come on account of money to come with and we cant phone you here we will be killed they dont want us to leave here & say if we dont go to war and fight for our country they are going to kill us and wants to get away if we can if you send 20 passes there is no doubt that every one of us will com at once. We are not doing any thing here we cant get a living out of what we do now some of these people are farmers and som are cooks barbers and black smiths but the greater part are farmers & good worker & honest people & up to date the trash pile dont want to go no where These are nice people and respectable find a place like that & send passes & we all will come at once we all wants to leave here out of this hard luck place if you cant use us find some place that does need this kind of people we are called Negroes here. I am a reader of the Defender and am delighted to know how times are there & was to glad to, know if we could get some one to pass us away from here to a better land. We work but cant get scarcely any thing for it & they dont want us to go away & there is not much of anything here to do & nothing for it Please find some one that need this kind of a people & send at once for us. We dont want anything but our wareing and bed clothes & have not got no money to get away from here with & beging to get away before we are killed and hope to here from you at once. We cant talk to you over the phone here we are afraid to they dont want to hear one say that he or she wants to leave here if we do we are apt to be killed. They say if we dont go to war they are not going to let us stay here with their folks and it is not any thing that we have done to them. We are law abiding people want to treat every bordy right. these people wants to leave here but we cant we are here and have nothing to go with if you will send us some way to get away from here we will work till we pay it all if it takes that for us to go or get away. Now get busy for the south race. The conditions are horrible here with us. they wont give us anything to do & say that we wont need anything but something to eat & wont give us anything for what we do & wants us to stay here. Write me at once that you will do for us we want & opertunity that all we wants is to show you what we can do and will do if we can find some place. we wants to leave here for a north drive somewhere. We see starvation ahead of us here. We want to imigrate to the farmers who need our labor. We have not had no chance to have anything here thats why we plead to you for help to leave here to the North. We are humane but we are not treated such we are treated like brute by our whites here we dont have no privilige no where in the south. We must take anything they put on us. Its hard if its fair. We have not got no cotegous diseases here. We are looking to here from you soon.

April 23, 1911
Alexandria, Louisiana
Gentlemens: Just a word of information I am planning to leave this place on about May 11th for Chicago and wants ask you assistence in getting a job. My job for the past 8 years has been in the

Armour Packing Co. of this place and I cand do anything to be done in a branch house and are now doing the smoking here I am 36 years old have a wife and 2 children. I has been here all my life but would be glad to go wher I can educate my children where they can be of service to themselves, and this will never be here.

Now if you can get a job with eny of the packers I will just as soon as I arrive in your city come to your pace and pay you for your troubel. And if I cant get on with packers I will try enything that you have to offer.

April 29, 1917
Atlanta, Georgia

Sir: I am a young man 25 years of age. I desire to get in some place where I can earn more for my labor than I do now, which is $1.25 per day. I do not master no trade but I have finished a correspondence course with the practical auto school of New York City and with a little experience I would make a competent automobile man, but I do not ask for your assistance on this line of business only. I am willing to do anything for better wages.

P.S. I would like if you knows if there is an auto school any where where colored men can go to and learn the automobile industry to give me their address.

Letters to the South from Recent Black Migrants

It is not surprising that many of the migrants found their first impressions of life in the North very satisfactory. In addition to greater personal freedom, women who had received $2.50 a week in domestic service in the South could now earn from $2.10 to $2.50 a day, and men who had gotten $1.10 or $1.25 a day found that in northern industry their daily wage was $2.50 or $3.75.[22] The emphasis on economic advancement and personal freedom in these letters encouraged many of those who received them to consider migration to the North. The letters below are from the Carter G. Woodson Papers, Library of Congress.

November 13, 1917
Chicago, Illinois

Mr. H——
Hattiesburg, Miss.

Dear M——: Yours received sometime ago and found all well and doing well, hope you and family are well.

I got my things alright the other day and they were in good condition. I am all fixed now and living well. I certainly appreciate what you done for us and I will remember you in the near future.

M ——, old boy, I was promoted on the first of the month I was made first assistant to the head carpenter when he is out of the place I take everything in charge and was raised to $95. a month. You know I know my stuff.

Whats the news generally around H'burg? I should have been here 20 years ago. I just begin to feel like a man. It's a great deal of pleasure in knowing that you have got some privilege. My children are going to the same school with the whites and I dont have to umble to no one. I have registered — Will vote the next election and there isnt any "yes sir" and "no sir" — its all yes and no and Sam and Bill.

Florine says hello and would like very much to see you.

All joins me in sending love to you and family. How is times there now? Answer soon, from your friend and bro.

September 25, 1917
Dixon, Illinois
Dear Sir: Time affords of writting you people now as we have raised to wages to three dollars a day for ten hours — eleven hrs. a day $3.19. We work two wks day and two wks night — for night work $3.90. This is steady work a year round We have been running ten years without stopping only for ten days repair. I wish you would write me at once.

October 7, 1917
Philadelphia, Pennsylvania
Dear Sir: I take this method of thanking you for yours early responding and the glorious effect of the treatment. Oh, I do feel so fine. Dr. the treatment reach me almost ready to move. I am now housekeeping again I like it so much better than rooming. Well Dr. with the aid of God I am making very good I make $75 per month. I am carrying enough insurance to pay me $20 per week if I am not able to be on duty. I don't have to work hard. dont have to mister every little white boy comes along I havent heard a white man call a colored a nigger you no now — since I been in the state of Pa. I can ride in the electric street and steam cars any where I get a seat. I dont care to mix with white what I mean I am not crazy about being with white folks, but if I have to pay the same fare I have learn to want the same acomidation. and if you are first in a place

here shoping you dont have to wait until the white folks get thro tradeing yet amid all this I shall ever love the good old South and I am praying that God may give every well wisher a chance to be a man regardless of his color, and if my going to the front would bring about such conditions I am ready any day—well Dr. I dont want to worry you but read between lines; and maybe you can see a little sense in my weak statement the kids are in school every day I have only two and I guess that all. Dr. when you find time I would be delighted to have a word from the good old home state. Wife join me in sending love you and yours.

I am your friend and patient.

Case Studies

The pages of the *Chicago Defender* were not the only source of information about the possibility of a better life. Some learned of opportunities up north from friends, and some had their horizons broadened by military service during the war. The speakers in the following excerpts came north to New York from one of the South Carolina sea islands; they suggest some of the many personal factors involved in the decision to migrate.

Male; left Island in 1918 at age 18:

Well, I tell you. Conditions is so indifferent down there. Little farms are so small that the average family just can' do mor'n exist by farmin' alone. You've got to have some other little job besides farmin' to work at several months of the year. Some goes to Savannah. Some to Beaufort. Then, there's a little work on the Island. That kind of arrangement didn't suit me. I want to do one thing and that thing specifically.

Then, another thing that caused me to leave was this: Over on Johnson plantation several people done lost their little farms to Mr. C. through mortgages. If I hadn't left, he'd been ownin' my little spot right now. Back in 1916, we borrowed $176 from Mr. C. to run us over a year. Hadn't made nothin' that year. Year went round' and all we had to meet his note was $25. I had been workin' for him at his saw-mill in Beaufort—goin' backward and forwards across the River every day. He was just payin' me $1.25 a day and I was payin' $1 a week out of my own wages on the mortgage. I says to myself, "Man, you ent gonna own this lan'." But things went mighty slow. He was chargin' 8 per cent interest, and the little weekly dollar payments he didn't consider as bein' paid so far as interest calculations went. Every week, though, when I handed him a dollar, he'd smile. One time he said, "Keep it up, Lester, drops of water'll wear away a stone." I say, "Yes, Mr. C. but it takes time!"

I worked for him, though, off and on two years. I just got too ambitious for him. I saw I never could get that paid by little dribbles like that. So, in 1918, I just picked up and went over to Savannah. Got a job helping around a construction camp. My pay was $12 a week. I took three out of that for my board, room, and laundry every week; so that left me nine clear. I began sending Mr. C. six and eight dollars a week. That was more like it. After several months, I took a trip back home. Went by to see Mr. C. "Why you leave me, Lester?" he ax. "More money. Twelve dollars a week. Takes money if I ever pay you off for that mortgage." "I'll give you nine dollars a week to come back to work for me," he said.

Well, I thought I'd better stay on the good side of him; so I worked for him a while till I had every cent of that bill paid. When I finished, I thinks to myself, "Old man, you've got enough out of me. Lan' paid for. I'm gone." Well, that's the reason I first left the Island for Savannah, and that's the reason I went back. Worked in Savannah several months again, n' went back to the Island. I'd saved up a little money, so I says to myself, "Well, it takes money to get a decent start farming. I got enough money here to take me to New York, pay my board a month, and come back if I don't like it." While I was in Savannah, a friend, Mr. Grier, wrote me a couple times to come up, an' I wouldn't have no trouble findin' a job. He wasn't doing public work himself, but said he was sure I could get located all right. Told me it was to the advantage of colored people to leave the South and come to New York. Well, as I was sayin', I didn't know whether I would stay or not. Main thing was my big notion to see New York.[23]

Male; left Island in 1925 at age 17:

The people had been livin' in the dark. They didn't know they was in reach of any place other than the cotton field. Then, when the war broke out and soldiers were carried away, they saw how easy it was to travel. They naturally would not be content to go back to the country to spend their days. Their eyes were opened. They tasted something better. They wrote to their friends after they came to New York, and opened their eyes. So the people began coming. When they get here and stay a while, maybe they have a relative or friend that wants to come up. So they send him money. And now, most every family, I guess, around Beaufort, Hilton Head, and St. Helena, has friends or relatives in New York. The young people have their faces turned this way. Soon as they get old enough, they'll come right up. Nothin' to stop 'em. I got a friend who is comin' up pretty soon himself.[24]

REACTION TO THE MIGRATION

Northern Newspaper Comment on the Migration

The reaction of the nation to the first great wave of black migrants was mixed. In the North and in the South, men of both races argued the matter. Many Caucasians in the North were concerned that the "Negro problem," formerly a southern monopoly, was now a matter for national concern. Editorials in white newspapers suggest the ambivalence and apprehension felt by many white northerners. The first editorial reprinted below is from the *Beloit* (Wis.) *News;* the second is from the *New York Globe.*

EDITORIAL I

The Negro problem has moved north. Rather, the negro problem has spread from south to north; and beside it in the South is appearing a stranger to that clime – the labor problem.

It's a double development brought about by the war in Europe, and the nation has not yet realized its significance. Within a few years, experts predict the negro population of the North will be tripled. It's your problem, then, or it will be when the negro moves next door.

Italians and Greeks are giving way to the negroes in the section gangs along northern railroads, as you can see from the train windows, and as labor agents admit. Northern cities that had only small colored populations are finding their "white" sections invaded by negro families, strangers to the town. Many cities are in for the experience that has befallen all communities on the edge of the North and South – gradual encroachment of colored folks on territory occupied by whites; depreciation in realty values and lowering of rents, and finally, moving of the white families to other sections, leaving the districts in possession of colored families with a small sprinkling of whites.

This means racial resentment — for the white family that moves to escape negro proximity always carries, justly or not, a prejudice against the black race. It hits your pocket too.

Negroes will enter trades now monopolized by white men, at first, perhaps, as strike breakers; later, as non-union competitors, working for smaller wages. It will take some time, probably to get them into the labor unions' way of thinking.

Politicians, both good and bad, will seek the ballot of a large new element, which will vote largely in the lump. Now, what will be the effect in the southern States? Already the offers of better jobs further north have caused strikes among southern negroes — something almost unheard of. The South gets no immigration, but the negro has been an ever present source of cheap labor. With the black tide setting north, the southern negro, formerly a docile tool, is demanding better pay, better food and better treatment. And no longer can the South refuse to give it to him. For when the South refuses the negro moves away. It's a national problem now, instead of a sectional problem. And it has got to be solved.[25]

EDITORIAL II

For more than a year a migration of men and women of color to northern States has been going on that has already deprived thousands of southern farmers of cheap labor. And the movement bids fair to continue. That it will have both good and bad effects is obvious. It will distribute the negro population more evenly throughout the States and thus tend to diminish race friction. But unless there is a change of spirit on the part of northern unions, it will increase the danger of labor troubles in case of industrial depression.[26]

Northern blacks generally welcomed the newcomers as brothers. They were welcomed in the churches and were sometimes met by organizations created to ease their way. Nevertheless, there was a hint of concern in black newspapers that the arrival of great numbers of poorly-educated rural Negroes might harm the welfare of earlier arrivals. Editorials in black newspapers suggest the mixture of pride, enthusiasm, and concern felt by many black northerners.

The editorials reprinted here are from the *Philadelphia Christian Recorder* and the *Chicago Defender*.

EDITORIAL I

1. The negro is an American. He speaks the language of the country and is, therefore, superior to the foreigner in this respect.
2. He knows the customs of the country and here again has the advantage of the foreigner.
3. He is a peaceable worker and is glad to have an opportunity to make good.
4. The negro is physically the equal and morally the superior of the immigrant from Europe.

There are reasons why the negro should succeed in the North. So we have no doubt that many will come.

Indeed, if a million negroes move north and west in the next twelve months, it will be one of the greatest things for the negro since the Emancipation Proclamation. And the movement of a million negroes should not alarm anybody, especially when we remember that a million immigrants were coming every year to this country before the war.

Let the good work go on. Let every community in the North organize to get jobs for our friends in the South. Let a million come. In coming the negroes will get higher wages.

They will get first class schools, running nine months a year—a thing worth leaving the South for, if there were no other advantages.

They will have a chance in the courts. If they should happen to have a difference with a white man, they will not take their lives in their own hands by standing up for their side.

They will be able to defend their homes, their wives and children in a way no negro can now protect them in the South.

They will have the right to vote. The foreigner must wait seven years for this—the negro only one year. If a million negroes come north, they will soon get sufficient political power, which combined with their economic power will be able to force the South to do some things she is now unwilling to do.

With labor competition for the negro between North and South with the North offering higher wages, better living conditions, better education, protection and a vote, the South must bestir herself if she would keep the best labor in the world. And southern statesmen will see that the South must cease to lynch, begin to educate and finally restore the ballot.

"But," says an objector, "these negroes coming north will increase prejudice." What if they do? Then the northern negro will sympathize more with his southern brother. But if prejudice increases, the negro has the ballot which is an effective way to combat it. If a million negroes come here we will have more negro businesses, better churches, more professional men and real political power, and the negro in the North will begin to get a social position not based on mere charity.[27]

EDITORIAL II

Laboring men who have been placed at shops and factories are urged to appear on the street cars and in public places in clean, decent clothes. They can leave their working clothes where they work and put on better ones when they leave. In the north a man is usually judged by how clean he is, and not how dirty and untidy. The Defender urges even riding on the street cars and elevated roads to keep themselves clean going to and coming from work. It is different here than in the south. There people don't care how they dress; here they make it a practice to look as well in the week as they do on Sunday. There are a number of southern women who wear boudoir caps. They don't seem to know when to wear them. To those who don't know, learn this: Don't wear them on the street or on the cars. If you see a woman with one on, tell her that it is to be worn in the house, where a kimona [*sic*] is worn. Women, don't wear boudoir caps and Kimonas [*sic*] on the streets.[28]

Southern Reaction to the Migration

In the South many whites saw the loss of black labor as a threat to the welfare of the region. In Chamber of Commerce speeches, in magazine articles, and in newspaper editorials, concerned whites called for examination of the situation and for justice.[29] The following editorial from the *Memphis Commercial Appeal* reveals that concern, and along with it a large measure of the racism in the South that made the North seem freer to so many blacks.

The enormous demand for labor and the changing conditions brought about by the boll weevil in certain parts of the South have caused an exodus of negroes which may be serious. Great colonies of negroes have gone north to work in factories, in packing houses and on the railroads.

Some of our friends think that these negroes are being taken north for the purpose of voting them in November. Such is not the case. The restriction of immigration because of the European war and the tremendous manufacturing and industrial activity in the North have resulted in a scarcity of labor. The negro is a good track hand. He is also a good man around packing houses, and in certain elementary trades he is useful.

The South needs every able-bodied negro that is now south of the line, and every negro who remains south of the line will in the end do better than he will do in the North.

The negro has been a tremendous factor in the development of agriculture and all the commerce of the South. But in the meantime, if we are to keep him here, and if we are to have the best use of his business capacity, there is a certain duty that the white man himself must discharge in his relation to the negro.

The business of lynching negroes is bad, and we believe it is declining, but the worst thing is that the wrong negro is often lynched. The negro should be protected in all his legal rights. Furthermore, in some communities, some white people make money at the expense of the negro's lack of intelligence. Unfair dealing with the negro is not a custom in the South. It is not the rule, but here and there the taking of enormous profits from the labor of the negro is known to exist.

It should be so arranged that the negro in the city does not have to raise his children in the alleys and in the streets. Liquor in the cities has been a great curse to negroes. Millions of dollars have been made by no account white people selling no account liquor to negroes and thus making a whole lot of negroes no account. Happily this business is being extinguished.

The negroes who are in the South should be encouraged to remain there, and those white people who are in the boll weevil territory should make every sacrifice to keep their negro labor until there can be adjustments to the new and quickly prosperous conditions that will later exist.[30]

In a number of places in the South more direct action was taken to stop the exodus. The City Council of Macon, Georgia, required of agents recruiting laborers a license fee of $25,000 and recommendations from ten local ministers, ten manufacturers, and twenty-five businessmen. The mayor of New Orleans is reported to have telegraphed the president

of the Illinois Central Railroad asking him to stop selling
tickets to blacks.[31] The following news reports describe
some of the efforts made to halt the black migration that was
threatening to deplete the South's source of cheap labor.

Jacksonville, Fla., August 11, 1916. A bill passed the city council
here where the emigrant agents must pay $1,000 in order that they
may sign labor for the northern fields and shops. It also provides a
penalty of $600 for those not having a license and 60 days in the
workhouse.

This heavy penalty was imposed last week after the Pennsylvania
railroad people swamped down and took all the members of the
Race they could find and sent them north, offering half as much
again as the men had been formerly paid and better housing and
living conditions and no "Jim Crow" schools.

The men hesitated at first, but the women got behind their husbands and insisted that they at once leave the south henceforth and
forever.

All the labor on one steamship line quit and it left the steamer
owners crippled.[32]

Atlanta, Georgia, August 11. So strong has the exodus of farm
and skilled labor been since the war that the southern whites have
begun to see that their treatment for the Race man has brought
about unsatisfied conditions and those who are trying to get away
from the "Jim Crow" and segregated part of the country are leaving
in large numbers owing to the shortage of white help in the north.
One hundred and fifty left for the tobacco fields of Connecticut
last week. The Baltimore & Ohio took 200 and about 50 more are
leaving for the steel mills in Indiana.

The mayor of the city spoke in the Methodist church Sunday
night, and urged the people not to quit the south. He tried to scare
them with the possibilities of them not being able to stand the win-
ters, which he claimed were dreadfully cold, and that they would
catch consumption, as they are not used to the change of climate.
His remarks were met without applause.

Every clew to a job in the north is being taken up and families
are preparing to leave on 12 hours notice. "Better living conditions
for my children" is the watchword in every household.[33]

Jacksonville, Florida, August 18. Owing to thousands of laborers
leaving for the northern mines and mills the white southerners

have become alarmed. They have held meetings pleading with the men not to leave the south and have enlisted the aid of some of the weak-kneed leaders of the Race to help them.

The mayor has ordered all men arrested that are not working. The southerners have gone so far as to have dodgers printed that the men were being used as strike-breakers, and had these dodgers passed out by members of the Race.

At a recent mass meeting held at the Chamber of Commerce notice was sent to the people begging them to stay and telling them that the whites were their best friends. These pleadings were signed by the following: Rev. John E. Ford, pastor of Bethel church; Dr. Meyers, who lives in his father's house; McGill, who poses as a lawyer; Lee, an ex-revenue collector; Ballou, an ex-judge; Mays, an old letter carrier; Scott, a big lodge man; Collier, a president of the Baptist Academy. They spoke also at length on the cold weather north.

The wages here are a dollar and ten cents to a dollar and a quarter a day, and then the laborer is cursed and dogged around. Thousands have left and many are planning to leave.[34]

Savannah, Georgia, August 18. During the past three weeks the agents of the Pennsylvania railroad have been sending thousands of laborers north to work on the railroad and in the factories. Train after train has been sent from Jacksonville, Fla., with as many as they could hold.

The officials of this city have been taken completely by surprise to find so many that are willing and ready to leave the south. Two and three trains have been leaving here with from ten to twelve coaches each. Two labor agents have been arrested for sending labor out of Georgia, but when the case came to trial the labor agents came way out ahead and resumed their work. The laborers lined up on West Broad and Margaret streets. When the labor agent passed he told them where to catch the train.

The men began to fill the West End car, going out to Central junction, which is four miles out of the city limits. The cars were crowded all day and the streets were lined with people.

When the city officials learned of it they sent a policeman out to arrest the agent. The agent proved he was a match for the policeman and refused to be arrested without a warrant.

The policeman then made all those aboard the train get off, but the labor agent told them to get on as he was ready to pull out. This they did and the train pulled away loaded.

The agent was arrested then and hustled to the jail, but soon gave bond and came back and laid plans for another train. Many of these men worked up till nearly train time for fear that they would be arrested if detected. Many wives brought suitcases to the train so that their husbands could leave. Women wanted to go, but they were ordered back as the management could not take care of them. Quite a few donned overalls. The agent was again arrested.

The plans of the Pennsylvania Railway Company are well laid and the men are well taken care of before they leave and if the letters are true that the men write back home they are well taken care of on the other end.

The agent made an address to the members of the Race on Monday, Aug. 7th, the day that crowds left the city for the Four Mill hill on the Louisville road. Farm hands and workers from rural districts are coming in from all parts of the country because they have been promised $1.80 a day with chance for advancement. They have their suitcases, some are only in jumpers and overalls, but declare that if once in the State of Pennsylvania they will never set foot in Georgia again.

They are determined not to live where taxation without representation is in vogue. The men here are not allowed to live in peace.

The white people have begun to sit up and take notice. They have tried every way to stop the exodus but have failed.[35]

Savannah, Georgia, March 23, 1917. Much has been said against members of the Race leaving this section of the country. Some of the would-be wise leaders are being paid by the whites to tell the laborer to stay, but little heed has been paid. Every train carries them "bound for the promised land," and although some agents have tried in vain to keep from selling through tickets to Chicago and Detroit the Race men have bought to smaller stations and from there to others and worked this scheme till they have been able to land in a town where a through purchase can be made.

The best class of southern people have not left yet and are waiting for the weather to break up north and then the general exodus or the "Great Northern Drive," as the Chicago Defender puts it, will begin. Last Thursday night at the West Broad street around the Union station all was excitement on account of so many members of the Race wanting to go north. They were NOT ALLOWED the privilege of even entering the station to wait for the train and were forced back by the bully police to the adjoining streets. The police had no respect nor regard for the women or children. They used their clubs freely and beat some people badly. Many suitcases and bundles were broken open and lost, so rough did the police become. Many of the people took the street car and rode three miles from here, and others fearing trouble, went eight miles to the next station. Some waited all night for the train which did not come. A Defender reporter later learned that the man in charge of the affair had been arrested by the police earlier in the day and could not carry out his plans. There were many sad scenes. Bleeding heads where the police had used their clubs, many camped out in the open air and ate their little food they had brought with them in the early hours of morning. No account of the arrest of this man has appeared in the papers. The whites here are up in arms against the members of the Race leaving the south.[36]

POETIC COMMENT

The human story of the Great Migration is one of courage and pathos, of obstacles standing in the way of a better life, of success and frequent failure. Langston Hughes, born in 1902 in Joplin, Missouri, became an important figure in the New York black literary renaissance of the middle and late 1920s. In a blues-style poem, Hughes emphasized the loneliness of the man who has cut himself adrift from past friends and associates and put himself on a road bound for the North.

BOUND NO'TH BLUES

Goin' down de road, Lord,
Goin' down de road.
Down de road, Lord,
Way, way down de road.
Got to find somebody
To help me carry this load.

Road's in front o' me,
Nothin' to do but walk.
Road's in front o' me,
Walk . . . and walk . . . and walk.
I'd like to meet a good friend
To come along an' talk.

Hates to be lonely,
Lawd, I hates to be sad.
Says I hates to be lonely,
Hates to be lonely an' sad,
But ever' friend you finds seems
Like they try to do you bad.

Road, road, road, O!
Road, road . . . road . . . road, road!
Road, road, road, O!
On de No'thern road.
These Mississippi towns ain't
Fit for a hoppin' toad.[37]

2

The Reality of Opportunity:
Living Conditions

As black Americans moved into the cities of the North, they found better homes than they had known, better neighborhoods, better recreation, and better schools.[1] They found that paying the fare on a streetcar entitled them to any seat; they found that the policeman directing traffic was sometimes himself a black man. Nevertheless, the color line in the North, although far less clear and less blatant than in the South, was nonetheless real. It was a ring of resistance against the freedom of those within.

HOUSING

Among the essentials of freedom is opportunity—to obtain the best job one's skills may afford, to live in the best neighborhood and the best house one's income may sustain, and to escape the social disorganization and disease of the slum. Most blacks in the North were without industrial skills, and as marginal workers in unskilled jobs they were forced to live in the least-desirable areas of the city. In this they were not unlike white workers of similar social class who lived in slums that were shocking in their squalor.[2] When hard work and good fortune, or simply the pressure of population congestion, caused blacks to seek housing in a hitherto white district, they found almost every white hand raised against them. Most blacks were therefore at a double disadvantage. They lived in undesirable and crowded areas because they were poor, and they usually could not get out because they were black.

When black migrants arrived from the South they generally moved into formerly white immigrant neighborhoods. Although often better than the run-down and neglected rural districts from which many came, these black housing areas were rarely effectively controlled by the health, building, zoning, and public service departments of the city.[3] Many such Negro districts were located on the edge of growing business or manufacturing areas. In such cases, landlords from whom the blacks rented held their properties until they could be sold for commercial use. Owners made little effort to maintain their residential properties while awaiting a profitable sale to those who would convert the property to business or manufacturing. Such was the case in the heavily black St. Antoine district of Detroit, where landlords allowed houses to become "so dilapidated that expenditure on the part of the owner to make them suitable for living purposes would [have been] useless."[4] Nevertheless the district was crowded, and the same was true in New York, Pittsburgh, Elizabeth, New Jersey, and most other cities.[5]

High rents were asked and population congestion was aggravated by the practice of taking in lodgers. This method of raising money to meet rent payments was widespread despite the danger to health and family stability attendant upon having strangers or even distant relatives in the household. In Philadelphia 37 percent of black families canvassed by one research team took in lodgers. In Indianapolis the figure was 25 percent, and in Buffalo (New York) it was 59 percent.[6] To the degree that overcrowding existed simultaneously with a limited area for Negro habitation, rents rose. In 1924, a particularly bad year for black tenants in Philadelphia, rents rose for 61 percent of the black population as compared with 53 percent of the white tenants.[7]

The following summary report by the Philadelphia Armstrong Association (Urban League) offers much that is common to such reports from other cities. In addition to deploring evil conditions, it refers briefly to good housing for a few of the more fortunate.

If the housing standard of a community is of the mud hut variety the fact of living in a mud hut is normal to it and need occasion no excitement or shame. If, however, the standard is higher, the assumption is that the community knows better and in order to maintain a proper balance it becomes the duty of all the units of that community to work together in the effort to maintain that standard.

In most of the cities of the North unofficial but effectively rigid lines are drawn prescribing the bounds of habitation for different racial groups. So long as the several groups remain within the bounds set, there is little disposition to regard them as a problem. It is the attempted emergence from these bounds which sets in motion the suggestion of social, economic and health problems.

In Philadelphia the same general housing deficiencies exist that in other cities lead to congestion in certain districts, overcrowding and its attendant evils in the poorer sections, due in turn to the shortage of houses and the enormous rents charged for those that are available. There are sections where the vast majority of the population is represented by a distinctive racial group; but as strange as it may seem Negroes are neither the only nor the worst sufferers from the adverse effects of bad housing.

The Whittier Center made a survey of Negro occupants in two districts in Philadelphia . . . . Of the very bad areas the report says: "Such areas differ in no wise from the bad housing districts occupied by other races. The Negro who has little or no income, or no steady or assured income, has to suffer from the same gross evils of insanitation that afflict his Italian or Jewish neighbor. He is the victim of the same greedy landlordism, the same municipal neglect, and he contributes to a like extent, through his own slovenliness, to the filth surrounding him . . . .

". . . It would not follow that because the less ambitious of the race are housed, as indeed they are, in insanitary rookeries, cellars and attics, in illegal tenements and amid pitiably demoralizing influences, that all Negro families are likewise situated. The conditions surrounding the homes of the very poor are not typical of the conditions surrounding the homes of the class above them . . . ."

Philadelphia received as its quota of the 500,000 Negroes who moved North during the period of the World War, about 35,000. This great number suddenly added to the large Negro population created maladjustments in housing which are even now being felt. In the South-Central part of the city there were most serious and frequent cases of overcrowding. The great industries, the railroads and shipyards were responsible for the large number of newcomers and having made no provision for their housing it became necessary to resort to many expedients in order that shelter of some kind might be provided. Houses long abandoned as unfit for occupancy were hastily put in a semblance of repair, stables converted into camps, shacks built of flimsy construction, and churches and other buildings were opened for temporary relief of the situation. All this is but to repeat the story of other cities . . . .

[A survey of 635 houses recently conducted by the Armstrong Association] shows that for the territory investigated there is very little evidence of overcrowding. It must be understood however, that many of the purely lodging and rooming houses could not be fairly investigated so there may be a larger proportion of overcrowding than our figures show. The largest number found occupying one room was five and this in only three cases. There were ten cases of four in one room and ten cases of two in one room . . . .

Special mention should be made of the sanitary condition of the majority of the houses investigated. The houses in the smaller streets, courts and alleys are breeding places for diseases. Two and three story houses, one and two rooms to the floor, dark and poorly ventilated, inadequate toilet facilities, cooking and sleeping in the same room, create a situation which is dangerous for the entire city. While overcrowding as it is commonly understood, was not in evidence, the fact that the houses are old and dilapidated and unsanitary offer a menace even without overcrowding. In the territory covered there are houses representing everything of comfort which one could wish, but these houses represent the exception rather than the rule . . . .

The foregoing . . . shows the great lack of an aroused public conscience on the menace to the whole community which bad housing produces. Philadelphia offers to both races an ideal type of home. In all directions there are and are being built two and three story single family dwellings. Unlike most metropolitan cities we are not being forced into multi-family houses. We have practically no tenement or flat houses. Such apartment houses as we have are of the more pretentious kind; but the great mass of both races is compelled, for reasons of economy primarily, to live in greatly inferior houses. The desire on the part of members of both races to get out of the "slum" districts offers a golden opportunity to the profiteer in real estate. Early in 1920, real estate operators began a campaign to encourage former renters to buy houses. In many cases notices were served on tenants to *buy or move*. Having nowhere to go many undertook the task of buying at greatly inflated prices. The evil of enforced ownership is summarized in a statement from the report of the Philadelphia Housing Association [of 1921]: "The increased percentage of owners in 1920 over 1900 is but a reflection of the state to which so many people were put to find a place to live. Owing to the housing shortage many bought who had only a small amount of money. This they paid and in order to meet the recurring payments have resorted to many expedients. In buying these houses prices were inflated. Houses selling in 1915 for $2,000 sold in 1920 for as much as $4,500. This enforced ownership has caused a congestion of mortgages which is the least of the evils the housing shortage has brought. The greater evils are: overcrowding, ill health from congestion, immoral evils due to indiscriminate contacts with lodgers or roomers. There is also the great evil of insanitary practices due to lack of water and removal of waste and garbage . . . ."

Reverting to the bad housing situation in Philadelphia, the report says: "One of the outstanding evils of bad housing is the inattention of owners and agents. This leads to neglect of general upkeep. Among the evils especially noticed are inadequate water supply, overdrainage, lack of sewers, open privies, broken drain pipes in cellars, flooded cellars, which cause damp walls: houses without cellars often have rotten floors caused by leaking or broken plumbing, lack of traps and vents, windowless rooms.

Housing shortage with increased rents has brought an increase in cellar living; subdivision of rooms which in most cases cause loss of windows. Owing to this arrangement it is necessary in many cases for occupants of one room to pass through rooms occupied by others."

The bad housing condition while not directed to the Negro as such affects the Negro in greater degree because of his greater percentage of families below the independent level. While it is true that many of them live in well appointed homes — some in luxurious homes — the great majority are compelled to live in houses which represent everything of discomfort and neglect.

While the reports above referred to seem to show lack of discrimination with regard to colored tenants or buyers the faot remains that *there is discrimination.* Owners not infrequently direct their agents to rent houses only to white people in certain areas while in other areas the same owner would direct his agent to rent only to colored tenants.

In the matter of purchase, discrimination is shown not only in the advertised lists but in the restrictive clauses in deeds. The following is a form of conveyancing found in Ladner's Volume on Conveyancing, page 71. It reads: "under and subject nevertheless to the express conditions and restrictions, that the said premises shall not within the period of five years from the date hereof, be sold or occupied by any persons other than of the Caucasian race," etc.

In order to perpetuate the restrictions above referred to in reconveyancing the property, the conveyancer copies the clause in the new deed. These restrictions have had much to do with holding properties unoccupied notwithstanding the housing shortage when the neighborhoods in which they are located change from white to colored.

Notwithstanding the assertions of the Whittier Center and the Philadelphia Housing Association that there is little evidence of colored renters or buyers paying more than whites, the reverse is so often true that it may safely be called the rule. Property depreciation is the commonly used excuse for making the extra charge but it is but an expression of the racial slant given. The idea of depreciation is in direct proportion to racial antipathy. In some neighborhoods white and colored people live in the same kind of houses but investigation discloses that invariably the colored tenant pays a higher rental or if a buyer he pays a higher price.

Some effort is being made to remedy both the extortionate rental charges and to improve housing conditions for those Negroes who are now forced in unsanitary homes. A pioneer in this field is the Octavia Hill Association. This Association buys or leases, on long time improvement lease, run down properties which they improve and re-rent to the former tenant, many times at a rental reduction of 25 to 40 per cent. This is a business concern with a philanthropic slant. Unfortunately the Association is limited in capital and cannot do very much in improving the general condition of housing, but it does show how it can be done, and too, without loss of revenue to the owner. The revenue of course is considerably reduced.

The Whittier Center follows somewhat the plan of the Octavia Hill Association with the exception that it builds houses to sell as well as to rent. It has a building and loan feature which makes home buying favorable to the purchaser. Numerous colored building and loan associations are in operation, some of which are close [sic] corporations maintained for the benefit of certain church organizations and such, but owing to limitation of capital and the difficulty in securing money from banks on second and third mortgages very little can be done through them to relieve the worst cases of housing. As a matter of fact it has been shown that most of these building and loan associations offer opportunity for the officers to use the capital for their personal advantage.

There are several private or semi-private schemes which are being promoted, not so much to benefit the unfortunate tenant as to exploit them. They represent some of the means by which Negroes are being deprived even by Negroes of the little capital they may have which could be used in financing the purchase of a home. What Philadelphia really needs is a well organized heavily financed organization whose purpose would be buying, or taking on long time improvement lease, the old dilapidated houses and converting them into homes of comfort and respectability, not for colored people, not for white people, but for all the unfortunate peoples who now inhabit the "slum" districts. This would not only prove a good investment, paying a good return in money, but would prove an investment in humanity that would have an ever widening influence upon the whole community.[8]

As the Philadelphia report indicates, really substantial housing for Negroes was the exception rather than the rule. In Elizabeth, New Jersey, investigators reported "no new houses built for occupancy by Negro tenants."[9] In Detroit the situation was similar. The following cases are brief descriptions from the notebook of the Detroit Board of Health investigator of conditions found in several Negro blocks.

A ONE-STORY FRAME HOUSE

The general condition of the outside of the house bad; porch falling down, window panes broken, foundation weak. The general condition of the interior: walls broken, floors bad. The plumbing out of order. Five rooms, rent $45. One sink and outside toilet. One room without ventilation. Stove heat. Water under house from leaking pipe in wall. Two roomers paying $6 per week. The landlord refused to make repairs. If repairs are made they will get a $10 increase.

A ONE-STORY FRAME HOUSE

Place used for a rooming house. Six rooms, of which five are used. Four couples, each paying $6 per week. General condition of the interior bad. Plastering off the walls. Walls smoked and very dirty. Floors bad. The kitchen is on the ground with linoleum for floor. Bath tub stopped up, pipes broken in wall, water under house. Kerosene lamps. Yard in bad condition. On the rear end of the lot a shed, renting for $25, used as a club with one door, one window, two people sleeping in it, and without water or toilet.

A DORMITORY HOTEL

A two story brick structure once a bakery. On the second floor 50 beds. Beds very dirty, using dark gray blankets as spreads. Men pay 25¢ per night for sleeping. Beds not changed often. Toilets stopped up, bath in a deplorable condition. In one corner of the dormitory about 35 or 40 dirty mattresses piled up, seemingly from a fire. The floors very dirty, walls bad. Men sleeping in their street clothes. On the first floor a restaurant without license selling soup and fish. Water in the back, flies very bad, no sink, foul air and poor ventilation.

A TWO-FAMILY HOUSE

Two family house, six rooms each. No bath, one outside toilet. Well in the yard. Stove heat, electricity. General condition of the house bad, roof leaks. Side and rear yard poorly kept. Men work at River Rouge; (time required to go to work, two hours and twenty minutes). House could be made very attractive by a few repairs and good housekeeping. Family complain of bad water.

A TWO-ROOM DWELLING AND BARBER SHOP

This particular family paid $1200 for the House. Down payment was $100 and monthly payments $12. In one room of the house the husband maintains a barber shop. The other room, living quarters. They have one bed, stove, table and three chairs. The barber shop has one chair, no means for sterilizing instruments, only with the tea kettle. Living quarters have no windows. Only ventilation one door. Husband earns $18 to $20 per week. General condition of the house is bad. Sanitary conditions bad, outside toilet about 15 feet from the well. Wife and child sick for four weeks. Cause of the sickness impure water. House is heated with a cooking stove. Kerosene lamps. Yard very poorly kept. Weeds allowed to grow around which makes mosquitos very bad.

RUSSELL STREET APARTMENT

Ten-family apartment. Apartments taken over in 1923 by colored. Place formerly rented for $30.00 and $35.00 per month. Rent raised $10.00. Apartments each of four small rooms. Steam heat and electricity. General condition of the interior bad. Needs redecorating. Paper on the walls very dirty and loose. Floors bad. Plumbing fair. Some apartments worse than others. Garbage and rubbish receptacles inadequate for the apartment house. Lawns bad.

SCOTTEN AVENUE RESIDENCE

A two story frame building on the west side of Scotten Avenue. The house is about 45 feet from the sidewalk with a front lawn, well-kept and attractively arranged with flowers and shrubbery. The house is newly painted with awnings on front. Flower boxes on the porch. Home consists of eight well ventilated rooms. Interior decorating artistically done. Housekeeping excellent. Plumbing and general repairs good. Home purchased in 1920 for $10,000; down payment, $1500, monthly payments $75.00. Monthly payments have been doubled for the last three years reducing the principal greatly. Husband died two years ago, leaving widow and three children.[10]

SOCIAL DISORGANIZATION AND HEALTH CONDITIONS

The deplorable housing conditions, lack of sanitation and of privacy under which the majority of the black migrants to northern cities lived contributed to family disorganization, illegitimacy, desertion, and disease. In Detroit during the first six months of 1926, for example, the arrest rate for blacks was 3.99 per 10,000 of adult population aged twenty and over as compared with 1 per 10,000 Caucasians.[11] In 1923, according to the United States Census Bureau, "Negroes formed 31.3 percent of the prison population and 23.3 percent of commitments as contrasted with 9.3 percent of Negroes among the adult population."[12] The situation was equally deplorable in regard to maintaining the stability of the black family, with the heritage of slavery and its deprecation of marriage an additional complication.[13]

So far as health is concerned, the situation was shocking and worse. The situation described in the following report had its counterparts in cities around the country.[14] The tragedy of the findings reported by the National Tuberculosis Association is underlined by their very succinctness.

SUMMARY OF FINDINGS

According to the Federal Census of 1930, North Harlem had 198,015 inhabitants, compared with 203,322 in 1920. Negroes who numbered 72,923 in 1920, or 35.9 per cent of the total population, had more than doubled in number by 1930, when they comprised 160,340 or 81.0 per cent of all the residents in the section.

In the twenty-one sanitary districts selected for this study, the estimated population for July 1, 1925, the mid-point of the five year period, 1923 to 1927, was 200,474. All birth and death rates have been computed on this estimate which is based on the population, as shown by the Federal Censuses of 1920 and 1930.

During this decade the total population of North Harlem decreased but 2.6 per cent, yet nearly 100,000 white residents moved out (or died), while an almost equal number of Negroes was moving in. This stupendous population upheaval in an area of one and one-half square miles has emphasized the inadequacy of the various civic, health, and social service agencies, both public and private, which aim to improve conditions in this section. At any rate, outrageously poor housing, frightful congestion, and extremely high death rates are being tolerated in this section of New York, the city which prides itself on its low mortality and fine health facilities.

In 1925, these residents of Harlem were living 198 to the acre, and even in 1930 one acre housed an average of 196 persons in squalid tenements, some of which were condemned forty years ago. But these figures are only averages. In one sanitary district the 1925 population density was 392 per acre; in another, 374, and in a third,

335. Such conditions call for immediate action on the part of those departments of the City of New York which control health and housing.

The crude general death rate for Harlem from 1923 to 1927 was 16.2 per 1,000, a rate 42 per cent higher than the annual average death rate of 11.4 for New York City. Since Harlem has a remarkable preponderance of young adult residents, its standardized general death rate is 18.2. This, again, is but an average for all the sanitary areas.

Organic heart disease caused 2,704 deaths in Harlem from 1923 to 1927. The annual average death rate for this leading cause was 270, compared with Manhattan's figure of 241 and New York's of 213.

Considering the respiratory diseases to which the Negro is most susceptible, deaths from pneumonia in all forms numbered 2,343 during the five years. The annual average rate of 244 doubled the city's pneumonia death rate of 124.

Pulmonary tuberculosis caused 1,839 deaths. While the annual average tuberculosis death rate for New York City was 76 during the five-year period, Harlem yields the rate of 183, two and a half times the rate of the city. This disease is not decreasing in Harlem. The 1923 death rate was 184, whereas in 1927 it had reached the figure of 191 per 100,000 population . . . .

Harlem's annual average birth rate of 21.9 is less than that of Manhattan, and somewhat higher than New York's rate of 20.3. Curiously enough, Harlem's birth rate was much lower for each of the five years than the rate for all colored people in New York. Stillbirths for Harlem residents numbered 7.2 per 100 live births, compared with 5.2 for Manhattan and 4.8 for New York City.

During the five-year period Harlem's infant mortality averaged 111 per 1,000 live births, whereas New York City's rate was 64, [and] Manhattan's 69. . . . All things considered, diarrheal diseases seem to have been controlled fairly well; on the other hand, the infant death rate from respiratory diseases should not be tolerated in any section of New York City.

One cannot fail to be shocked by Harlem's maternal mortality rate of 10.1 per 1,000 live births, twice that of New York City [5.1 per 1,000] and more than twice the Manhattan rate [4.8 per 1,000]. Certain districts with fairly good records in other respects have extremely high maternal mortality.

If the annual average death rates for Harlem are high, those for the small sanitary areas or census tracts are at times alarming. In spite of the fact that numbers are small in certain instances, this is a five-year study which brings out some strikingly high mortality rates for which there can be no plausible excuse. Unfortunately, the study must of necessity be inconclusive because so many factors of importance have not been touched upon. Nevertheless, for every important cause of death, the Harlem rates exceed those of New York City in spite of the fact that Harlem has a much higher proportion of young adult residents.

It is a tenable theory to suppose that the mercenary rights of the few should be subordinated to the good of the many. The ultimate effect of improved housing and better living conditions pays many times over, not only in better citizenship and in a vastly greater enjoyment of life with reduced misery, morbidity, and mortality, but in a great saving to the city of assets that must otherwise be expended ultimately in curative and relief institutions. An almost immeasurable loss of time, energy, and efficiency may be obviated through improved living conditions.[15]

CASE STUDIES

Great numbers of black people living under conditions of bad housing, overcrowding, and the omnipresent threat of illness found that they were unable to extricate themselves. Handicapped by lack of adequate education, physically weakened by the poverty they had endured in the South, and impeded by inability to find other than marginal jobs, many were forced to turn to the municipality for assistance. The following three cases are illustrative of the families that needed such assistance. The first two were characterized as typical by the Detroit Department of Public Welfare, and the third was similarly described by the Mother's Pension Department of Detroit. The M. and W. in these reports signify Man and Woman.

CASE 1

W. was an only child. Her father was a houseman and drove a buggy for a doctor. She was married at the age of 21, had one child. This husband deserted and she was married to M. at the age of 23.

There were eight children ranging in age from 14 years to the infant born 9-27-25. There are twins born 8-11-24. The man's father came to Detroit in October 1919, secured work at good wages and the man followed in two months and brought his family. All family normal.

M. third grade W. sixth grade. Fourteen year old boy is in the 6-A grade, 12 yr. old girl in 6-B grade, 10 yr. old girl in 4-B, 6 yr. old girl in 2nd. Protestant.

Before coming to Detroit M. was a skilled laborer in a plough factory. Wages $13.50 week. Rent $7. month. On coming to Detroit December 1919 he worked for the Kelsey Wheel Company earning $28.80 a week for the first month and $40.00 a week after that. He was employed until April 1920, then out of work for a year and a half. He returned to the Kelsey Wheel Company. Wages were cut from 75¢ to 60¢ an hour. Since then his wages have averaged from $30.00 to $35.00 a week. His longest layoff since April 1922 has been three months. There have been several layoffs of 2 or 3 weeks. M. is at present employed at the Kelsey Wheel Company working 2 and 3 days a week. W. did cooking and laundry work before marriage.

Soon after coming to Detroit family started buying a home for $4,900. They had paid . . . over $700 when the man was unemployed and lost the home. They have never been able to start buying again.

Family pays $45 a month rent for five rooms and bath. House in good locality, good condition. They have lived there one year and month. There are no roomers or boarders. Family has two adults and eight children.

From December 1920 to April 1921 and from August 1921 to February 1922 the family received continuous relief in the form of a grocery order. The man did unpaid work for the city in return for this. Their income was supplemented by milk tickets during the fall and winter of 1924 and 1925 with five grocery orders of $10.00 each during the winter when the man was laid off. The income was again supplemented in August 1926. The only problem in this family has been unemployment and insufficient income for so large a family. They are self-respecting, good type of family, children clean and well kept. Relief given. M. worked for city in exchange. Food $253.74, shoes $12.75, coat $24,00—Total $290.49. Relief given, no work done, Food $70.00, Milk $62.16, coat $28.13, shoes $5.00—Total $165.29.

M. states that in Columbus, Georgia, where he grew up the colored people can vote for president but not for any other office unless
they own $1500 property or more. M. has always paid his poll tax
but did not own property enough to vote. Always voted for president and has always voted since coming to Detroit. Mentioned the
fact that in the factories the foremen bring pressure to try and make
the colored people vote the Democratic ticket. Said many of the
colored votes are bought up that either because of being bought or
freightened [*sic*] into it almost all the colored votes are Democratic
though at heart they are Republicans.

CASE 2

M. was born in Georgia in 1875. Was one of four children. The
father worked the farm on shares. A younger brother went to school
a little but M. and the other three never went.

W. was one of eight children. Her grandmother was sold away
from her husband and two children in Virginia and was brought to
Georgia with two babies. W's father being one of these two. The
grandmother always pined for the other children, but when freedom came W's father and his brother were settled in Georgia, and
she never went back or learned what became of them. W's father
also worked a farm on shares, grew cotton and corn. Of the eight
children only two are living. Six died after growing up. Two of
T.B., one of 'fever.' Some went to the 3rd grade in school, some the
5th.

M. died in 1921 in a little place ten miles from Bethlehem, Georgia, where he worked a farm on shares. W. worked out. Came to
Detroit in June 1922 to be with a niece who had T.B. and who returned to the South and died April 1924. W. brought only the
youngest child, Essie Mae, born October 1920, when she came to
Detroit July 1923. Left the three older ones with M's mother near
Atlanta. W. returned and got them in March 1925 and soon after
that M's mother and sister joined her, and are still living with her.

W. is at middle age and not very well. M's mother is 70 years old
and feeble. M's sister about 59 years old, has been 'afflicted' for
four years. Refuses to have medical attention, possibly has some
internal growth. Children not very rugged—as there has been so
much T.B. in the family they are to be examined.

M. no education. W. 3rd grade. Protestant.

W. does day work when she can, which is very irregularly. The aged mother-in-law does an occasional day's work and cares for the sick sister-in-law.

Family occupy a little cottage of four rooms and toilet. Rent $25. month. Family keep it neat and clean. The occupants are three women and four children.

W. should be eligible for a Mother's Pension, but has been unable to prove two years residence in Michigan. Also has given uncertain information as to M's death and we have not succeeded in verifying it. W. appears to be truthful but illiterate. Has received relief continuously since August 1925. Whole family to be examined at T.B. Clinic and 'afflicted' sister-in-law to be examined at Clinic.

Total Relief Given

Food	505.50
Rent	171.00
Coal	15.40
Shoes	15.00
Dentures	10.00
	$716.90

CASE 3

M. was born in Florida, worked in a brick yard in Cleveland, when W. first knew him. Followed to Detroit when she came here to stay with her mother. While in Detroit M. worked longest for the Michigan Copper and Brass works, then was out of work for a long time except for small irregular jobs. Was unable to support family but never had any special quarrel with W. He left on February 24, 1923 and has never been heard from since. W. thinks he left because of his inability to support family.

W. was born in Georgia, went to the fifth grade in school, began to work in a laundry in Macon, Georgia when 12 years old. Went to Cleveland with her parents in 1915, worked here in a laundry. Emma was born when M. and W. were married. W. has no marriage certificate. States she was married in Cleveland in September, 1916. After her marriage W. did not work outside of her own home until M. was out of work in Detroit. She then did laundry work in her mother's home, which was in the City. Was able to support herself and the five children in this way. Moved to the Eight Mile Road in May, 1924 and is unable to do as much work as when she lived in the city. Her mother cares for the children two days a week while W. does day work and W. cares for the children the rest of the week; has received help from the Public Welfare since.

W. and the children are living with her parents south of the Eight Mile Road and west of Livernois on Greenfield Township in a settlement made up of Negroes. The shack is set upon posts and has four very small rooms. Sleeping conditions are crowded. There is almost no furniture except beds. The house is a long ways from the bus line and from school. The housekeeping is indifferent. W's brother is buying the lot and in May, 1924 put up a shack for his mother and sister to live in.

W. is very large, easy going and good natured. She was frank and truthful in her statements. Children were poorly clothed. W. is well. Florence, her child, has been ill for several months, and is under the care of Woman's Hospital Clinic and is probably tubercular. School report stated that Marie had naval [*sic*] hernia. W. promised to take her to Woman's Hospital Clinic.

W. doesn't have anyone upon whom she can depend but the brother with whom she lives. She is able to work two or three days a week. All the children should be given physical examination, and medical care for Florence should be followed up closely. Standards of living should be raised. W. has been granted a pension and every possible effort is being made to safeguard the health of the children.[16]

Not all black migrants, of course, lived on the edge of disaster. The following three cases are illustrative of those who met with greater success in life, the last one particularly so. The case descriptions were drawn up by the Chicago Commission on Race Relations from a five page questionnaire and a two hour interview with Negro interviewers.[17]

AN IRON WORKER

Mr. J——, forty-nine years old, his wife, thirty-eight years, and their daughter twenty-one years, were born in Henry County, Georgia. The husband never went to school, but reads a little. The wife finished the seventh grade and the daughter the fifth grade in the rural school near their home.

They worked on a farm for shares, the man earning one dollar and the women from fifty to seventy-five cents a day for ten hours' work. Their home was a four-room cottage with a garden, and rented for five dollars a month. They owned pigs, poultry, and a cow, which with their household furniture, were worth about $800. The food that they did not raise and their clothing had to be bought from the commissary at any price the owner cared to charge.

They were members of the Missionary Baptist Church and the wife belonged to the missionary society of the church and the Household of Ruth, a secret order. Their sole recreation was attending church, except for the occasional hunting expeditions made by the husband.

Motives for coming to Chicago. Reading in the *Atlanta Journal,* a Negro newspaper, of the wonderful industrial opportunities offered Negroes, the husband came to Chicago in February, 1917. Finding conditions satisfactory, he had his wife sell the stock and household goods and join him here in April of the same year. He secured work at the Stock Yards, working eight hours at $3 a day. Later, he was employed by a casting company, working ten hours a day and earning $30 a week. This is his present employment and is about forty minutes' ride from his home. Both jobs were secured by his own efforts.

The family stayed in a rooming-house on East Thirtieth Street. This place catered to such an undesirable element that the wife remained in her room with their daughter all day. She thought the city too was cold, dirty, and noisy to live in. Having nothing to do and not knowing anyone, she was so lonely that she cried daily and begged her husband to put her in three rooms of their own or go back home. Because of the high cost of living, they were compelled to wait some time before they had saved enough to begin housekeeping.

Housing experience. Their first home was on South Park Avenue. They bought about $500 worth of furniture, on which they are still paying. The wife then worked for a time at the Pullman Yards, cleaning cars at $1.50 a day for ten hours' work. Their house leaked and was damp and cold, so the family moved to another house on South Park Avenue, where they now live. The house is an old, three-story brick, containing three flats. This family occupies the first flat, which has six rooms and bath. Stoves are used for heating, and gas for light and cooking. The house is warm, but dark and poorly ventilated. Lights are used in two of the rooms during the day. The rooms open one into the other, and the interior, as well as the exterior, needs cleaning. There are a living-room, dining-room, and three bedrooms. The living-room is neatly and plainly furnished.

The daughter has married a man twenty-three years old, who migrated first to Pittsburgh, Pennsylvania, then to Chicago. He works at the Stock Yards. They occupy a room and use the other part of the house, paying half the rent and boarding themselves. A nephew, who was a glazier in Georgia, but who has been unable to secure work here, also boards with Mr. and Mrs. J——, paying $8 a week. He is now unemployed, but has been doing foundry work. Mrs. J—— occasionally does laundry work at $4 a day.

How they live. The cost of living includes rent $25; gas $5.40 a month; coal $18 a year; insurance $9.60 a month; clothing $500 a year; transportation $3.12 a month; church and club dues $3 a month; hairdresser $1.50 a month. Little is spent for recreation and the care of the health. The family carries insurance to the amount of $1,700, of which $1,200 is on the husband.

The meals are prepared by the wife, who also does the cleaning. Greens, potatoes, and cabbage are the chief articles of diet. Milk, eggs, cereals, and meat are also used. Meat is eaten about four times a week. Hot bread is made daily, and the dinners are usually boiled.

Relation to the community. The whole family belongs to the Salem Baptist Church and attends twice a week. The wife is a member of the Pastor's Aid and the Willing Workers Club, also the Elk's Lodge. The husband is a member of the Knights of Pythias. He goes to the parks, bathing-beaches, and baseball games for amusement. The family spends much of its time in church and helped to establish the "Come and See" Baptist Mission at East Thirty-first Street and Cottage Grove Avenue. They have gone to a show only once or twice since they came to the city. During the summer they spend Sunday afternoons at the East Twenty-ninth Street Beach.

Heavier clothes were necessary because of the change of climate, and more fresh meat is used because of the lack of garden space and the high cost of green vegetables.

The wife thinks that northern Negroes have better manners, but are not as friendly as the colored people in the South. She says people do not visit each other, and one is never invited to dine at a friends house. She thinks they cannot afford it with food so high. She thinks people were better in the South than they are here and says they had to be good there for they had nothing else to do but go to church.

She feels a greater freedom here because of the right to vote, the better treatment accorded by white people, the lack of "Jim Crow" laws. She likes the North because of the protection afforded by the law and the better working conditions. "You don't have an overseer always standing over you," she remarked.

Life here is harder, however, because one has to work all the time. "In the South you could rest occasionally, but here, where food is so high and one must pay cash, it is hard to come out even." The climate is colder, making it necessary to buy more clothes and coal. Rent also is very much higher here. They had to sell their two $50 Liberty bonds.

Economic sufficiency. With all this, Mrs. J—— gets more pleasure from her income because the necessities of life here were luxuries in Georgia, and though such things are dear here there is money to pay for them. Houses are more modern, but not good enough for the rent paid. They had to pay $2 more than the white family that moved out when they moved in.

Sentiments on the migration. Mrs. J—— says "some colored people have come up here and forgotten to stay close to God," hence they have "gone to destruction." She hopes that an equal chance in industry will be given to all; that more houses will be provided for the people and rent will be charged for the worth of the house; and the cost of living generally will be reduced. She does not expect to return to Georgia and is advising friends to come to Chicago.[18]

A MISSOURI FAMILY

Mr. and Mrs. T—— came to Chicago in 1919, the wife arriving one month before her husband. They had been living in St. Louis, Missouri, where Mr. T—— was employed as a roller in an aluminum works. Prior to that time he had been a houseman, and before that a teamster.

There are two children. One is fourteen years old and in the first-year high school, and the other is seven and in the first-grade grammar school.

Mrs. T—— has always been a substantial aid to her husband, and, as she says, she "doesn't always wait for him to bring something to her, but goes out herself and helps to get it." Accordingly, when reports were being circulated that Chicago offered good jobs and a comfortable living, she came up to investigate while her husband held his job in St. Louis.

Home life in Chicago. The family lives on State Street over a store. They have moved four times since coming to Chicago in 1919, once to be nearer work, once to get out of a neighborhood that suffered during the riot, and twice to find a more desirable neighborhood for their family. They are not satisfied with their present home and are planning to move again as soon as a more suitable place can be found. With them live a sister-in-law and her child, who are regarded as members of the family. The house is in poor sanitary condition. The toilet is in the yard and used by two families. There is no bath. The sister-in-law is a music teacher but does not earn much. She pays board when she can afford it.

Mr. T—— is forty-seven and his wife forty-six years old. He is employed at the International Harvester Company and earns $35 a week for a nine-hour day. He consumes an hour and a half each day going to work.

Although Mr. T—— lived on a farm and too far from school to attend, he taught himself to read and write. Mrs. T—— went as far as the eighth grade in grammar school.

Community participation. The entire family belongs to a Methodist church. Mr. T—— is a member of the Knights of Pythias and Mrs. T—— is a member of the Sisters of the Mysterious Ten. They have no active recreation. For amusement they attend motion-picture shows in the neighborhood. The children regularly use the playground near their home and the Twenty-sixth Street Beach.

Adjustment to Chicago. Their most difficult adjustment has been the housing. They think landlords should be forced to provide better homes for the people in view of the high rents.[19]

A MIGRANT PROFESSIONAL MAN

Mr. and Mrs. F—— lived in Jackson, Mississippi, until 1917, the year of the migration, when they moved to Chicago. He followed his clientele and established an office on State Street near Thirty-first Street. Mr. F—— received his commercial and legal training at Jackson College and Walden University. Mrs. F—— is a graduate of Rust College and the University of Chicago.

Home life. The F—— home evidences their economic independence. It contains ten rooms and bath and is kept in excellent condition. They own six houses in the South, from which they receive an income. Mr. F—— is the president of an insurance company incorporated in Illinois in 1918, which has a membership of 12,000. He has also organized a mercantile company, grocery and market on State Street, incorporated for $10,000, of which $7,000 has been paid.

They have two sons, nineteen and twelve years of age, and three adult nephews living with them. One nephew is a painter at the Stock Yards, another is a laborer, and the third a shipping-clerk.

Community participation. They are members of the Baptist church and of the People's Movement, while Mr. F—— is a member of the Appomattox Club, an organization of leading Negro business and professional men. In addition to membership in three fraternal organizations, they are interested in and contribute to the support of the Urban League and United Charities.

Opinions on race relations. Concerning housing, Mr. F—— feels that some corporation should build medium-sized cottages for workingmen. He thinks that the changes in labor conditions make it hard for Negroes to grasp immediately the northern industrial methods. Patience will help toward adjustment, he thinks.

He thinks that colored women receive better protection in Chicago than in the South. His experience in the courts leads him to believe that Negroes have a fairer chance here than in the South. Agitation by the press in his opinion can have no other effect than to make conditions worse. [20]

RESIDENTIAL RESTRICTION

Not every black district was a slum, nor was every street in a run-down district a slum street. Toledo, Ohio, had its own middle-class black community,[21] and part of West 139th Street in Harlem, known as "Striver's Row," was the home of well-to-do Negroes. But middle-class islands in northern black districts were not sufficient. As more and more migrants arrived, crowding forced out the boundaries of black districts and adjoining white areas were "invaded" by one, then a handful, and then scores of blacks as whites retreated.

The black pioneers in white areas were often middle-class people simply seeking good housing not readily available elsewhere. They should have made fine neighbors. Often, however, black occupancy in a white area, or even the possibility of it, brought strong reaction from whites: attempts to fix racial boundaries through ordinances and covenants, intense social pressure, and, sometimes, violence.

Prohibiting the purchase of property by blacks in a white area through legislation was invalidated by the United States Supreme Court in 1917,[22] but other attempts to legislate segregation continued to be made. Indianapolis, for example, followed the lead of New Orleans in restricting the right of purchasers to occupy their property — without restriction on purchase or sale — in a neighborhood across the color line.[23] This arrangement was rejected by the United States Supreme Court in 1927.[24]

Restrictive Covenants

One of the most effective ways of maintaining residential segregation was through the use of restrictive covenants. As late as 1944, more than eleven square miles of Chicago were covered by race restrictive convenants,[25] thus legally segregating blacks and implicitly branding them as undesirables. Well established in law by the 1920s, restrictive covenants were generally of two types. Deed covenants, placed in title deeds, prevented the purchaser of a piece of real property from subsequently selling it to those classes of persons designated in the restriction. There were also separate covenants in which a group of property owners agreed to restrict the sale of their properties. Documents establishing either form of restriction customarily were filed in the Office of the County Clerk or the Register of Deeds and were enforceable in the courts.[26] The following case, decided in the Supreme Court of Michigan in 1922, held race restrictive covenants to be compatible with the interests of the State.

The chancellor who heard this case filed a written opinion therein which so clearly states the questions involved that we reproduce it here:

"At the time the Ferry Farm addition to the city of Pontiac was platted [i.e., plans were drawn that established boundaries and subdivisions], the lots were sold subject to the following uniform restrictions:

" 'No building shall be built within twenty feet of the front line of the lot. Said lot shall not be occupied by a colored person, nor for the purpose of doing a liquor business thereon.'

"Defendant Morris, and Anna Morris, his wife, both colored, have entered into a contract to purchase a lot in the subdivision, and the bill of complaint was filed by plaintiffs, who are owners of lots on the same subdivision and residents of the neighborhood, to restrain defendants from violating the restriction by occupying the premises in question. The record presents the sole question as to whether or not the restriction against the occupancy of the premises by a colored person is void as contravening the provisions of the Thirteenth and Fourteenth Amendments to the Constitution of the United States, while plaintiffs insist that the provisions of the federal Constitution have no application and that the restriction is a matter of a purely personal action of the owner of the premises and is valid and enforceable.

"Every owner of land in fee is invested with full right, power, and authority, when he conveys a portion away, to impose such restrictions and limitations on its use as will in his judgment prevent the grantee, or those claiming under him, from making such use of the premises conveyed as will impair the use or diminish the value of the part which he retains. The only limitation on this right is the requirements [sic] that the restrictions be reasonable; not contrary to public policy and not create an unlawful restraint on alienation. These rights have been repeatedly recognized by our Supreme Court....

"The reasons urged on behalf of defendants ... are:

"(1) ... [T]he restriction contravenes rights granted to defendants by the Thirteenth and Fourteenth Amendments to the Constitution of the United States.

"(2) ... [T]he restriction is contrary to public policy.

"These reasons will be discussed in their order.

"1. Since the days of the civil rights cases, the law has been regarded as settled that the provisions of the Thirteenth and Fourteenth Amendments applied to legislative acts of the state rather than the actions of individuals....

"[T]he United States Supreme Court, in passing upon the scope of these amendments, said:

" 'It is state action of a particular character that is prohibited. Individual invasion of individual rights is not the subject-matter of the amendment; it has a deeper and broader scope.' ...

"In an exhaustive opinion in Plessy v. Ferguson . . . the court said:

" 'The object of the amendment (Fourteenth) was to enforce the absolute equality of the two races before the law, but in the nature of things it could not have been intended to abolish the distinction based upon color, or to enforce social, as distinguished from political equality, or a commingling of the two races upon terms unsatisfactory to either. Laws permitting and even requiring their separation in places where they are liable to be brought in contact do not necessarily imply the inferiority of either race to the other, and have been generally, if not universally recognized as within the competency of state legislatures in the exercise of their police powers.'

"It is interesting to note that in the foregoing case the Supreme Court of the United States sustained the validity of a statute of Louisiana providing for the separation of races in passenger cars as not being repugnant to the provisions of the Fourteenth Amendment.

"It would seem settled by the foregoing decisions of the highest court of our land that the provisions of the Thirteenth and Fourteenth amendments cannot be invoked in the present case. The issue presented arises out of individual rather than state action and is to be determined wholly as a domestic issue. . . .

"2. Is the restriction contrary to public policy?

"It has been said that certain acts are contrary to public policy so that the law will refuse to recognize them when they have a mischievous tendency so as to be injurious to the interests of the state. This brings up the question as to what interests of the state are likely to be injured if an owner of property, for reasons which are satisfactory to himself, refuses to sell himself, or permit his assignors to sell, to certain persons who may be distasteful to him as neighbors. Are there any interests of the state which will be promoted or advanced compelling the creation of such a condition in the community? The law is powerless to eradicate racial instincts or to abolish distinctions which some citizens do draw on account of racial differences in relation to their matter of purely private concern. For the law to attempt to abolish these distinctions in the private dealings between individuals would only serve to accentuate the difficulties which the situation presents.

"The precise issues presented have been squarely before the courts of last resort of several states, and have been decided adversely to the contentions of defendants. . . .

"One of the purposes of the restriction in the instant case was apparently to preserve the subdivision as a district unoccupied by negroes. Whether this action on the part of the owner was taken to make the neighborhood more desirable in his estimation or to promote the better welfare of himself and his grantees is a consideration which I do not believe enters into a decision of the case. So far as I am able to discover, there is no policy of the state which this action contravenes. Were defendants' claim of rights based upon action taken by the authority of the state, an entirely different question would be presented.

"Defendants motion to dismiss the bill of complaint will therefore be denied. The injunction heretofore issued is, however, broader than warranted by the provisions of the restriction. The restriction covers the occupancy of the property by a colored person only. In terms at least it would not be violated by leasing the same to a colored person so long as such person did not occupy it. The temporary injunction heretofore issued will therefore be modified to the extent of prohibiting defendant from occupying the premises himself, or from permitting the same to be occupied by a colored person, and, as so modified, will be made permanent.

Glenn C. Gillespie, Circuit Judge."

A decree was made in accordance with the opinion. The case is brought here for review by appeal.

Counsel urge the same defenses that were urged in the court below....

Counsel say in the brief:

"Under the theory of our American democracy and citizenship, negroes, or any other race or class, ought not now be forced to stand and plead for right, justice and equity which ought to be the common heritage of all men by virtue of their citizenship and domicile within the jurisdiction of the United States. If the opinion of the learned trial judge is affirmed, it will open a wedge to all kinds of discrimination, wrongs and injustice to a vast number of American citizens of African descent. Slavery was once defended by church and statesmen, but who to-day would want to be classified as an upholder of such a vile institution?

"Such a restriction as the one referred to, if upheld, would place the negro and people of other sects and creeds in the same category as slaughter houses, livery stables, tanneries, garages, etc., and brand them as a nuisance, loathsome and undesirable in neighborhoods...."

"Would the learned trial judge's decision stand the test of time? Will there always exist in this country conditions whereby judicial decision will band 10,000,000 of people, as it affects the negro, 3,000,000 as it affects the Jew, and about 30,000,000 as it affects the foreigner, and equally as many as it affects the Catholic, thus placing all of these classes in the list of undesirables? . . .

"We think the learned trial judge's decision in this case, if affirmed, would in a short period of time take the course of the Dred Scott Decision written by Mr. Justice Taney."

We think the counsel has entirely misapprehended the issue involved. Suppose the situation was reversed, and some negro who had a tract of land platted it and stated in the recorded plat that no lot should be occupied by a Caucasian, and that the deeds that were afterwards executed contained a like restriction: would any one think that dire results to the white race would follow an enforcement of the restriction? In the instant case the plat of land containing the restriction was of record. It was also a part of defendant's deed. He knew or should have known all about it. He did not have to buy the land, and he should not have bought it unless willing to observe the restrictions it contained.

The issue involved in the instant case is a simple one, i.e., shall the law applicable to restrictions as to occupancy contained in deeds to real estate be enforced, or shall one be absolved from the provisions of the law simple because he is a negro? The question involved is purely a legal one, and we think it was rightly solved by the chancellor under the decisions found in his opinion.

The decree is affirmed, with costs to the appellees.[27]

Agitation

Having received the official sanction of the state in regard to race restrictive covenants, whites felt free to proceed in an atmosphere of moral approval to organize neighborhood "improvement associations," one of whose major purposes was to keep the blacks out. Such groups were prone to disregard the primary motive of blacks seeking houses in white neighborhoods—better housing—and attributed such behavior to a wish to mingle with whites. The racist rhetoric employed by the neighborhood associations sometimes alarmed white residents who, although opposed to permitting blacks into the area, feared racial violence. Such was the case with the Kenwood and Hyde Park Association in Chicago, who published the following in their *Property Owners' Journal*.

There is nothing in the make-up of a Negro, physically or mentally, which should induce anyone to welcome him as a neighbor. The best of them are insanitary, insurance companies class them as poor risks, ruin alone follows in their path. They are proud as peacocks, but have nothing of the peacock's beauty. Certain classes of the Negroes, such as the Pullman porters, political heelers and hairdressers are clamoring for equality. They are not content with remaining with the creditable members of their race, they seem to want to mingle with the whites. Their inordinate vanity, their desire to shine as social lights caused them to stray out of their paths and lose themselves. We who would direct them back where they belong, towards their people, are censured and called "unjust." Far more unjust are their actions to the members of their race who have no desire to interfere with the homes of the white citizens of this district. The great majority of the Negroes are not stirred by any false ambition that results only in discord. Wherever friction arises between the races, the suffering is usually endured by the innocent. If these misleaders are sincere in their protestations of injustice, if they are not hypocritical in their pretence of solving the race question, let them move. Their actions savour of spite against the whites, whose good will can never be attained by such tactics. The place for a Negro aristocrat is in a Negro neighborhood.[28]

In the same issue, under the heading *Caveat Vendor* (Let the Seller Beware) appeared the following:

People who sell their property to Negroes and take first and second mortgages and promises to pay monthly sums do not know what risks they are taking in trying to collect the money. Mrs. Nora F—— of —————— sold her house to some niggers and when she went to collect she was assaulted and thrown down a flight of stairs. This is not a case of saying it served her right because more than seven of her neighbors sold before Mr. F—— did, but it does serve as a splendid example of the fact that niggers are undesirable neighbors and entirely irresponsible and vicious.

The Negroes' innate desire to "flash," to live in the present, not reckoning the future, their inordinate love for display has resulted in their being misled by the example of such individuals as Jesse Binga and Oscar de Priest. [29] In their loud mouthing about equality with the whites they have wormed their course into white neighborhoods, where they are not wanted and where they have not the means to support property.

Keep the Negro in his place, amongst his people and he is healthy and loyal. Remove him or allow his newly discovered importance to remove him from his proper environment and the Negro becomes a nuisance. He develops into an overbearing, inflated, irascible individual, overburdening his brain to such an extent about social equality, that he becomes dangerous to all with whom he comes in contact, he constitutes a nuisance, of which the neighborhood is anxious to rid itself.

Another building which has been polluted by Negro tenancy is to be renovated on May 1st. . . . Either the Negro must vanish or decay sets in. Who is next?

Misleaders of the Negro, those flamboyant, noisy, witless individuals, who, by power of superior gall and gumption, have blustered their way into positions of prominence amongst their people, wonder why this district resents their intrusion. To allow themselves an opportunity to parade their dusky persons before an audience of their followers, these misleaders held a meeting of the Protective Circle (composed, no doubt, of Negro roundheads), at which a varied assortment of Negro preachers, politicians and other what nots exposed our methods and organization work. With much comical oratory, they dangled our association before the spellbound eyes of their sable dupes and after extreme fuming and sweating appointed about fifteen committees to annihilate all Hyde Parkers.[30]

Violence

Racial violence, although far from an everyday occurrence, erupted often enough to make an attempt by a black man to enter a white neighborhood that had no race restrictive covenants an undertaking that was at best uncertain and at worst physically dangerous. In Chicago, for example, from July 1, 1917, to March 1, 1921, there were fifty-eight bombings, with two blacks killed and numbers of whites and blacks injured.[31] In Detroit, in 1925, in addition to a cross burning, one black newcomer in a white neighborhood had his house vandalized and his furniture loaded in a van and carted away. Another had a load of coal dumped in front of his house and the house pelted with coal chunks. In the ensuing uproar a bystander was shot.[32]

Perhaps the best-known incident involved Dr. Ossian Sweet. On September 8, 1925, Dr. Sweet and his wife moved into their new house at the corner of Charlevoix Street and Garland Avenue, Detroit, a white neighborhood. Fearing trouble, the Sweets left their small daughter with relatives and were joined in their new home by Sweet's two brothers and seven friends. They came armed and determined to protect the Sweets in their own home.

On the night of September 9, a mob of between one hundred and one thousand attacked the house.[33] In the ensuing melee one Leon Breiner, white, was shot and killed. The Sweets and their friends were soon charged with murder. The National Association for the Advancement of Colored People quickly entered the case and was able to persuade famous criminal lawyer Clarence Darrow to take charge of the defense. He was joined by attorney Arthur Garfield Hays, chairman of the American Civil Liberties Union. The claim of self-defense was the legal issue when the case came to trial in the Detroit Recorder's Court, but the larger social issues were a black man's freedom to live where he chose and to defend his right to do so against attack. The following account of Dr. Sweet's testimony is taken from the extensive newspaper coverage given the trial.

Attorney Arthur Garfield Hays turned the searchlight of his legal mind, Wednesday afternoon [November 18, 1925], on the past of Ossian M. Sweet, Negro doctor, and wrote into the records of Judge Frank Murphy's court a biography of the man's life from the day he was born 30 years ago, the son of a poor minister-farmer in Florida, until the night of September 5, [34] this year, when it is alleged he and nine other defendants barricaded themselves in the new home of Dr. Sweet, on Garland avenue, and fired a volley of shots that resulted in the death of Leon Breiner.

By clever questioning he traced the defendant-witness through Wilberforce and Howard universities, working his way as a porter, bellhop, waiter and what-not, disclosed his struggles to get a foot-ing in the medical profession in Detroit, pictured his courtship and marriage, his studies in Vienna and Paris and his subsequent pur-chase of the Garland avenue home.

And having done this, he switched to the picturization of the man's mind as it developed, throwing onto the screen what he had seen, heard, read and thought of race riots. Slowly he dramatized the fear that he maintains became inculcated into the man's con-sciousness as a result of what he had experienced and what he had learned, and what he had thought.

In pursuing this course, which to the casual listener seemed far removed from the Garland avenue crime, Hays and Clarence Dar-row, chief of counsel for the defense, were following along the lines set down by Darrow . . . that a man's present has been shaped by his past, and that his past should be considered before passing judgment on his present acts.

Darrow stated the proposition as follows in opposing an objection to the admission of the testimony made by Prosecuting Attorney Robert M. Toms:

"This is the question of the psychology of a race — of how every-thing known to a race affects its actions. What we learn as chil-dren we remember — it gets fastened in the mind. I would not claim that the people outside the Sweet home were bad. But they would do to Negroes something they would not do to whites. It's their race psychology. Because this defendant's actions were predicated on the psychology of his past, I ask that this testimony be admitted."

Well educated and an acute student of the race problem, Dr. Sweet, under the adroit prompting of Attorney Hays, gave a graphic account of the disturbances ranging geographically from Washing-ton, D.C., to Chicago, and going back to the days when he was at-tending school. He recited the facts of the Chicago race riots, hold-ing the jury and spectators silent and immovable by his vivid pic-turing of morbid details, and the fear that gripped him as a result of what he read.

Speaking clearly and without hesitating for word or phrase, he told of seeing a Negro carried through the streets of Washington in an automobile and badly beaten by a group of white men. He told of reading in a magazine how a number of Negroes were evicted from their homes, near where he was born, of how others were riddled with bullets — of how his people had long suffered without chance of redress, as a result of racial intolerance.

The scenes were then shifted to Detroit, and he described a number of disturbances which, the defense attorneys maintained, were admitted solely to show the state of his mind on the night of the crime.

Skillfully the attorney led him up to the time when he purchased the Garland avenue home from Mrs. Edward G. Smith, the wife of a Negro.[35] He recited several conversations he had had with her in which she told of threats made by neighbors, of how they had told her they "would get her if they had to follow her to California," and of how they would "kill the Negro" if he dared to move into the district.

He admitted he purchased part of the firearms found in his house because of fear.

"What did you do when you got home the evening of September 9?" he was asked.

"The first thing I remember is of my wife telling me about a telephone conversation she had with Mrs. Butler, in which the latter told her of overhearing a conversation between the motorman of a street car and a woman passenger."

Asked to recite the conversation, he said the woman remarked that a Negro family had moved in and that they would be out before the next night.

He stated the other nine defendants were in the house and that he took them through the place showing them the various rooms, including the closet in which the firearms and ammunition was stored.

"When did you first observe anything outside?"

"We were playing cards; it was about 8 o'clock when something hit the roof of the house."

"What happened after that?"

"Somebody went to the window, and I heard them remark 'The people; the people!' "

"And then?"

"I ran out to the kitchen where my wife was; there were several lights burning, I turned them out, and opened the door. I heard someone yell: 'Go and raise hell in front; I'm going back.' I was frightened and after getting a gun ran upstairs. Stones kept hitting the house intermittently. I threw myself on the bed and lay there a short while—perhaps 15 or 20 minutes—when a stone came through the window. Part of the glass hit me."

"What happened next?"

"Pandemonium—I guess that's the best way of describing it—broke loose. Everyone was running from room to room. There was a general uproar. Somebody yelled 'There's someone coming.' They said, 'That's you[r] brother.' A car pulled up to the curb. My brother and Mr. Davis (one of the defendants) got out. The mob yelled, 'Here's niggers! Get them; get them!' As they rushed in, the mob surged forward 15 or 20 feet. It looked like a human sea. Stones kept coming faster. I was downstairs. Another window was smashed. Then one shot—then eight or ten from upstairs. Then it was all over."

Questioned as to who was downstairs at the time of the firing beside himself, Dr. Sweet said his wife, his brother, Davis, and he thought Morris. [William E. Davis and Leonard C. Morris were two of the defendants.]

The rest of his recital dealt with the appearance of the police and the arrest of the defendants. He said that on the way to the police station an officer asked him why he had moved into a white neighborhood when he knew he was not wanted. His answer was that there wasn't anywhere else to move.

"State your state of mind at the time of the shooting," Hays instructed.

"When I opened the door and saw the mob I realized I was facing the same mob that had hounded my people throughout its entire history. In my mind I was pretty confident of what I was up against, with my back against the wall. I was filled with a peculiar fear—the kind no one could feel unless they had known the history of our race."

. . . Dr. Sweet was still on the stand when the case adjourned. It is expected that several hours will be spent by the prosecution in his cross-examination. . . . [36]

Forty-six hours after Clarence Darrow's closing argument, the jury reported that agreement could not be reached. A second trial was scheduled, but this time only Henry Sweet, who had admitted firing his gun, was tried. Henry Sweet's acquittal caused the weaker cases against the other defendants to collapse—and it confirmed the right of black men to defend themselves and their homes.

3

The Reality of Opportunity:
Employment Conditions

With the decline in immigration and the general labor
shortage of World War I, blacks had a real opportunity to
enter industry in sizable numbers. From 1910 to 1920, according to census records, the number of blacks in manufacturing and mechanical industries increased by 40 percent,
from 631,280 to 886,810.[1] A new wave of black workers entered industrial employment in the early 1920s. Opportunities became available with the end of the depression of
1921 and the beginning of European immigration restriction. Most of these new black workers were unskilled or at
best semiskilled in industrial occupations.

Although the great majority of black Americans continued
to work in agriculture and in personal and domestic service,[2] sizable numbers of Negroes entered the steel mills,
automobile plants, packing houses, and commercial laundries of industrial towns and cities. Others swelled the ranks
of the transportation industry and the extractive industries.
Not surprisingly, since so many were unaccustomed to the
regimentation of factory life, they faced problems of ad-
justing to waiting attendance on a machine and reporting to
the job punctually day after day. In this respect the problems

of the unskilled black worker differed little from those of his white counterpart. In a profoundly important way, however, race prejudice compounded his problems.

When blacks made up a large proportion of the work force in a particular plant, the general wage scale was often lower than in similar plants having but few blacks. Generally speaking, there was in the North no distinction in wage rates between black and white workers doing the same job in the same plant.[3] The exceptions to this statement, however, were numerous and often unconcealed, as in the case of a notice from New York which read: "Wanted: Factory Helpers; experienced only; white $24.00, colored $20.00. Apply...." [4]

Hostility to a particular ethnic group on the part of employers, foremen, or fellow workers was not confined to blacks, but the frequency of occurrence combined with the intensity of the hostility was greater in the case of blacks than in any other. The attitude of Caucasian workers was indicated by the "white only" policies of more than a dozen unions and by the workers' willingness to walk off the job at the first appearance of a black face. Not surprisingly, black workers failed to view unions as their protectors. Black workers often saw the employer as filling that role, perhaps in part because of the tradition of white paternalism in the South, but also because job opportunities were opened to them if they were docile, loyal workers or even strikebreakers.

Employers seek harmony in their labor force, and harmony rarely followed the promotion of black workers to positions of authority over whites. The situation in the meat-packing industry was typical. Because of refusals by Caucasians to work under Negroes, "the companies avoid the issue as much as possible by giving Negroes supervisory positions only in rare instances. Negroes have seldom advanced beyond the rank of 'strawboss,' " that is, one rung below assistant foreman.[5] Sometimes employers presented the white workers with a "take it or leave" proposition, but such a move was made only with the prospect of successful acquiescence.

Black workers were in a difficult position. Acceptance of

employer paternalism usually meant acceptance of a job ceiling—except in rare cases. Seeking the protection of a union often meant rebuff, although there were notable exceptions like the International Longshoreman's Association. Even here instances of local discrimination were numerous, and it is fairly clear that the ILA's choice was limited by the very large number of black longshoremen that could have constituted a threat to the union if they had remained outside it.

Radicalism might have seemed an answer to black workers. Radical groups, such as the Socialists and the Communists, welcomed blacks into their ranks to join an attack on the entire capitalist structure.[6] The response from black Americans was far from enthusiastic,[7] although Philip Randolph and Chandler Owen proclaimed the Socialist creed in the pages of the *Messenger* for over half a decade after the founding of that magazine in 1917, and a number of other black intellectuals called themselves Socialists.

There are several reasons for the failure of the radical appeal. The black workers who were least aware politically had trouble grasping the meaning and purpose of radical doctrines and were understandably suspicious of the white radicals who offered them. And the white radicals rarely recognized the unique identity created by black experience, generally seeing black workers merely as whites with black skins. In addition, many Negro workers saw that being black was often enough a source of difficulty without their being Red as well. And Negro leaders who already had a stake in the existing system made vigorous efforts to convince black workers that their best hope lay in following the path of loyalty to the employer, hard work, and striving.[8]

Some of the black middle class had made their way by just such attention to duty. The National Negro Business League, founded in 1900 by Booker T. Washington, was able to boast in 1924 that the number of small businesses owned by blacks had grown from twenty thousand to seventy thousand in twenty-five years.[9] Admirable as this growth was, it must be noted that many black-run businesses prospered by attending to needs that had been neglected by white enterprise, as in the case of cosmetics for black women and insurance for black Americans. Sometimes, as was true of Caucasians, good luck lent a helping hand. Jesse Binga, founder of the Binga State Bank in Chicago, acquired part of his fortune through his marriage to the sister of "Mushmouth" Johnson, notorious Chicago gambler.[10]

Black business efforts were made as well by groups seeking more than the rewards of business enterprise. The Universal Negro Improvement Association, Marcus Garvey's separatist organization, promoted grandiose projects such as the Black Star Steamship Line, as well as smaller enterprises developed on a cooperative basis. These included a chain of grocery stores, a restaurant, a steam laundry, a tailor and dressmaking shop, a millinery store, and a publishing house.[11]

Important as the development of Negro business was, the vast majority of urban blacks still faced the necessity of earning their bread through physical labor. Opportunity for advancement up the occupational ladder was hindered by race prejudice, lack of training, and lack of seniority. Although the concept of "last hired—first fired" may have been too often attributed to racism, the fact that black men were so often the new men on the job made job security a problem.

THE EMPLOYMENT SITUATION IN THE CITIES

In 1910 the National Urban League was founded. Its central concerns were to give assistance to new arrivals from the South, to help black workers prepare for jobs in industry, and to convince Caucasian employers to open job opportunities to Negroes. From time to time the Urban League published progress reports in its journal. The following excerpts from that journal include a summary statement and representative reports from New York City, Pittsburgh, Philadelphia, Columbus, and Milwaukee.

SUMMARY STATEMENT

Since early in 1925 the National Urban League has maintained in New York a Department of Industrial Relations. During the fifteen years the League has operated, it has maintained offices in various parts of the country (mostly Northern communities where the population of Negroes has grown out of proportion to previous increases) in which emphasis has been placed upon securing occupations for Negroes. The local Leagues are still vigorously pressing this service. The large numbers throughout the North make placements difficult now when there appears to be no great demand for laborers.

The capacity of the Negro is no longer in question. Too many instances of success in industry are of record to enable the charge of inefficiency to stand. Employers may be provided with proof of fitness in many lines of work in which until recently Negroes never had experience. There remains, however, a very definite and necessary "over-head" task which will inure to the benefit of the whole problem of the Negro and his work. We have not yet popularized the idea of the use of Negroes. An employer needing help is still prone to think of white and never of black labor. Many of them are not aware of the excellent quality of service Negroes have rendered. Others who use their labor still resort to the old system of limiting them to certain occupations without regard to fitness for better positions and meritorious service which should earn promotion.

White workers still intimidate employers who might otherwise hire colored men and women. There are threats of strikes, riots and boycots [sic] if colored workers are employed. Labor unions have as yet given only partial recognition and little or no attention to annexing Negro wage-earners.

Interracial harmony will have gained a greatly advanced position, from which it will be difficult to recede, should we attain a mutually satisfactory adjustment of the differences between black and white labor.

Our plan includes a third feature. Much must be done to equip the race to fit it to hold the occupations it has thus far acquired and to obtain new ones. It will be possible to destroy the common belief of race inferiority only when we have succeeded so often as to make failure exceptional. This will take training and concentration, plus the proper attitude of mind that senses the value of success and the danger of failure—not to the individual alone, but mainly to the whole problem of Negro industry. The schools must perform a very definite service here. There must be articulation between the training for the job and the job itself. Finished tradesmen are far too few. Labor turn-over, due too often to matters which the schools may find a way to improve, must be reduced.

Here then, are the three major factors in the industrial equation of the Negro—the employer, the white employee, union and non-union and the Negro himself. The Industrial Relations Department of the Urban League is applying its energy to them. Many other considerations, by no means unimportant, involving the problems incident to migration, employment agencies, vocational guidance, agricultural opportunities in the North and the like will be given attention. It needs and solicits the aid of all who have counsel to offer. It is free to extend its service to owners and employees, individually and collectively. Through its affiliated movement in various parts of the country it touches the problem in many places and is positioned to serve on the basis of fact and experience. . . .

NEW YORK

. . . Thus lies New York. Many of its problems have a similarity to, yet a divergence from, the difficulties of other industrial centers. Rendered complex by its diversified industries, the city has many industrial problems including those provoked by the clash of racial and economic interests.

Despite the fact that the main source of the City's labor supply has been curtailed, no scientific effort has been made to study the industrial status of the Negro. Those capable of promoting such a step financially have not thought it necessary.

There are 125,000 gainfully employed Negroes in New York, the bulk of whom are engaged as personal and domestic servants, elevator operators, porters, and laundry workers. Within the last decade many have found employment in the factories of New York, but are so widly [sic] distributed as to make no outstanding impression as a group. As public laundries move northward into Harlem, there is an increasing demand for colored workers. It is estimated by labor groups that the number of colored workers now exceeds 10,000. Longshoremen and laborers form a similarly large group.

Negro men and women come to New York experienced and inexperienced. They find the lure of the city deceiving. The experienced find few opportunities open; the inexperienced see little chance for improvement. Clerical workers with enviable records come from the West Indies seeking a position. Eventually they are elevator operators. Industries do not have time to train the inexperienced. Thus skill and brawn grovel at the bottom of the industrial ladder hoping for an opportunity.

Colored workers receive lower wages than white workers in similar occupations, except when both are members of trade unions. The want ad given is indicative of the situation. Another instance may be noted in this case of profit and loss:

"A large laundry recently moved into North Harlem and replaced its white help with colored. Wages were reduced $3.00 on the week, and the Saturday half-holiday given to white workers substituted by a mid-day lunch and four hours extra work."

Organized labor is at last making an effort to enlist Negroes. A "boring from without" has merited from trade unions some consideration for the Negro workers. It was at the instance of the New York Urban League that the Trades Union Committee for Organized Negro Workers was organized. A paid secretary works daily on this one phase of our industrial life.

One notices improvements specific as well as general. The Negro Press encourages the patronage of stores employing Negroes. One month's work by this organization netted the employment of ten stenographers in publication offices. A Long Island shoe factory is successfully using fifty colored men. A Harlem department store has employed three colored salesladies. A national chain grocery has employed its first colored clerk. A coal company uses a Negro salesman and statistical worker. Through such a maze of situations we may hope to reach the fact that the Negro is thoroughly absorbed into New York's industrial life.

There exists an unparalled field for patient, assiduous, and earnest effort which is certain to produce more competent, satisfied, and progressive workers. Ira DeA. Reid

PITTSBURGH

Pittsburgh has had several periods of greater unemployment than now, but during the last six months a greater number of Negroes have been under-employed than ever before. The workman counts himself fortunate who averages four (4) full days of work each week. Hence, the industrial situation as it affects Negroes in the Pittsburgh district is serious.

Many Union Coal Mines in this district closed as a result of the wage dispute which has brought many Negro families into the city. Negro families direct from the South are still coming into our city. In one school during September were entered the children from five Negro families who moved into that district direct from the South during the summer months. The Negro population (now estimated at 65,000) increased about 9 per cent since 1923. It must find work in the major industries here, whose production averages about 20 per cent less than what it was in 1923. In addition to this automatic increase in the supply of Negro labor, it appears that fewer men are now used in each unit of production than in 1923. None of the few Steel Mills which claim a hundred per cent production at the present time, employ within 15 per cent of the total number of men they employed in 1923. Employers attribute this mainly to more regular and better service that workmen give today and to improved organization and some new patent processes. Hence, the industrial situation is bad among Southern Negroes in this district who have been trying to establish their family life here during the frequent periods of depressions of the last few years. John T. Clark

PHILADELPHIA

Philadelphia ranks first among the great textile industries in the United States. In fact, almost every section of the city has one or more textile mills but in none of them are Negroes employed in a productive capacity, and only recently in any capacity at all.

In one of the largest steel fabricating plants, there has been a shortage of machine hands. It was suggested to the management that Negroes be employed as is being done in several other plants. He refused to employ Negroes on the ground that they have developed a welfare program which brings together in social contact the employees, their wives, sisters, etc., and that if Negroes were employed they would expect to participate in the social activities which would not be tolerated by the white employees. In this plant nearly 75 per cent of the machine hands are of foreign birth.

A situation which is both humorous and tragic is shown in the method of discrimination against Negroes on jobs controlled by white contractors and the ease with which white union mechanics will work with Negro mechanics, non union at that; when the job is controlled by a Negro contractor.

There are in Philadelphia two or three Negro contractors who are

among the largest in their lines in the city. One a building contractor is now erecting a large church building. The bricklayers,
carpenters, plasterers, etc., are all Negroes. The structural steel
work, plumbing and steam fitting are being done by white union
mechanics. The construction engineer and the general foreman are
Negroes. From the beginning till the present, the best relations
exist between the two race groups. The other case is that of a Negro
reinforced concrete contractor who in competition with white contractors has been awarded some of the largest contracts in this line
in the city. He also employs a Negro engineer but his employees
are both white and Negro. On the other hand, there was being
erected a large office building. At the time of excavation, Negro
portable engineers were employed. The portable engineers are
members of the A.F. of L. When the steel erectors – union men –
came on the job, they refused to work with Negro hoisters and the
Negro engineers were displaced and white engineers were employed to take their places.

Very few Negroes are employed in machine shops as machinists
or machine hands; to operate machines which are almost automatic
and which are absolutely stationary; yet among the most ordinary
occupations for Negroes is that of chauffeur who drive high-powered complicated machines, with the families of these same owners, through crowded streets without accident or trouble.

Another paradox is the refusal to employ competent Negro girls
as clerks in stores and offices and colored men as workers in mills
or factories, but the employment of colored girls as nursemaids,
governesses and housekeepers or colored men as porters and
messengers.

There have occurred one or two labor disputes in recent years
from which the Negro had greatly benefitted although not a parti-
cipant in the strike nor a conscious strike breaker. In a large shipyard where a few Negroes were employed as laborers the rivetting
[sic] gang struck. The striking rivetters [sic] automatically threw
everybody else out of employment. One of the Negro laborers told
the foremen that he was a rivetter and asked permission to organize the Negro laborers into rivoting [sic] gangs and take over the
job. After trying to settle the dispute with the white riveters the
management decided to try out the Negro gangs. It was soon discovered that almost every Negro who was working as a laborer was
an experienced shipyard worker, some from Hog Island, some from
Norfolk, some from Baltimore and others from New Port News and

for the first time in a hundred years Negroes were employed in this plant actually building ships. It wasn't long before the white workers were willing to come back, a condition being that the Negroes would be discharged. The management refused to discharge the Negro shipworkers and they are there yet. Writing to us recently the manager said: "We find the colored men in our employ equal in every way to any others. We do not know how many we employ as we made no distinction in employment because of race, creed, or nationality."

While in many plants there is still prejudice against the employment of Negroes except in the hardest and poorest paying jobs, this prejudice is giving way as employers are shown the capability of the newest migrant to quickly understand industrial processes and to master intricate machinery. Prejudice is giving way as Negro contractors are brought more and more in contact with white contractors on a competitive basis. A. L. Manley, Armstrong Association of Philadelphia.

INDUSTRY IN COLUMBUS

Until 1917, the Negro earned his livelihood generally in personal and domestic service. The Buckeye Steel Casting Co., one of the largest, at that time employed 10 percent Negroes, 40 percent foreign, and 50 percent native white. The war gave the Negro his chance. Now, with few exceptions, all of the leading manufacturers in this city employ Negroes. This same Company that employed 10 percent in 1917 now has 40 percent Negroes. In the Jeffrey Manufacturing Company, the Secretary to the Vice President is a colored man. This plant employs Negroes in both skilled and unskilled work and as clerks. In the retail business, except where the Negro conducts his own, he has not been able to rise above the personal service jobs. The largest house moving business in the city is conducted by a colored man. Practically all of his trade is white. Several hairdressing establishments and barber shops are owned by Negroes with all white trade. N.B. Allen

MILWAUKEE

The industries of Milwaukee, on account of a relatively small Negro population, have never used them to the extent that they are used in other large industrial cities.

During the last three months the Urban League induced one of the large canneries to employ 35 new apprentices on a certain operation where they had not been employed previously. Another plant enlarged the number of its colored employees and at our suggestion employed their first Negro foreman. In another industry, a young Negro was placed in a position having the timing operation of every department in the plant, — an exceptional position.

In some instances it has been found that the heads of industries were sympathetic to Negro labor but the department foreman and straw bosses were doing all in their power to make conditions intolerable for them. In one industry the turnover of Negro employees was 65 per cent higher than other groups. Several of the men were interviewed and facts revealed which warranted investigation. It was found that the foreman was opposed to Negro workers; that his language was so abusive that the men resented such treatment, and made it a practice to give all small jobs to Negroes instead of so planning that all men would have some large and some small jobs, which would more equalize their wages.

This particular foreman was transferred to another department and the president sent word to every department in the plant that Negroes were to be employed by that plant, and in larger numbers when conditions warranted, concluding by saying that any man who objected [to] working with Negroes were at liberty to find employment elsewhere.

Two weeks ago employment managers from 22 industries employing large numbers of Negroes were invited to a round table discussion on the question of Negroes in the industries which was held at Urban League headquarters. Negro ministers, prominent persons in the local Negro Business League, heads of fraternal and social organizations were also present.

The principal complaint was not the quality of the Negroes' work — for in many cases it was superior — but their instability. One employer whose firm employs more than 2,000 men, about 175 being Negroes, stated that in the next five years under present immigration laws Negroes and labor saving machinery must be relied on to meet the ever increasing demands.

Our experience has taught us that through selection placements, private and group conferences with employers very definite results have been made. James H. Kerns [12]

Lest the emphasis on progress cast too rosy a glow over the prospects of black workers in the 1920s, consider a newspaper account of an incident that took place in Buffalo, New York, at the beginning of the decade.

IDLE NEGROES OUSTED AFTER BUFFALO RAIDS

Thousands Arrested and Exiled by the Police —
Many Pawn Clothing and Flee City

Buffalo, Nov. 29. Within the past forty-eight hours more than 1000 negroes, discharged during the recent business depression, have been forced out of Buffalo by the police. Raids have been conducted in the negro districts and those who are unemployed are arrested.

Many negroes, becoming frightened, have left of their own accord. Some of these withdrew liberal amounts from savings banks and departed for the South. Pawnbrokers report that many pawned clothing and jewelry to enable them to get away. Employers are not disturbed, as there has been a surplus of labor in Buffalo for several months.[13]

In like manner, the personal story of George S. Schuyler reveals some of the difficulties facing an ordinary black workingman. Schuyler later became a well-known journalist. He served on the editorial board of the *Pittsburgh Courier* and wrote a column widely syndicated in black newspapers.

New York is the Mecca of America. The steps of plutocrat and proletarian alike turn toward this great metropolis. Like some huge magnet it attracts young and old, male and female, clever and stupid, black and white. It is not strange, therefore, that I, too, sought my fortune among its caves and canyons of steel and stone.

Like most strangers who enter this great city, I was not overburdened with a supply of this world's goods. Hence, I was on a still hunt for work a very short time after I arrived. Having had considerable experience as a clerk in the government service, both civil and military, and armed with excellent references, it was only natural that I should seek that sort of work.

Day after day I tramped the streets answering advertisements out of the newspapers. Day after day I was met with refusal. Sometimes I was frankly told that no colored help was wanted. More often I was met with evasions, excuses or profuse apologies. On two or three occasions I *almost* succeeded in getting excellent positions by mail, but the inevitable interviews were sufficient to kill my chances for those jobs. I was soon forced to seek for other work.

Although I was reluctant to leave the city, I was finally forced to take a shipment to a railroad camp from a Bowery agency. I went out as a waiter. The wages offered were sufficiently large to arouse suspicion. When I asked pertinent questions concerning the conditions obtaining at the place I was gruffly told to take the job or leave it. Hungry men seldom ask many questions, so I accepted.

That afternoon we left, ten of us, for the camp in Pennsylvania, where we arrived late that night. The "camp" was a railroad yard with repair shops, roundhouses, etc., in a narrow valley alongside a river, with steep bluffs on each side. There is a large town overlooking the yards. On the edge of the bluff was a barb-wire fence about ten feet high with sentry boxes at intervals in which reclined the heavily armed "guards" of the railroad. The shops were built against the bluff. Near the river was a large shed where the commissary and dining coaches were situated. Between these and the river were the long lines of coaches converted into sleeping cars; three for the Negro workers and about eight cars for the whites. These sleeping cars were steam-heated, unventilated and unsanitary. Fourteen double-deck iron beds were in each car, used alternately by the day and night shifts. A little observation and questioning confirmed my earlier view that it was a scab job. Next morning, despite the threats of gunmen of the company and the refusal of transportation back to the city, I left on foot.

My one night's stay afforded me an opportunity to obtain the views of the Negro strikebreakers. Nearly all of them were dissatisfied and were only staying long enough to "make a stake." Many considered it an excellent opportunity to learn a trade, saying, "If there wasn't a strike, we couldn't get a job at this shop work." There were English-, Spanish- and French-West Indian Negroes there, but the majority of the Negroes were from the South. They were not surprised to learn that I was leaving in the morning. I learned that many Negroes had left as soon as they discovered what sort of job it was.

Three days later I was back in New York. This time I sought only restaurant and hotel jobs. Even here I found my color against me in many instances. Some establishments hired no colored help. No Negroes were wanted as countermen or cashiers. Here and there I would find a place that hired Negro waiters. But one must have a certain uniform to wait on table. After a night or two at the Municipal Lodging House, with its pedigree-taking and other prison-like humilities, I finally succeeded in getting a $14-a-week dish-washing position.

Ten or twelve hours a day, standing over a tub of steaming, soapy water in an oven-like kitchen is not calculated to endear one to the profession of "pearl diver." So, after a few weeks of that sort of thing I sought other fields of employment. On several occasions, however, I have had to return to it.

I have found that more and more factories, plants, and industries cater to Negro labor, but generally for Negro unskilled labor. With the exception of the civil service, there is little opportunity for the Negro clerk, stenographer, accountant or executive; his greatest opportunity is with Negro business concerns. It is seldom that one finds him employed in any other establishments.

Even in the civil service some subtle methods are at times used to keep the successful Negro applicant out of the higher positions. For instance, in 1919 I successfully completed an examination at the Customs House in New York City for first grade clerk in the field service. A month later I got an appointment as timekeeper at the Port of Embarkation at Hoboken. I called at the latter place for interview, as directed, and was sent across the river to the main offices on Broadway. After some questioning by an official at that office, I was told that I would not "do" for the position and that the district secretary of the civil service would be notified accordingly. A day or two later I received a letter from the latter announcing that "In view of the fact that you *refused* the position offered your name has been taken from the eligible list"! Of course, there are many Negroes in the civil service, and this may only be an excep-tional case. Still, I have been told of similar experiences.

I have also experienced the inconveniences of carrying a hod. As a member of the union I generally received a square deal. Once a contractor refused to rehire me when a strike was settled. Imme-diately my white fellow-workers refused to return to work unless I also was allowed to return. Needless to say, the boss was forced to give in. I have worked as a straw boss over white laborers with-out any difficulty whatever, although a great deal of tact is required in such cases.

As the supply of foreign labor diminishes and the migration of Negro labor in the North continues, both white employees and their employers are being forced to change their traditional attitude toward their black brothers.... [14]

THE BLACK WORKER

Problems with Unions

By 1930 black union membership was estimated at 56,000 out of a total black work force of 1.3 million in transportation, extraction of minerals, and manufacturing. About 4.3 percent of black workers were organized in labor unions as against 20.8 percent of all American wage earners.[15] Part of the reason for this disproportion was the fact that black workers were so often among the unskilled and semiskilled workers hardly touched by unionization. Even skilled black workers, however, faced the fact that as late as 1930 no fewer than twenty-four national and international unions, ten of them affiliated with the American Federation of Labor, excluded blacks either by constitutional provision or by their ritual.[16] The AFL barred racial discrimination in membership; however, power over admission resided not in the Federation but in its component unions. The following excerpts from union constitutions illustrate only the tip of the iceberg of discrimination, much of it practiced informally.

CONSTITUTION OF THE BROTHERHOOD OF RAILWAY CARMEN OF
AMERICA, 1921

Subordinate Constitution, Section 6, Qualifications for Membership.

Clause (a). Any white person between the ages of 16 and 65 years, who believes in the existence of a Supreme Being, who is free from hereditary or contracted diseases, of good moral character and habits, who is employed at the time he or she makes application for membership as railroad, electric or motor car builder or repairer on any class of cars, wood or steel, car inspector, car oiler, coach, gas and steam pipe work, steel cabs, steel pilots, pilot beams and steel running boards, millwrights, drill press men, air brake and triple valve work, upholsterer, pattern maker in car department, planing mill work, bench, coach, locomotive, tender and tank work . . . and all helpers employed in any of the classifications above mentioned, shall be eligible to membership in this Brotherhood. Providing that any person making application for membership who is not a citizen of the United States or Canada must present his or her first naturalization papers or make affidavit that he or she has applied to the proper authorities for same.

CONSTITUTION OF THE BROTHERHOOD OF LOCOMOTIVE FIREMEN AND ENGINEMEN, 1925

Article 12, Section 22. Qualification of Applicants

(a) Applicant for membership shall have served at least thirty days as a locomotive engineman, engine hostler, hostler helper, engine dispatcher, employed handling engines in or about round house or ash pit, in shop yards, locomotive works, industrial plants, motorman or helper or electric engines. . . .

(b) He shall be white born, of good moral character, sober and industrious, not less than eighteen years of age, and be able to read and write the English language and understand our Constitution. . . .[17]

CONSTITUTION OF THE COMMERCIAL TELEGRAPHERS UNION OF AMERICA, 1928

Article III, Eligibility to Membership

Section 1. Any white person who is actually employed as a commercial telegrapher, or as an operative connected with an automatic telegraph machine, and maintenance of lines, bookkeeper or clerk in the commercial telegraph service, or in the operation of a telephone, shall be eligible to membership: Provided, any commercial telegrapher, although not actually so employed is eligible to membership.

Certain unions had separate locals for blacks, among them the hotel and restaurant employees, cooks and waiters, laundry workers, barbers, textile workers, and musicians. Sometimes it was the practice of unions organized with separate locals to allow blacks to be represented only by white delegates to the councils of the union.

CONSTITUTION AND BY-LAWS OF THE BROTHERHOOD OF MAINTENANCE OF WAY EMPLOYES, 1925[18]

Article XII, Section 1, Membership. Any Maintenance of Way Employe or Railway Shop Laborer not above the rank of foreman who is sober, moral and otherwise of good character is eligible to membership in the United Brotherhood of Maintenance of Way

Employes and Railway Shop Laborers. Rights of membership of the colored Maintenance of Way Employes and Railway Shop Laborers in the United States shall be under the direct control of the System Division or System Federation. They shall be entitled to all the benefits and protection guaranteed by the constitution to its members and shall be represented in the Grand Lodge by delegates of their own choice selected from any white lodge on the System Division or System Federation where employed. Nothing in this section operates to prevent the colored employes from maintaining a separate lodge for social purposes and to receive official communications and information from the Grand Lodge and the System Division or System Federation.

CONSTITUTION AND BY-LAWS OF THE INTERNATIONAL BROTHERHOOD OF BLACKSMITHS, DROP-FORGERS AND HELPERS[19]

Article XVII.

Section 1. Where there are a sufficient number of colored helpers, they may be organized as an auxiliary local; and shall be under the jurisdiction of the white local union, having jurisdiction over that locality; and minutes of said auxiliary local must be submitted to duly authorized officers of said white local for their approval;

Section 2. In shops where there is a grievance committee of the white local, grievances of members of said auxiliary local will be handled by that committee;

Section 3. Members of auxiliary locals composed of colored helpers shall not transfer, except to another auxiliary local composed of colored members, and colored helpers will not be promoted to blacksmiths or helper apprentices; and will not be admitted to shops where white helpers are now employed; and

Section 4. Auxiliary locals will be represented in all conventions by delegates elected from the white local in that locality.

Not surprisingly, informal exclusion of blacks from unions was widely practiced. In a survey of employment opportunities in Buffalo, New York, for example, investigators found that of twenty-one unions studied, nine practiced exclusion informally. "Some are quite frank," wrote the investigator, "in admitting that they can easily find some excuse to prevent the admission of Negro workmen."[20]

The sense of frustration experienced by black workers in

dealing with unions led to strikebreaking and to the formation of separate black-led unions. Blacks often also opposed laws that restricted the power of the courts over union activities. When the Shipstead Anti-Injunction Bill was under consideration by the Senate in 1928, blacks quite logically saw little benefit to themselves in limiting the power of injunction used by the courts so effectively against organized labor in the 1920s. The following affidavit was introduced in testimony before the Senate subcommittee holding hearings on the anti-injunction bill.

AFFIDAVIT

State of Ohio,
Cuyahoga County, ss:

I, Charles E. W——, being first duly sworn, say that I reside at —— Street, Cleveland, Ohio; am 34 years old, and am an electrician by trade.

I am a colored man. When I was 16 years old I was office boy for Myron H——, and later for some of his associates who were interested in the Cleveland Electric Illuminating Co. While working as office boy I studied electricity and finally became an electrician, at which trade I have worked for the past 17 years.

The electrical work of Cleveland is done almost wholly by union men. In 1914 I applied to become a member of the Electricians Local Union in Cleveland. At that time the initiation fee was between $40 and $50. However, they demanded $100 initiation fee of me and of another colored man—Elmer B. T——. I gave the union secretary my check for $200 to cover the initiation fee of Mr. T—— and myself. The secretary handed it back to me and said I would have to see Mr. H——. I called repeatedly for the next three months at the union office and was always told that Mr. H—— was out.

I continued to work until 1916 or 1917, in which two years 25 different jobs of wiring which I had done were destroyed by cutting the wires throughout the work. Then I called on Mr. Clarence S——, business agent of the same electricians' union, and told him that I could not continue working because of the damage done to my work and asked him if he could see that a union card or permit was given to me by my joining the union. Mr. S—— said:

"Well, I might just as well tell you now that we will not take colored men in as members of the union. Our charter forbids it."

He asked me to return that evening to the executive committee meeting. The committee met behind closed doors and after waiting some time I noticed them dispersing. I went to them and repeated what I said to Mr. S——. There were present at this meeting in addition to Mr. S—— some eight or nine other members of the committee, all white men. Mr. S—— said:

"We are willing to let you and your partner, Mr. T—— continue to work if you will agree not to teach any more colored men the electrical trade."

I told him that the colored men working with us had studied in colleges outside of Cleveland and were largely men who came from outside of Cleveland, together with some who had graduated from Case School of Applied Science.

After that some more of our jobs were destroyed and I again went to Mr. S——, business agent. I told him that some more of our work had been damaged and asked him if he would permit union electricians to work for us so as to satisfy the union. He said he would bring it up before the union and I returned to him about a week later. Mr. S—— said:

"Our men won't work for a colored man."

I said, "I know some of the men who will work for us if the officers will let them work."

Mr. S—— denied this. Then I said, "Now, Mr. S——, you won't let the union men work for us and you won't take us into the union. What shall we colored electricians do?"

Mr. S—— said, "There must be some other work besides electrical work that you can find to do."

I told him that I had given so many years to studying electricity that I would not want to give up the trade.

In the following two years contractors reported to me that the business agent of the electricians union had come to them and said:

"If W—— comes here for work, don't give that nigger any work."

One of these contractors was Mr. A——, who told me that the business agent of the electricians' union had told him that if I did the electricians' work, there would be trouble. Mr. A—— then took away from me the electrical work on a nine-suite apartment house which had been previously contracted to me. A little later this same thing occurred with a contractor, Tony V——.

The same occurrences have happened time and again during the past few years. Finally, last year I was working on a contract . . . on Sandusky Avenue in Cleveland, when Mr. Fred B——, the business agent of the electricians' union, appeared on the job. Mr. B—— said:

"You have a nonunion electrician working here."

I said, "You know why I am not a union man. I can't get into the union."

Mr. B—— said, "I have not a thing to tell you, W——. I am here looking after the work to see that only union men work."

There was present . . . a contractor, who was building some houses on the same street and for whom I had work. [He] said to Mr. B——:

"Mr. W—— has explained to me that you will not take him into the union, and I have no sympathy with the union about Mr. W—— because he is a good workman."

After working a few days, I had to quit.

Immediately after that I completed the electrical wiring for a Mr. E—— in Garfield Heights, a suburb of Cleveland. The work was finished and approved by the city inspector, who placed his seal on the work. The day after it was finished there was a meeting on the job between Mr. E——, B——, the union business agent, a union electrical workman and myself. Mr. B—— said to Mr. E——:

"Mr. W—— is a non union electrician, and you must take this work out and let this union electrician do it over."

Mr. E—— said: "The work is all finished and approved by the electrical inspector of Garfield Heights."

Mr. B—— said: "It makes no difference. We will show you who is running this town. We will tie up all the rest of your jobs."

Then the union electrician tore out all the wires and did the work over. I was not paid anything for my work.

Upon a change of officers of the electricians' union in July, 1927, I asked . . . the new business agent, if I could sign up as a contractor and obtain union men. [He] sent me to [a] bonding firm . . . to secure a bond that I would pay the wages. I went to the office . . . and made my application for a bond. I signed an application showing a net worth of much in excess of the bond. Then the representative of the bonding company said:

"Before we can write the bond, we must have the approval of the Electrical Contractors' Association."

After that I was told by the bonding company that they would not write the bond, and then I discovered that the business representative of the Electrical Contractors' Association was the Mr. S——— mentioned above, a former officer and still a member of the electricians' union.

There are no colored union men in the electrician's union except one man who is so light in color that he is not suspected by the union members as being a colored man.

Through all of these affairs I have lost all of my property, consisting of my home and another piece of property which I owned and rented.[21]

With such evidence as background, Harry E. Davis, prominent black lawyer and member of the Ohio legislature from a Cleveland district, gave his testimony to the subcommittee.

STATEMENT OF HARRY E. DAVIS, ATTORNEY AT LAW AND A MEMBER OF THE HOUSE OF REPRESENTATIVES OF THE STATE OF OHIO, CLEVELAND, OHIO

MR. DAVIS. I am an attorney of Cleveland, Ohio, and I have just completed my fourth term as a member of the Legislature of Ohio, and during my last two terms it was my fortune to serve as chairman of the codes committee in the Ohio House, which occupies the same relative position in the Ohio House as the Judiciary Committee occupies in the Senate.

I appear here as a representative of the legal committee of the Cleveland branch of the National Association for the Advancement of the Colored People.

In appearing before this subcommittee in opposition to the so-called Shipstead bill, I want to make it clear that I am not primarily interested in the constitutional or legal phases of the measure nor am I at all concerned in the controversy between employers and labor unions regarding this measure. My sole interest in being here is to prevent what I believe is a gross injustice to a submerged group of people, the colored people, 12,000,000 in numbers, 95 per cent of whom are of the working classes. That is the class I want to speak for because for the most part they are inarticulate.

The bill would deny the right of equitable intervention of our courts in all cases except where tangible and transferable property was concerned. I take it that physical property is the easiest thing in the world to protect by the police power of the State.

The group I represent has not got very much physical or tangible property and their biggest asset is their right to a job, recognized as a contract, but an intangible right, and I maintain that if this bill becomes a law it would affect very materially their right to the biggest thing which they have, the right to earn a living.

I think it is a matter of common knowledge that labor unions do directly and indirectly discriminate against colored men belonging to the unions. I could pile up oceans of evidence on that if necessary. . . .

It logically follows that if the colored workers, who by the way may want to join a labor union and can't, it logically follows that a colored worker who is denied the protection and the benefits of organized labor because they will not take him in, has only one place of redress in case his right of employment is assailed, and that is in our courts, and that, in my judgment, is the inherent vice and inequity of this bill, and that is why I am here talking about it.

Colored people are not as yet aware just what this bill means to them. If they were, they would be here in greater numbers, and still will be here yet I think in greater numbers, letting you know what they think about it.

I do not want the committee to think we are conjuring up hypothetical or academic objections about this. It is a very real thing in the life of the colored workers and I want to say parenthetically I have no particular feeling one way or the other about labor unions.

If I were a craftsman or an artisan, I would join a union. I have from time to time, advised clients in my home city to join unions, just like I joined the bar association.

This is not a hypothetical objection which we are conjuring up and I want to refer to [a] case . . . [that] is typical of a great many cases which happen.

This is the case of Willis v. Local No. 106 of the Hotel and Restaurant Employees International Alliance, et al., decided July 2, 1927.

The syllabus reads: "Injunction lies against the boycott of an eating place by a branch of the Hotel and Restaurant Employees International Alliance, where the sole ground of the boycott is that the place is employing colored help, and it appears that the application of these colored employees for a charter for a Waiters and Restaurant Employees [local] has been denied on racial grounds."

And the opinion by Judge Irving Carpenter reads as follows:

"This is an action seeking an injunction to restrain the defendants from picketing plaintiff's place of business, a country roadhouse, with from three to five automobiles in the highway in front, all bearing banners saying that plaintiff's place is 'unfair to organized labor.'

"The admitted and undisputed facts reveal a very unusual situation. It differs in several respects from most cases of this character.

"Plaintiff's property is located in the village of Valley View, one of the numerous suburban municipalities in this county, and is 11 miles from the Cleveland Public Square. . . .

"Plaintiff's property consists of about 3 acres of land on which is located a building used by the plaintiff and his family the year around as a residence and a large restaurant, capable of serving 275 to 300 guests at once. The business is only operated in the summer and during the mild weather of spring and fall. The week-day patronage is very small, and some evenings of the week slight. Saturday night and Sunday and holidays are the only time business is brisk.

"Plaintiff began the business four years ago last spring, and since then has purchased the property paying for it, he says, $18,000 and since has made some improvements and additions to it.

"The first three years of plaintiff's operation of the place he employed union waiters and cooks exclusively, but he says, that owing to the distance of the place from the city of Cleveland and his intermittant and irregular demand for such help that the union waiters and cooks were dissatisfied and did not render service satisfactory to plaintiff or his patrons. Hence a year ago last spring he did not employ union help, but instead hired nonunion colored waiters and cooks. He paid them the same scale of wage as fixed by the union, and the conditions under which they were required to work conformed to the union standard in every respect. He employs four regular waiters and five extras who only come on special occasions when crowds are expected. The number of cooks employed are not shown by the evidence, but from the number of waiters it can be inferred it is not large.

"Last year the union said nothing to him about his employees, and at the beginning of this season, by verbal contracts, he reemployed substantially the same group of colored waiters and cooks for this reason. About two days before he planned to reopen his place, the first part of last April, defendant Edward W——, business agent of defendant Local No. 106, the Waiters Union, and Martin S——, the vice president of that local, called upon him and demanded of him that he employ white help and members of their union. He told them they were too late, that he had already reemployed his help of last season, that it had been satisfactory, and that the union help in years before had not been. They told him he might take his choice of any of their unemployed members. This he refused under the circumstances, and they told him they would 'give him a battle.'

"Some time later they began the picketing by the use of automobiles upon the road in front of his place at the times when his customers would be going there, particularly Saturday nights. The automobiles bore on the back thereof large cloth banners which said in large letters in substance that 'Will's Terrace Garden is unfair to organized labor,' and was signed by the initials of the union. There is some dispute about the conduct of the drivers of the automobiles and the persons riding with them.

"In all about 25 men and women, all members of the defendant unions or their wives, participated in driving or riding in these automobiles.

"After this agitation started, at the request of plaintiff, two of his colored employees went to Cincinnati, to the international headquarters of the union, and saw the secretary of the supreme body, and asked if a charter for a colored local for Cleveland could be granted to them and other colored waiters there. He told them to see defendant W——, and if he would consent to it the charter might be arranged, but not unless approved by W——. They saw Mr. W—— and he told them 'Nothing doing,' and their efforts to form a union ceased. It should be added that the constitution of defendant Local No. 106 restricts its membership to white persons.

"At this length these facts have been here stated, and from them it appears that there existed no real trade dispute; both the employer and his employees are satisfied with each other, the standards of the union, both as to wages and working conditions, are being observed.

"The employees wanted to affiliate with the union and the employer wanted them to, and they went to no little trouble trying to do so, and were refused by these defendants solely because of their race.

"This court recognized the very well established rights of union labor under certain conditions to inform the public of the fact that an employer does not employ union labor, and the employer who chooses not to do so can not complain if such information causes loss to his business. There are many precedents, in Ohio and elsewhere, supporting this proposition. . . . The ideal of all union efforts is and must be the improvement of the social and economic conditions of those who work, and the law seeks to protect the union in the fair accomplishment of such ideal.

"The boycott does not appeal to this court of equity as conforming to this standard. In its last analysis it is a case of white men opposing colored men. As this court sees it the only information these defendants could properly and truthfully give the public about plaintiff is that he employs colored people, and I do not believe these defendants care to advertise that fact as such. . . .

"The motive prompting this attack on the plaintiff under these circumstances can not be justified by this court. . . .

"This court feels that under all these circumstances justice requires that the temporary restraining order prayed for be granted. . . ."

This is a typical case, your honor. We are not trying to conjure up anything hypothetical or academic. We are not trying to construct this thing out of thin air or ether. This is what is actually going on in the city where I was born and raised, not in a section where it might be attributed to local prejudice or conditions. I challenge anybody to justify the attitude of that labor union. It is impossible to conceive of anything more inequitable, unjust, arrogant or unfair than the attitude of that labor union. This is only one case, and I am citing it because it is typical.

I can pile them up, I believe, if this committee cared to hear them.

Colored workers want just as good wages and just as good working conditions as anybody else. Don't let anybody think colored labor is cheap labor. They are just as much interested in getting the best out of life as anybody else and are striving toward that end daily and they want that right protected and they are willing to join unions to secure that protection but in so many of the unions that we can almost call it a rule they are unfair to colored men. There are isolated cases where unions do admit colored men and some cases where they are treated fairly and with no difficulty over racial disputes. I think the Longshoremen's Union is principally the fairest in the country in that respect. Colored and white men work together and socialize together to some extent and they allow no race prejudice to get in there. It has been attempted but they will not listen to it, and absolute harmony prevails and colored men would be good union men if they would let them be and while this action which I have mentioned was started by the employer, yet I think you will all agree with me that any one of these aggrieved colored waiters could have taken the same action. I want it kept in mind all through that if this bill passes the Federal Congress, it will become a model and a pattern for State legislation all over the country and within 10 years every State in the Union will have substantially the same law.

What position is a colored worker in, willing to join a union, and he can not, and yet they say to an employer, "You can not hire these colored men because they are not union men," and they say to the colored men, "You can not work because you are not a union man"? What is he going to do? Does anyone mean to tell me the strong legislative arm of the United States Government is going to lend sanction to a bill which will take from a man the only remedy or redress which they could have under such circumstances, the right to appeal to a court to protect their right to work, and my protest is brought on behalf of that submerged group who have no one to appeal to, who do not get the protection or benefits of organized labor and as a last resort must come to our courts.

Courts are primarily intended for the protection of minorities. Majorities are not oppressed, but minorities may be, and these courts of equity which have grown up with a background of thousands of years are here to protect minorities and to protect the submerged group of 12,000,000 colored people who have no protections, strength or power, and can not get in the union, and it seems to me absolutely unjust for Congress to even think of passing a law which would deny their only appeal, an appeal to the courts for their redress. I thank you.[22]

Recognizing a seemingly logical potential alliance between black workers and organized labor, the National Association for the Advancement of Colored People at its 1924 Annual Conference appealed for cooperation on the basis of mutual advantage.

OPEN LETTER TO THE AMERICAN FEDERATION OF LABOR, THE
RAILWAY BROTHERHOODS, AND OTHER GROUPS OF
ORGANIZED LABOR

For many years the American negro has been demanding admittance to the ranks of union labor.

For many years your organizations have made public profession of your interest in negro labor, of your desire to have it unionized, and of your hatred of the black "scab."

Notwithstanding this apparent surface agreement, negro labor in the main is outside the ranks of organized labor, and the reason is first, that white union labor does not want black labor and secondly, black labor has ceased to beg admittance to union ranks because of its increasing value and efficiency outside the unions.

We thus face a crisis in interracial labor conditions; the continued and determined race prejudice of white labor, together with the limitation of immigration, is giving black labor tremendous advantage. The negro is entering the ranks of semiskilled and skilled labor and he is entering mainly and necessarily as a "scab." He broke the great steel strike. He will soon be in a position to break any strike when he can gain economic advantage for himself.

On the other hand, intelligent negroes know full well that a blow at organized labor is a blow at all labor; that black labor to-day profits by the blood and sweat of labor leaders in the past who have fought oppression and monopoly by organization. If there is built up in America a great black block of nonunion laborers who have a right to hate unions, all laborers, black and white, eventually must suffer.

Is it not time, then, that black and white labor get together? Is it not time for white unions to stop bluffing and for black laborers to stop cutting off their noses to spite their faces?

We, therefore, propose that there be formed by the National Association for the Advancement of Colored People, the American Federation of Labor, the Railway Brotherhoods and any other bodies agreed upon, an interracial labor commission.

We propose that this commission undertake:

1. To find out the exact attitude and practice of national labor bodies and local unions toward negroes and of negro labor toward unions.

2. To organize systematic propaganda against racial discrimination on the basis of these facts at the great labor meetings, in local assemblies and in local unions.

The National Association for the Advancement of Colored People stands ready to take part in such a movement and hereby invites the cooperation of all organized labor. The association hereby solemnly warns American laborers that unless some such step as this is taken and taken soon, the position gained by organized labor in this country is threatened with irreparable loss.[23]

Strikebreaking

Appeals like that of the NAACP were hardly sufficient to alter very much the life of the black worker. With union membership on the decline in the 1920s, economic factors joined racial antipathy to keep the union door closed except where black workers were of great numerical significance in an industry. Sometimes blacks formed separate organizations, such as the short-lived American Negro Labor Congress, or the Brotherhood of Sleeping Car Porters which, despite a shaky beginning, grew to become a major union in the transportation industry.[24] Often, however, union hostility to black workers led to an increase in strikebreaking among Negroes. William Z. Foster, radical labor organizer and a leader of the 1919 steel strike, estimated that thirty or forty thousand black strikebreakers entered the steel mills during the great strike of 1919, contributing to its failure.[25] At the end of the strike, those who had been taken on as scabs lost their places. Those blacks who had been employed before and who had remained at work in the better jobs of the men who struck were returned to their old places when the strike ended.[26]

Black strikebreakers were used in the coal strike in Pennsylvania in 1927-28 and in the longshore strike in Boston in 1929, and elsewhere as well, but the number of black strikebreakers is perhaps not so important as their visibility and the hostility they aroused among white workers. Among Negroes, to scab or not to scab was a source of controversy. Claude McKay, in his naturalistic novel, *Home to Harlem*, had his characters confront the issue.

One week when they were not working, Zeddy came to Jake with wonderful news. Men were wanted at a certain pier to unload pineapples at eight dollars a day. Eight dollars was exceptional wages, but the fruit was spoiling.

Jake went with Zeddy and worked the first day with a group of Negroes and a few white men. The white men were not regular dock workers. The only thing that seemed strange to Jake was that all the men ate inside and were not allowed outside the gates for lunch. But, on the second day, his primitive passion for going against regulation urged him to go out in the street after lunch.

Heaving casually along West Street, he was hailed by a white man. "Hello, fellow-worker!"

"Hello, there! What's up?" Jake asked.

"You working in there?"

"Sure I is. Since yestidday."

The man told Jake that there was a strike on and he was scabbing. Jake asked him why there were no pickets if there was a strike. The man replied that there were no pickets because the union leaders were against the strike, and had connived with the police to beat up and jail the pickets.

"Well, pardner," Jake said, "I've done worked through a tur'ble assortaments o' jobs in mah lifetime, but I ain't nevah yet scabbed it on any man. I done work in this heah country, and I works good and hard over in France. I works in London and I nevah was a blackleg, although I been the only black man in mah gang."

"Fine, fellow-worker; that's a real man's talk," said the white man. He took a little red book out of his pocket and asked Jake to let him sign him up in his union.

"It's the only one in the country for a red-blooded worker, no matter what race or nation he belongs to."

"Nope, I won't scab, but I ain't a joiner kind of a fellah," said Jake. "I ain't no white folks' nigger and I ain't no poah white's fool. When I longshored in Philly I was a good union man. But when I made New York I done finds out that they gived the colored mens the worser piers and holds the bes'n a' them foh the Irishmen. No, pardner, keep you' card. I take the best I k'n get as I goes mah way. But I tells you, things ain't none at all lovely between white and black in this heah Gawd's own country."

"We take all men in our union regardless." But Jake was haunching along out of hearing down West Street. . . . Suddenly he heard sharp, deep, distressful grunts, and saw behind some barrels a black man down and being kicked perilously in the rear end by two white men. Jack drew his hook from his belt and, waving it in the air, he rushed them. The white men shot like rats to cover. The down man scrambled to his feet. One of Zeddy's pals, Jake recognized him.

"What's the matter, buddy, the peckawoods them was doing you in?"

"Becaz they said there was a strike in theah. And I said I didn't

give a doughnut, I was going to work foh mah money all the same.
I got one o' them gif! in the eye, though. . . ."

"Don't go back, buddy. Let the boss-men stick them jobs up.
They are a bunch of rotten aigs. Just using us to do their dirty work.
Come on, let's haul bottom away from here to Harlem."

At Dixie Red's pool-room that evening there were some fellows
with bandaged arms and heads. One iron-heavy, blue-black lad
(he was called Liver-lip behind his back, because of the plankiness
of his lips) carried his arm in a sling, and told Jake how he happened to be like that.

"They done jumped on me soon as I turned mah black moon on
that li'l saloon tha's catering to us niggers. Heabenly God! But if
the stars them didn't twinkle way down in mah eyes. But easy, easy,
old man, I got out mah shaving steel and draws it down the goosey
flesh o' one o' them, and, buddy, you shoulda heah him squeal. . . .
The pohlice?" His massive mouth molded the words to its own
form. "They tooks me, yes, but tunned me loose by'n'by. They's
with us this time, boh, but, Lawdy! if they hadn't did entervention
I woulda gutted gizzard and kidney outa that white tripe."

Jake was angry with Zeddy and asked him, when he came in,
why he had not told him at first that the job was a scab job.

"I won't scab on nobody, not even the orneriest crackers," he
said.

"Bull Durham!" cried Zeddy. "What was I going to let on about
anything for? The boss-man done paid me to git him mens, and I
got them. Ain't I working there mahself? I'll take any job in this
heah Gawd's country that the white boss make it worf mah while
to work at."

"But it ain't decent to scab," said Jake.

"Decent mah black moon!" shouted Zeddy. "I'll scab through
hell to make mah living. Scab job or open shop or union am all the
same jobs to me. White mens don't want niggers in them unions,
nohow. Ain't you a good carpenter? And ain't I a good blacksmith?
But kain we get a look-in on our trade heah in this white man's
city? Ain't white mens done scabbed niggers outa all the jobs they
useter hold down heah in this city? Waiter, bootblack, and barber
shop?"

"With all a that scabbing is a low-down deal," Jake maintained.

"Me eye! Seems lak youse gettin' religion, boh. Youse talking
death, tha's what you sure is. One thing I know is niggers am made
foh life. And I want to live, boh, and feel plenty o' the juice o' life

in mah blood. I wanta live and I wanta love. And niggers am got to work hard foh that. Buddy, I'll tell you this and I'll tell it to the wo'l'—all the crackers, all them poah white trash, all the nigger-hitting and nigger-breaking white folks—I loves life and I got to live and I'll scab through hell to live."

Jake did not work again that week. . . .[27]

The Job Ceiling

When the black worker did find work, and when he did succeed in gaining some desirable skill if he had not one already, he was faced with breaking through the job ceiling that did not exist for whites. In their survey of employment conditions in Buffalo, New York, investigators offered the somewhat plaintive opinion that "there must have been *some* Negroes employed in these various establishments capable of rising to the rank of foremen, and more than a scant handful able to do skilled labor."[28]

Evidence of the existence of a job ceiling was not restricted to Buffalo. In 1930, for example, a vice-president of the Metropolitan Life Insurance Company, which employed blacks as menials, wrote that it was "inadvisable to include colored people" as employees in the company's offices because anticipated objections by white employees "would result in an uncomfortable situation for both white and colored employees."[29] The following report reprinted from the Railway Mail Association's journal typifies the situation facing many Negro employees throughout the nation.

ILLINOIS BRANCH, SIXTH DIVISION

At regular session of the Illinois Branch, Sixth Division, Railway Mail Association, held at the Hotel Sherman on the evening of January 28, 1929, the following resolution was unanimously adopted by the Branch:

Resolution

WHEREAS a colored clerk in charge has been appointed in the Chicago, Ill., Terminal R[ailway] P[ost] O[ffice] and

WHEREAS said clerk in charge has direct supervision over 33 clerks of Caucasian birth;

WHEREAS this does not create harmonious relations between

clerks and clerks in charge, nor would it in any other case similar in character, nor can the best interests of the service be attained under such conditions; and

WHEREAS we believe that no colored clerk in charge can supervise the work of clerks of Caucasian birth to the best advantage, nor to the best welfare of the employes:

Therefore be it

Resolved, That the Illinois Branch, Sixth Division, R. M. A., in regular session assembled, vigorously protests this assignment, or any future assignment of a clerk in charge who will have direct supervision over a crew any of whom are of Caucasian birth; and be it further

Resolved, That a copy of this resolution be spread upon the minutes of this Branch of the Railway Mail Association, a copy sent to each Branch of the Railway Mail Association, a copy sent to each Division President of the Railway Main Association, a copy sent to each of the National Officers of the Railway Mail Association, a copy to each clerk in charge of a Terminal R.P.O. in the United States, a copy to THE RAILWAY POST OFFICE for publication, and a copy to each of our Representatives in Congress from the States of Illinois, Iowa, Indiana, and Wisconsin. B. E. Bachmann, Secretary, Illinois Branch, Sixth Div., R.M.A.[30]

The Black Businessman

Although by far the greater number of Negroes in urban America were employed by Caucasians in the 1920s, black businessmen in black enterprises were becoming increasingly important. From 1888 to 1934, for example, 134 banks were organized by blacks. The greatest increase in banking resources took place in the decade 1918-29, with total resources reaching nearly $13 million in 1926.[31] Aside from the lack of a strong entrepreneurial tradition, black businessmen were hampered by difficulties in securing credit and, despite their growth, black banking remained a pygmy in the shadow of white banking. Nevertheless, despite a proverbial belief held by whites that Negroes lack business and managerial ability, black businessmen were to be found most often engaged in financial enterprises, such as banking and insurance, amusement enterprises, real estate, retail trade, and personal service, the last having the largest number of concerns.[32]

The entering wedge for a black businessman was often the failure of Caucasians to exploit a potentially profitable area. Consider the following account of the Black Swan Record Company of New York.

THE MAKING OF PHONOGRAPH RECORDS OF NEGRO VOICES
By Mr. H. H. Pace of the Pace Phonograph Company

The making of Phonograph Records is so unusual and so wide a departure from the beaten paths of Negro business that many people who are accustomed to unusual things were startled when the project was first announced.

To those of us who have been connected with the business side of Negro music, the need for such a company has been apparent for a long time. Although Negroes throughout the country are owners of phonographs and talking machines in large numbers, and although we are heavy buyers of phonograph records of every description, yet none of the larger companies making records have appreciated the Negro patronage it received sufficiently to permit Negro voices to make records for them. This too, despite the fact that 65 per cent of one Company's Southern business has been colored people.

For many years Bert Williams has made records for the Columbia Company, but it was only after an overwhelming demand on the part of the public for his records that the Company took him on, and at first at very meager pay. Now he is one of their biggest assets and colored people are among the heaviest buyers of his records.

Last year a small company, after repeated efforts on my part to persuade them, took up a colored girl to sing Blues. They did not believe in her nor the kind of records she put out. But within six months Mamie Smith became the biggest hit the Okeh ever had and made them more money than any other Artist ever made them in the same time. The biggest buyers of her records were our people who appreciated the recognition of one of our own.

Afterwards every other company wanted a colored girl to sing Blues, but they did not want nor would they accept singers who could do any other class of music. Personally, I attempted to persuade some of the managers that there were wonderful Negro voices that were superior to many of the so-called artists they were featuring but I was advised that "prejudice of the white people in this country would not admit the Negroes singing anything else than ragtime, comic songs or Blues." "It would ruin their business to have a colored person record high class music," etc., etc.

Then I decided to start a company that would permit Negroes to do the same kind of recording and singing that white men and women were doing, believing that there are enough of us in this country who want to preserve the best voices and musical talent among us to make it pay. I, therefore, spent several hundred dollars experimenting until I was absolutely convinced that Negroes could make any kind of a record white men and foreigners could make. I experimented with singers who could sing grand opera and Spirituals, and popular songs and Blues and I picked out of hundreds of voices the most capable ones I could find.

When I announced my plans in the newspapers it brought two results. Hundreds of our people from everywhere wrote and wired me commending the step and assuring me of their desire to purchase the records. Hundreds of dealers, more white than colored, wrote and telegraphed for agencies and several actually came to New York in person from as far away as Virginia to secure their agencies in person.

On the other hand I incurred the great displeasure of the white companies making records, who thought and so expressed themselves that no Negro had any business going into any occupation like this. Because I was connected with the music publishing house of Pace and Handy, and music publishers depend for their largest income on phonograph records and piano rolls, that concern was threatened that it would be cut off the lists and no more records made of music published if I did not desist. Instead of desisting, I determined to go ahead with the recording and making of records and resigned the presidency of Pace and Handy.

I was determined that the kind of records we were determined to make should be made, and after all sorts of obstacles and delays which were placed in my way, including the purchase of a pressing plant by a large company to keep me from getting out records there, I was enabled early in May to place on the market the first records ever sung, played, recorded and manufactured by colored people.

The business has been established first as a business proposition operated on safe sound business principles and dedicated to the proposition that it must return a reasonable dividend to its owners.

In the second place, it is dedicated to racial service along a new line. And it might as well be stated that no institution deserves to succeed that has for its object merely the making of money. A very prominent man of the race wrote me in the early days of its conception as follows: "The more I think over your scheme of phonograph records of colored artists, the more I am convinced that it is a great and feasible undertaking. It fulfills two indispensable considerations. First, it is a great social service for the race and its art. Secondly it is a good business proposition."

We have accepted the task of developing the possibility of making records of our artists on that basis and we believe that the ultimate success of the concern will be beyond the fondest dreams of those who helped to establish it.

I found in the beginning that the rank and file of our race were not awake to the discrimination that has been practiced by the phonograph companies. People who were otherwise well versed in all things pertaining to music were under the impression that we were given chances commensurate with our abilities. Some told me of various singers who had recorded for the white companies and insisted that I was wrong when I stated that colored artists were not accepted on the same basis as other singers and players unless they sang "Blues" or comic songs. They told me of Roland Hayes' records for the Columbia and Pattie Brown's records, and thought there were others I did not know. But the truth is they did not know the difference I was calling attention to, and that is that when Caruso sang for the Victor Company he got paid and when Roland Hayes and Pattie Brown sang for the Columbia Company, they had to pay for the privilege. Surely there is quite a difference between getting paid for singing and having to pay somebody to sing. . . .

Naturally I protested against such unfair practices as I observed, and when I saw that some of these things could be overcome and the colored artist given a fair chance and at the same time that it would pay, I started the manufacture of BLACK SWAN RECORDS.

In the four months that we have been issuing records we have created a demand that has surprised our white competitors, and we have sold more records in a dull season of depression than some white companies have sold in prosperous times, with a steadily growing sale amounting now to over 1,200 records daily. We sold of one Blues record alone in less than thirty days over 18,000 records. During October we will have ready for sale and shipment, a new and modern phonograph which we shall begin to market under the trade name of "Swanola" which will play all records, as our records now can be played on all machines.

Every dollar of the capital stock of the Company has been subscribed for and nearly all paid in, and there is no more stock for sale. We have issued twelve records, six of them standard high class numbers, three of the popular type and three Blues. We have had to give the people what many of them wanted in order to get them to buy what we wanted them to want. While our sales have naturally been larger for the last two kinds of records, it has been extremely gratifying to us the way the public has received and bought the records of Revella Hughes and Carroll Clark to whom we have given nation-wide prominence. This month we have added to our list of artists two tenors of exceptional promise in Harry A. Delmore of Boston and J. Arthur Gaines of New York. We expect in the near future to release instrumental records from other artists and to continue our lists of vocal artists to take in many others we have been unable to reach. In fact, we plan to open the doors of voice reproduction to every artist without regard to the question of whether his grandfather could vote. . . .

Already our success has been the cause of every white Company adding at least one colored singer of the Blues type to their list, and one company has even issued a Jim Crow catalogue of specially selected "Blues" for the "Colored trade" as they express it. If they have gone this far in three months, surely, if we continue as we have done, there must be some permanent effect on the musical art of the race. . . .

I could make more money if I subscribed to the theory that Negroes want only one kind of music. But I believe that we want every kind of music that other people want, and if we do not want it, we ought to want it, and it behooves some of us to undertake the job of elevating the musical taste of the race. And in keeping with this work, BLACK SWAN RECORDS are trying to do their part.[33]

Black businessmen organized for mutual benefit into such groups as the Associated Negro Press, the National Bankers Association, the National Negro Insurance Association, and the National Negro Business League. The last, a federation of state and local business leagues, observed its twenty-fifth anniversary with a speech both retrospective and prospective by its president, Robert R. Moton.

. . . Twenty-five years ago Booker T. Washington, whose name we delight to honor and whose memory we deeply revere, called together at Boston a group of business and professional men and women with a view of devising ways and means by which they could fix attention not less on the moral and intellectual development of the Negro race, but at the same time on the importance and absolute necessity for greater business progress.

There was organized at that meeting the National Negro Business League.

In and out of season, sprang [sparing] neither time, means nor energy, the great Founder of this organization with his prophetic vision preached the gospel of business development for the Negro people as a fundamental necessity to their general development. His great personality drew to his aid always many of the leading spirits of the races. The inspiration and impetus which he gave to business development and the results that have been accomplished in the years following cannot be adequately measured. The change and progress that have come to the race during these years is marvelous, possibly beyond the dreams of the most sanguine well wishers, within as well as without the race.

We meet now in the great metropolis of the Middle West in our Twenty-fifth Annual Meeting, our "Silver Jubilee." For sixteen years the Founder and President of this organization, with consummate tact and wisdom, indomitable force and courage, sought to overcome what seemed almost an obsession with our people — business fear and timidity; a lack of faith and courage to go into business. In large measure as individuals, and even more so in groups, partnerships, and other corporate efforts, we have very largely overcome this timidity. The need for the present, therefore, is not to overcome timidity and lack of courage as such, but to stress the need for honest, capable, expert management as a basis for credit and a warrant of confidence on the part of the business world in the ability and the competency of the American Negro to handle financial and commercial affairs, corporate and otherwise, in a thorough-going, genuinely efficient, business-like fashion.

In the future we should give no less attention to the inspirational aspect of business development, but we should also, if we are true to the ideals and aspirations of Booker Washington, emphasize more the business efficiency aspect, and share more largely and effectively in the financial affairs of the nation, especially as touching and affecting our group; for whatever affects in a business way one group of American citizens must of necessity affect other groups.

There is no need today for discouragement; rather there is every reason for hopefulness from whatever angle we may view our situation, notwithstanding the back currents and eddies in our political and social progress. The Business League has had a very large share in the astounding progress that the race has made. Let me give a few concrete examples of this progress. When the League was organized twenty-five years ago, there were in existence about 20,000 Negro business enterprises, little and big; now there are quite 70,000. Twenty-five years ago, there were 250 drug stores; there are today over 900. Then 450 undertaking establishments were conducted by Negroes; there are 1558 today. When the League was organized there were but two banks, now there are 74. We boasted, and properly, twenty-five years ago, of 10,000 retail merchants; we can boast today of 25,000. [34] In 1900 we paid taxes on property valued at three hundred million dollars; our realty holdings alone today are worth one billion seven hundred million dollars, and if we should add the value of church property and educational institutions owned and operated by the race and for the race, and the progress in education in all of its phases, including music, art, and literature, we can properly say as the prophet of old, with the profoundest reverence and thankfulness, "What Hath God Wrought!"

Then, it is entirely fitting that we should hold our twenty-fifth session, our "Silver Jubilee," here in Chicago, a city which I have been told was founded by a Negro [35]; this much is certain, the first home on this spot was erected by a member of our race. One cannot view the great industrial plant of James S. Kirk and Company, which marks the location of the first home in Chicago, without thinking of what Chicago owes to the Negro. And some of us who live in other parts of the country are inclined to think that the Negro, too, owes something to Chicago, for in this city the progress of the race does not suffer in comparison with any other city in the country, with its multifarious business enterprises, with two great banking institutions — the Binga State Bank, and the Douglass National Bank — owned and operated by our people; the Liberty Life and other successful insurance companies, with taxicab companies, not to mention the great printing establishment of Mr. R. S. Abbott and the Chicago Defender, the headquarters of the Associated Negro Press, with scores of successful professional men and women, and the unnumbered beautiful Christian homes.

We should and do rejoice that, in spite of difficulties, in spite of injustice here and there, in spite of discrimination, nowhere in the world has the Negro made so much progress along so many lines, on so large a scale as is the case of the United States of America — our United States of America, the country which we love and for which we have fought and bled and died, and for which we would even now give our lives if need be. . . .

We have been all too long placed in the category of the five foolish virgins who slumbered and slept, and when the bridegroom came, tried to borrow oil but could not, and the door was shut in their faces. We must, with all earnestness and sincerity in the future by intelligent industry and thrift, by rigid economy and by careful, confident cooperation, place ourselves in the class of the five wise virgins who had oil in their lamps, who at the night time were able to go to them that sold and buy for themselves and thus were ready to go into the marriage feast. This we can do if we awake to our opportunities.

Let us see what the possibilities are. It is conservatively estimated that there are twenty million dollars of Negro money hidden under mattresses, behind bricks in the arch, buried in earthen jars, and in other ways hidden around the home. I know of one family where the wife and children knew that the father had at least six thousand dollars. He was taken ill and went out one night, telling his wife he was going to hide it. They had good reason to believe he had a good deal more hidden away somewhere. He died the next day; and though they scoured the place inside and out, they were never able to locate that money.

It is also estimated conservatively that Negroes have in banks not owned or operated by colored people, between seventy and a hundred million dollars. Upon a great deal of this they draw no interest, it not being in the savings account. Suppose half of this money were deposited in Negro institutions, what a big difference it would make in furnishing employment to Negro boys and girls. This would mean no loss to white institutions because most of our own banks, for obvious reasons, carry large accounts in white banks. . . .

Now if the League along with all the other organizations of the Negro in the country, including churches, Sunday schools, secret and benevolent societies and the like could set up a continuous joint campaign, say for five years, a crusade, as it were, with a view to getting the race to save, not the entire amount, that would be impossible, — but without curtailing in any appreciable degree our pleasures and recreations, to set aside an aggregate of ten per cent of the amount we spend for luxuries which would total at least $100,000,000 — think what it would mean to our financial and commercial standing in the nation. Two percent of that total, if combined in a strong, well conducted financial organization would make it impossible for any worthy business enterprise among our group to fail, and at the same time would create a business confidence and support, in fact a financial credit, which would not only mean greater prosperity for business organizations, but the churches and educational institutions as well would enter upon an era of prosperity, the like of which has never before been witnessed by any single group in this country.

Our speakers are accustomed to saying, and I think rightly, that the Negro can do what any other group in America can do if given a chance. His accomplishments here seem to justify that. There is a Jewish relief organization, with headquarters in New York that in the past twenty years has accomplished what would appear to the casual observer to be startling results by the combining of small sums in a partnership. The Chinese have done the same thing by what is known as the Chinese Six Society. Six years ago, Dr. Frederick C. Howe, former Commissioner of Immigration, a most competent writer and investigator and a most successful organizer, who knows banks and banking and has no superior in the knowledge of real cooperation, whom we are expecting for this session, was asked to organize for the Federation of Labor a cooperative banking institution, not with a view to making money for the organization as such, but with a view to helping labor along lines of thrift and the pooling of their interests for benefit primarily of their own group. He did so and out of that bank, which Mr. Howe organized six years ago in Cleveland, the Federation of Labor today has developed fifty banks, scattered all over the country with combined assets of over a million dollars. Can we do the same? We have the money in our race to do it, and friends, we have the ability within our race to do it. . . .

Sentiment is necessary and valuable, and we must have sentiment in this movement, but sentiment must not control the movement. We must place at the disposal of local business organizations expert advice and counsel as well as financial assistance when the conditions warrant it. We must help in cooperative buying and selling, in up to date methods of bookkeeping and inventories; in

neat, orderly, attractive places of business and courteous service.
We must take away from Negro business enterprises the all too
characteristic ear marks of shiftlessness, disorder, discourtesy,
uncertain weight, unbusiness-like as well as unethical methods of
dealing with customers. In other words, we must, in business par-
lance, sell the Negro merchant to his own race as well as to other
races.

We need also to establish a central bureau from which may be
sent the latest information regarding Negro business and corporations, a sort of clearing house of helpful information on worth-
while enterprises. . . .

The time is rapidly approaching when all of us, wherever we are,
whatever our social or educational status, whatever our profession
or business, and whatever may be our differences of opinion, must
in a larger measure than ever before sing [sink] personal differences and prejudices and stand together, work together, strive
together, that our race shall have an equal share in all the bless-
ings and privileges of American civilization without regard to creed
or condition or habit, and having secured these privileges, we must
together use them unselfishly for the good of our race and our
glorious country and to the glory of God, so that all may fully share
in that "far-off divine event to which the whole creation moves." [36]

Mr. Moton's remarks, the *Minutes* reveal, were greeted
with "a whirl of applause." Heir to Booker T. Washington
in both the principalship of Tuskegee Institute and the presidency of the NNBL, Moton was also heir to what Abram
Harris has called Washington's "optimistic naïveté." To
deny that Negro business had made great strides would be
both foolish and incorrect; but Moton's vision of the power of
the black purse must be set alongside some depressing
statistics. Total receipts for the NNBL for the fiscal period
August 15, 1923, to August 1, 1924, were $2,080.84. [37]

A 1928 survey of the 1,534 black retail businesses in thirty-
three large cities found that 15.8 percent did an annual gross
business of less than $2,000.00 and 63.2 percent less than
$10,000.00. Only 8.9 percent showed an annual gross busi-
ness of $25,000.00. And on the average only 3.9 persons were
employed in each establishment. [38] In 1930, the Department
of Commerce reported 28,243 Negro retail stores employing

12,561 persons with an annual payroll of $8,523,306. At the same time there were 6,432 Oriental store owners employing 8,916 persons with an annual payroll of $9,253,000.[39]

One must surely applaud Robert Moton's hopes, but the black middle class was minuscule, and the black working class faced enormous obstacles.

BRASS SPITTOONS

Langston Hughes was able to capture in a number of his poems some of the feeling of the black man at the bottom of the economic ladder. For such a man the way up often did not exist, or, as black sociologist Charles S. Johnson once put it, "Once a porter, barring the phenomenal, always a porter."[40] The following poem is a view from the bottom.

BRASS SPITTOONS

Clean the spittoons, boy.
   Detroit,
   Chicago,
   Atlantic City,
   Palm Beach.
Clean the spittoons.
The steam in hotel kitchens,
And the smoke in hotel lobbies,
And the slime in hotel spittoons:
Part of my life.
   Hey, boy!
   A nickel,
   A dime,
   A dollar,
Two dollars a day.
   Hey, boy!
   A nickel,
   A dime,
   A dollar,
   Two dollars
Buys shoes for the baby.
House rent to pay.

Gin on Saturday,
Church on Sunday.
   My God!
Babies and gin and church
and women and Sunday
all mixed up with dimes and
dollars and clean spittoons
and house rent to pay.
   Hey, boy!
A bright bowl of brass is beautiful to the Lord.
Bright polished brass like the cymbals
Of King David's dancers,
Like the wine cups of Solomon.
   Hey, boy!
A clean spittoon on the altar of the Lord.
A clean bright spittoon all newly polished, —
At least I can offer that.
   Com' mere, boy! [41]

4

View Across the Color Line: White

Although racial demographic patterns in the United States changed significantly as a result of the black migration during World War I and after, vast numbers of white Americans had little personal contact with blacks. Many whites still lived in smaller cities and towns with negligible black populations. Even in centers with a large black population, restrictive employment patterns and residential segregation, not to mention the American tradition of racial separateness, were effective barriers preventing significant interracial contacts for a great many whites. The situation was quite otherwise for most blacks, who, as members of a minority group with relatively little power, were confronted on every hand with white employers, white landlords, white shop owners, white policemen, and white city officials.

For many white Americans, then, a significant ingredient in their mental conception of a black American was the product of what they learned about blacks from secondary sources: newspapers, magazines, radio, moving pictures, and other whites. Even for whites who lived or worked near blacks, widespread social intercourse was not common; for these whites also popular media were the significant sources of information about blacks.

Under these circumstances what is arresting about white attitudes toward blacks is not that they were so often hostile or indifferently contemptuous, but that there were some who raised their voices in protest against that hostility and that contempt. Sometimes these protesting voices were those of independent thinkers who saw racism as a pernicious evil, inhumane, unfair, and detrimental to the public good.[1] Sometimes they were the voices of aldermen, mayors, and congressional representatives, politicians dependent upon constituencies with a growing number of black voters.[2] Sometimes they were the voices of reformers who set themselves against many of the inequities and wrongs in American life,[3] and sometimes they were those of religious leaders who deplored all that was iniquitous or uncharitable.[4]

At the other extreme from the protesters against racial injustice were its perpetuators, those who doted on white supremacy and black subservience. Often enough, the spokesmen for white supremacy were also spokesmen for Anglo-Saxon superiority, heaping their contumely on Catholic southern and eastern Europeans and on Jews as well as on Negroes.[5] The best-known organization devoted to the dubious cause of white Anglo-Saxon superiority in the 1920s was, of course, the Ku Klux Klan,[6] an organization that had somewhat less than one and a half million active members at its high point, an organization strong not only in the small towns and villages of America but in the large cities of the North as well.[7] The great mass of white Americans, however, including many of the Klansmen, were passive recipients of the idea of white supremacy carried by the movies and radio, in which blacks were so often portrayed as lazy, shiftless, good humored, stupid, and childlike, that is, when they were not ruffians lusting after white women.[8]

Black criminality was a major concern of white newspapers. One study of the press in Philadelphia reveals that from 1908 to 1932 newspapers in that city gave between 51.1 percent and 73.6 percent of Negro news space to crime reporting, with accidents, suicide, divorce, civil suits, sports, jokes, comic strips (with black characters), photographs, and stories, added to crime news, making up an average of three-quarters of all space given to blacks. Only the remaining quarter of the space given to blacks contained material on such matters as education, religion, health, and science.[9]

SCIENTIFIC SUPPORT FOR RACISM

In the early 1920s popular assumptions about white supremacy received widespread support from scientific studies. Psychologist George Oscar Ferguson, Jr., for example, was able to state that "psychological study of the Negro indicates that he will never be the mental equal of the white race."[10] This kind of conclusion followed logically from the results of intelligence tests conducted by the United States Army during World War I. The tests, widely publicized and widely misunderstood, quite clearly found a hierarchy of intelligence with the Anglo-Saxon type at the top of the ladder and the black person at the bottom, with various European "races" distributed between the two. It was not for several years that scientific critics of the army intelligence tests began to make their objections known, and even then the critics were unable to obtain immediately so large an audience as had those who supported the conclusions of the army tests.[11] The tests were described and the testers praised, for example, in the pages of the *Atlantic Monthly*, a popular magazine noted for its intelligence and taste.[12] The project was more fully explained in a volume by Carl C. Brigham, then assistant professor of psychology at Princeton University, excerpts from which follow.

Our results showing the marked intellectual inferiority of the negro are corroborated by practically all of the investigators who have used psychological tests on white and negro groups . . . .

Some writers would account for the differences found between white and negro by differences of educational opportunity alone. The army tests showed the northern negro superior to the southern negro, and this superiority is attributed to the superior educational opportunities in the North. The educational record of the negro sample we are studying shows that more than half of the negroes from the southern States did not go beyond the third grade, and only 7% finished the eighth grade, while about half of the northern negroes finished the fifth grade, and a quarter finished the eighth grade. That the difference between the northern and southern negro is not entirely due to schooling, but partly to intelligence, is shown by the fact that groups of southern and northern negroes of *equal schooling* show striking differences in intelligence.

The superior intelligence measurements of the northern negro are due to three factors: first, the greater amount of educational opportunity, which does affect, to some extent, scores on our present intelligence tests; second, the greater amount of admixture of white blood; and, third, the operation of economic and social forces, such as higher wages, better living conditions, identical school privileges, and a less complete social ostracism, tending to draw the more intelligent negro to the North. It is impossible to dissect out of this complex of forces the relative weight of each factor. No psychologist would maintain that the mental tests he is now using do not measure educational opportunity to some extent. On the other hand, it is absurd to attribute all differences found between northern and southern negroes to superior educational opportunities in the North, for differences are found between groups of the same schooling, and differences are shown by beta as well as alpha [intelligence tests].

At the present stage of development of psychological tests, we cannot measure the actual *amount* of difference in intelligence due to race or nativity. We can only prove that differences do exist, and we can interpret these differences in terms that have great social and economic significance. The intellectual superiority of our Nordic group over the Alpine, Mediterranean, and negro groups has been demonstrated. . . .

If these four types blend in the future into one general American type, then it is a foregone conclusion that this future blended American will be less intelligent than the present native born American, for the general results of the admixture of higher and lower orders of intelligence must inevitably be a mean between the two. . . .

We must face a possibility of racial admixture here that is infinitely worse than that faced by any European country to-day, for we are incorporating the negro into our racial stock, while all of

Europe is comparatively free from this taint. It is true that the rate of increase of the negro in this country by ten year periods since 1800 has decreased rather steadily from about 30% to about 11%, but this declining rate has given a gross population increase from approximately 1,000,000 to approximately 10,000,000. It is also true that the negro now constitutes only about 10% of the total population, where he formerly constituted 18% or 19% (1790 to 1830), but part of this decrease in percentage of the total population is due to the great influx of immigrants, and we favor in our immigration law those countries 35% of whose representatives here are below the average negro. The declining rate of increase in the negro population from 1800 to 1910 would indicate a correspondingly lower rate to be expected in the future. From 1900 to 1920 the negro population increased 18.4%, while the native born white of native parents increased 42.6%, and the native born white of foreign parents increased 47.6%. It is impossible to predict at the present time that the rate of infiltration of white blood into the negro will be checked by the declining rate of increase in the negro blood itself. The essential point is that there are 10,000,000 negroes here now and that the proportion of mulattoes to a thousand blacks has increased with alarming rapidity since 1850.

According to all evidence available, then, American intelligence is declining, and will proceed with an accelerating rate as the racial admixture becomes more and more extensive. The decline of American intelligence will be more rapid than the decline of the intelligence of European national groups, owing to the presence here of the negro. These are the plain, if somewhat ugly, facts that our study shows. The deterioration of American intelligence is not inevitable, however, if public action can be aroused to prevent it. There is no reason why legal steps should not be taken which would insure a continuously progressive upward evolution.[13]

The next selection is an excerpt from an article that raises some pertinent questions about the significance of the army intelligence scores. Its appearance in a learned journal meant, however, that its distribution was limited.

It is an easy matter for a people occupying a position of social, economic, and political advantage to imagine themselves superior by nature to a less fortunately situated group. Such a belief also serves to fortify their position—it gives them security. Down-trodden peoples will trudge along if it is "God's will," but they resent being held down by their equals. Hence, this feeling of race superiority is not new. The "Nordic myth" is no different essentially from the Hebrew myth, the Greek myth, the Roman myth. The emotional bias which assigns the Negro in America to an inferior position biologically rests upon the same basis as that in the feudal system in Europe which made the lord of finer clay than the peasant.

So it turns out to be not a matter of actual race differences so much as a matter of cash and clothes, a matter of superior advantage giving rise to biases and prejudices. I am not saying here that no racial inferiorities and superiorities exist. I am simply saying that the arguments for their existence have always been made by peoples who happen to occupy, for the time, a favorable position; and that these arguments have had an emotional, rather than a scientific and rational background. Some of the arguments remind me of the reasonableness of the southern mountaineer who, when asked why he thought the black man "lower down" than the white man, replied: "Cuz I don't like 'em."

. . . Certainly there are racial characteristics which clearly set the Negro off from the white man. He has kinky hair on his head; no hair on his body; a broad low nose; his jaws also appear to be slightly prognathous. There are biological differences, but are they marks of inferiority? It is easier to believe a priori than to demonstrate. The broad low nose and prognathous jaws are more simian-like than the narrow high nose and the straight jaws of the Caucasian. These characteristics thrust themselves upon our attention. But what about the kinky hair and the absence of hair of the body? In these traits the white man is more apelike than the Negro. The lips of the ape are also thin and grayish, like those of the Nordic, in contrast to the thick red lips of the Negro.

The Negro is black. When, however, one attempts to make out a scientific case against blackness of skin, the facts are not so accommodating as he would like. Researches have already demonstrated that the body covered with dark skin does not produce heat so rapidly as in the case of a light skin. This means, apparently, that black skin is an advantage on a tremendously hot day, whereas the light skin gives an advantage on a cold day.

In the light of present knowledge—or lack of knowledge—it is impossible to make any reliable statement of inferiority on the basis of purely anatomical differences.

. . . Some studies have been made with view to determining whether or not there are any significant differences in the psychological actions of different races.

A high temperature accompanied by a quick pulse beat and a high respiration rate might suggest a restless and excitable disposition, but I am unable to find any record of significant differences being reported in these conditions between races living under similar environment. Further, no suggestive differences in races have been observed in their simpler reaction to stimuli, such as would indicate, for example, a keener sense of pain, or sight, or hearing, by one race than another. It must be remembered, however, that studies of this kind have been far too limited to warrant any conclusions of a generalized sort. Besides, the investigations that have been reported were made by white men, according to methods familiar to white men and with instruments of their own devising; all of which conditions would be likely to affect the results in a way favorable to the white race, if at all.

. . . It may be argued that the Negro, as shown by a high mortality rate and a greater frequency of physical maladies, is not equipped racially to resist disease germs. He is, consequently, unable to measure up to the demands of civilization. Here again environmental influences as conditioning factors would have to. be eliminated before any claims based upon susceptibility to disease are worth anything. We know that the general living conditions of the Negro averages very much lower in America than the living conditions of the whites. The Negro lives generally in the most unhealthful parts of the city. He has very little training, comparatively, in matters of health preservation or sanitation. Because of his economic circumstances, and ignorance concerning the importance of disease, he does not take precautions as does the white man. It follows naturally that his mortality rate will be high, just as it is comparatively high among disadvantaged classes of whites, and for the same reason that the death-rate was higher among whites in the sixteenth century than among whites today. . . .

. . . The army and other intelligence tests have been interpreted by many in such a way as to indicate that the Negro is an inferior. But here again the environmental factor has not been given the weight that it deserves. If social and economic factors play so large a part in the matter of health and physical fitness, it naturally follows that these conditions influence directly the development of the individual's mental powers. Their effects upon the mind might be expected to be greater, for normal mental development depends not only upon the normal and vigorous action of the body, but also upon opportunities for acquiring and organizing and analyzing information. That is to say, the individual's environment — social and otherwise — plays in upon his intellectual life from two directions. The importance of opportunity in the unfolding of mental ability is not known, but that it is great is shown by the fact that some Negro groups in the northern states far surpassed those in the southern states, and made higher scores than the whites in some southern states. Table I gives the comparison.

TABLE I: MEDIAN SCORES *

Whites		Negroes	
Mississippi	41.25	Pennsylvania	42.00
Kentucky	41.50	New York	45.02
Arkansas	41.55	Illinois	47.35
Georgia	42.12	Ohio	49.50

* For discussion of results of Army testing see Article by James E. Gregg, *Scientific Monthly*, March, 1925.

It has been held by some that the northern Negroes were a selected group in the sense that the more richly endowed mentally were the ones who pushed out from the South to seek the opportunities to be found in the North. This is a mere assumption and nothing more. It might as logically be assumed that the superior Negroes would most likely remain in the South, since they would be the ones to have acquired property and thus have some permanent attachment to that region.

The preponderance of evidence is on the side of superiority of opportunity rather than superiority of inborn race equipment....[14]

VIEWS ON RACE: FROM THE RIGHT

To the extent that scientific inquiry supported white superiority, racists found aid and comfort. Ku Klux Klan Imperial Wizard Hiram W. Evans, for example, might have found a considerable measure of support among social scientists for his assertions that Negroes entering the cities were a "retrograding" influence. Evans argued that even though assimilation of Negroes was an impossibility, white America was honor bound to promote the well-being of those who had been brought forcibly into slavery.[15] Other spokesmen for white supremacy, however, urged recolonization of blacks in Africa. The following selection is from the *American Standard*, a newspaper highly supportive of the Klan that was published in New York City during 1924-25. The article responds to the efforts of Marcus Garvey, leader of the Universal Negro Improvement Association, to encourage the development of a free Africa.

BACK TO AFRICA

The powers that be are after Marcus Garvey. They do not want him to carry out his plan of taking all the Negroes back to Africa.[16] Garvey is a real prophet and his philosophy will some day find its way.

The Negro is not at home in America. He does not feel and think in terms of Anglo-Saxon civilization. As an ape of such civilization he is equally a failure. His very contention for equality is an acknowledgment of deficiency along, not his own lines, but Anglo-Saxon lines.

It is also true that white man must direct and handle his own civilization. How can the Negro master and control that which he did not produce? That is to say, the Negro does not and cannot know what to do with the white man's civilization. The same is true if you turn it around the other way. The white man would be equally lost in adapting himself to a Negro civilization.

Suppose New York City with its tubes, tunnels, skyscrapers, banks, culture, business, all were left today entirely to Negroes. They could not maintain it for an hour. The wheels of the metropolis would stop within thirty minutes and within one year they would be revolutionized. On the other hand, raze the city to the ground today and leave it in the hands of those who produced it at first and within twelve months they will restore it.

That is to say, Anglo-Saxon people know what to do with Anglo-Saxon civilization. Other people do not and cannot know what to do with it.

And just there is where Marcus Garvey is correct. The Negro can never be himself in America. In Africa, his native home, surrounded by his kind, moved by his ideals, instincts, traditions and surroundings, he can build a civilization of his own. What he builds will be different from that which white men build, to be sure. But it would be an expression of his own inner soul. And in expressing himself as a race in producing his own civilization, the Negro would grow and become strong and useful in the world. Moreover, he would thus make his distinctive contribution to the world.

Divine law declares that "God made the nations (races) and hath set the bounds of their habitation." To disregard God's law is tragic. No race can attain unto its highest and best when surrounded by and handicapped by another race. This is true for both white, black or yellow peoples. The rule works every way. The white race would be lost if it were required to fit into and adopt as its own the civilization of a colored race.

In taking this stand we certainly do not disparage the Negro race. To do so would be to question God's wisdom and plans. Remember, God made the races. Nor are we here to compare the achievements of the different races. We do not declare one to be good and the other bad. "All are architects of fate." "Each one in his place is best." Our appeal is in behalf of and in the higher interest of the Negro race. When he is free to function in history in his own God-appointed way, the result will be pleasing to the Supreme Architect. That should satisfy us.

The American Standard wishes Marcus Garvey well, as it wishes the Negro race well. This is strange, plain talk for America. But it is the truth. And the truth will make us free.[17]

VIEWS ON RACE: IN THE CENTER

Probably far more significant to most white Americans than the writings of self-proclaimed white supremacists was the vast body of material in the popular media that created the stereotypical Negro, the black man who shuffled when he walked, rolled his eyes, scratched his head before he spoke to get his brain operating, stumbled over words of more than three syllables, and laughed good-naturedly over his own childishness. Stepin Fetchit made him famous in the 1930s. This was merely one of several stereotypes, the others including, for example, the lustful scoundrel or the faithful servant. Each of the stereotypes had some variations. The dice-shooting preacher was sometimes a head-scratcher, sometimes a faithful servant, sometimes both.

Blacks were not, of course, the only objects of humorous ridicule during the 1920s. Dialect comedians had a field day with the Irish, the Germans, the Jews, the Italians, the Swedes, and others as well. But for black Americans, unlike all the other groups, there was no counterbalance. In the popular media white Americans did not find blacks treated as real human beings who had loves and hates, who were capable of sincere aspirations or deeply felt emotions. To the extent that blacks were not *really* human in this sense in the popular media it became very difficult indeed for whites to conceive of them as friends, coworkers, or neighbors. Relatively few whites were acquainted with the writings of Countee Cullen, Langston Hughes, Claude McKay, or other black writers of the 1920s.

One of the most popular portrayals of black Americans in the 1920s was that of a fictitious pair of friends who had come north to Chicago where they had established them-selves in business as "the Fresh-Air Taxicab Company of America, Incorpulated." Amos 'n' Andy were the creations of two white men, Charles Correll and Freeman Gosden, who broadcast a ten-minute-long serial episode each night in Chicago. Syndication made possible a nationwide audi-ence, an audience so enthusiastic that by 1929 the National Broadcasting Company was ready to pay Correll and Gosden $100,000 a year for their services.[18] "Amos 'n' Andy" con-tained no overt racism; it was really a very funny radio show. But that is precisely the point. In the absence of any sub-stantial evidence to the contrary in the popular media, Cor-rell and Gosden's assertion that their characters were based on "a thorough understanding of the colored race" must have seemed quite believable to many Caucasians.[19] Black writer William Branch remembered how his family had laughed at "Amos 'n' Andy." All except his father. Only gradually did the son learn why. These people were supposed to be "us."[20]

Following is an excerpt from radio script number 250, an

episode in the lives of "Amos 'n' Andy." It begins with the voice of the announcer giving a synopsis of the events leading up to this episode.

The battle is on. Again we find the boys in court, while the breach of promise suit is going on. Today Mrs. Parker testified on the witness stand, much to the embarrassment of Andy. She told how he came into her life, how he led her on and then threw her down. She wept and cried, and at the end of her testimony she was carried from the witness stand after fainting. The Judge called a short recess in order to allow Mrs. Parker time to revive. As we find the situation now, Amos and Andy are seated with their attorney. Directly across from them Mrs. Parker's attorney is holding smelling salts under his client's nose. The Judge has not returned to the bench. Here they are:

AMOS: Andy, it ain't no use to worry now. Jus' do de best you kin, dat's all.

ANDY: Dat gal git up on de witness stand dere an' tell all dat stuff. It's enough to make me worry. . . .

SPIELMAN: Now I think you'll be the next one on the stand to be cross examined by Mrs. Parker's attorney. When you get there, sit down very quietly, and, whatever you do, don't show any signs of nervousness.

AMOS: Git dat in yo' head now.

ANDY: (to Amos) — Shut up!

AMOS: 'Scuse me. I was jus' trying' to he'p yo'.

SPIELMAN: (confidentially to Andy) — And Brown, when you get on the witness stand, admit nothing.

ANDY: Do whut to nuthin'?

SPIELMAN: I say, when you get on the witness stand, admit nothing.

ANDY: Admit nuthin' where?

SPIELMAN: On the witness stand.

ANDY: Oh, in otheh words, don't let nothin' git on de witness stand.

AMOS: Why don't you listen, Andy?

ANDY: (resentful of Amos) — Is you gonna shut up, or is I gotta kick you out de cou't room? De mo' you talk, de worse off I is.

SPIELMAN: Now, Brown, you can occasionally use the expression "I don't remember." Don't make it noticeable, but occasionally say, "I don't remember." Now, don't forget that. Now, what are you going to say?

ANDY: "Now, don't fo'git dat."

SPIELMAN: No, no; "You don't remember."

ANDY: Oh, dat's right; "You don't remembeh."

SPIELMAN: No, no; "*I* don't remember."

ANDY: (mixed up) — You don't rememberh whut?

AMOS: No, no, Andy. Listen, "*You* don't rememberh."

ANDY: Oh, Oh! Who is my lawyeh?

SPIELMAN: Now, Brown, just say, "I don't remember."

ANDY: Ain't it some way dat I kin keep off o' dat chair again up dere? All dese peoples in the cou't room looks at me when I git up dere. I feels rebarrassed.

SPIELMAN: No, no, you *must* get up there, but remember, "I don't remember."

ANDY: "Rememberh I don't rememberh." I got-cha.

AMOS: Stop shakin' now, Andy. Don't let 'em know dat you is nervous. You act like you is scared to death.

ANDY: (disgusted with Amos) — Dey is gonna be tryin' me fo' bustin' yo' head open in a minute if you don't shut up.

SPIELMAN: Here comes the Judge now. Don't over do it. But remember to say "I don't remember," and don't say anything that will incriminate you.

ANDY: Dey ain't goin' to *cremate* me, is dey?

AMOS: De Judge is gittin' ready to staht — look at him. . . .

JUDGE: We will proceed with the case — Parker versus Brown. Andy Brown to the witness stand for cross examination by attorney for the plaintiff.

ANDY: (in low tone to himself) — Oh, oh! I gotta git up dere again.

SPIELMAN: All right, Brown; get on the witness stand.

ANDY: (to bailiff, who is waiting to administer the oath) — I'se comin', Misteh, I'se comin'.

BAILIFF: (in quick, jerky tone) — Raise your right hand.

ANDY: (shaking head as if making a positive reply) — I don't rememberh.

BAILIFF: Raise your right hand!

ANDY: Yessah, yessah.

BAILIFF: (rattling off the oath in quick, inaudible tone) — Do you solemnly swear that the evidence you are about to give in this case is the truth, the whole truth, and nothing but the truth, so help you God?

ANDY: I don't remembeh.

BAILIFF: Say "I do."

ANDY: I do.

BAILIFF: Sit down!

JUDGE: (in distance) — Attorney for the plaintiff will proceed with the cross examination.

ATTORNEY RADA: (fading in to cross examine Andy) — Your name is Andrew Brown?

ANDY: I don't remembeh.

JUDGE: (raps twice) — The witness will answer the attorney for the plaintiff. Proceed with the cross examination.

RADA: Your name is Andrew Brown. Is that correct?

ANDY: Yessah, dat's right.

RADA: You are president of the Fresh-Air Taxicab Company?

ANDY: (boastfully) — Yessah — yessah.

RADA: Do you know Mrs. Parker?

ANDY: I *did* know her, but I ain't speakin' to her now.

RADA: Brown, how long have you been in Chicago?

ANDY: Well-a, we left Atlanta, Georgia, last March, an' I been up heah evah since.

RADA: Brown, when did you first meet Mrs. Parker?

ANDY: I met Mrs. Parker over at Ruby Taylor's house one night.

COURT CLERK: What was that last statement?

ANDY: I met Mrs. Parkeh oveh at Ruby Taylor's house one night, but I'se sorry I eveh went oveh dere.

RADA: That's neither here nor there.

ANDY: Yes, 'tis. It's oveh dere.

RADA: (impatiently, to Andy) — Just a minute!

ANDY: (settling in seat) — I don't remembeh.

RADA: Brown, did you ever write Mrs. Parker a letter? . . .

RADA: (To Court) — I would like to read the Court the last two lines of the poem written by Andrew Brown. "Come fly with me and we will hide — Just Popsy-boy and his little bride." (Repeating in flowery manner, with much affection in voice.) "Come fly with me and we will hide — Just Popsy-boy and his little bride." (To Andy.) Brown, do you know what the word bride means?

ANDY: I don't remembeh.

RADA: (shaking finger in Andy's face) — Is it true that you went to the Easy Buying Furniture Company and signed a note for the balance which Mrs. Parker owed on her furniture?

ANDY: Yessah, an' dat man done called me up 'bout dat.

RADA: In other words, that was just a shield.

ANDY: Nosah, it wasn't no shield. She owed fo' chairs an' a table an' a lot o' otheh stuff.

RADA: (more high pressure) — Is it true that you have called up Mrs. Parker as often as ten times in one day?

ANDY: I guess it is.

RADA: (pounding fist on palm of hand in front of Andy) — Then you admit that you led this little girl within a few feet of the altar, leading her to believe that she was to be Mrs. Andrew Brown? Before answering that question I want you to look at Mrs. Parker, seated there crying.

SPIELMAN: (in distance) — I object.

JUDGE: Objection overruled.

SPECIAL DEPUTY: (in distance, to crowd) — Order in the court room.

RADA: Andrew Brown (slow and deliberate), I want to ask you one question.

ANDY: I don't remembeh.

RADA: (to Judge, pleading for assistance as if impatient) — Your honor, how can I cross examine this witness (start fading out) when he evades the question before I even ask him (and other similar wording until fadeout is completed).[21]

The pages of mass circulation magazines often offered their own version of Andy Brown. Perhaps the most famous of the magazine characters was J. Florian Slappey, created by Octavus Roy Cohen. Cohen's popularity may be attested by the appearance of over seven dozen of his pieces in the *Saturday Evening Post* between 1920 and 1928, as well as numerous others in *Collier's* and the *American Magazine*. A case in point is the story of J. Florian Slappey's adventure as unofficial talent scout and agent for the Midnight Pictures Corporation, Inc.[22] As a result of Slappey's recommendation, movie director J. Caesar Clump and Midnight Pictures president, Orifice J. Latimer, discover the talented boy comic Excelsior Nix, a potential "cullud Jackie Coogan." Clump and Latimer seek to prevent Slappey from cashing in on the discovery, but Slappey gets the child under contract to himself by playing up to his mother. He then deals with Midnight Pictures from a position of advantage.

The story line is simple, but what a message of genial contempt it conveys. The characters almost without exception are seen to be scheming rascals acting under a moral code of "Do others before they do you." The reader is invited not to take this peculiar morality too seriously, of course, for who can take seriously the actions of characters whose words are utterly ridiculous? "Jes look at that boy," says Orifice J. Latimer. "Fling yo' eyes on him an' keep 'em flang." The chief schemer, J. Florian Slappey, acknowledges the perceptive grasp of a neat bit of reasoning by little Excelsior Nix's mother. "Presac'ly," he says. Was black dialect ever like this?

Readers of popular magazines were seeking fiction that was entertaining—fiction that was divorced from social commentary, simply fun in its own right. And caricature is legitimate entertainment. But the fact is that caricature does contain social commentary and in this instance the implicit comment was that blacks do not deserve the consideration accorded "real" human beings. The popular white magazines offered little to balance the values contained in this view.

Motion pictures were still another source of popular information about Negro life. White America had the opportunity to learn from several Florian Slappey shorts made by Octavus Roy Cohen during the 1920s. Jungle films made in this period revealed that the Negro's ancestral home, Africa, was peopled by ignorant savages, cannibals, and head hunters. D. W. Griffith's *Birth of a Nation* portrayed the Ku Klux Klan of Reconstruction as having saved the South from the ghastly depravity of lustful blacks. Griffith's *One Exciting Night* (1922) had the black character (played by a white man in blackface) that began the long line of black clowns, good darkeys all, that occupied the silver screen for many years thereafter. Stepin Fetchit made an appearance in *Hearts in Dixie* in 1929 as a lazy, good-for-nothing but good-natured slave in the same tradition.[23]

Hallelujah, also a 1929 film, was decidedly better from the point of view of realism, but its melodramatic story of a black cottonfield worker and part-time preacher dazzled by a good-time woman left ample opportunity for gospel shouting, spiritual singing ("they got rhythm"), and crap shooting. The following selection from the film script deals with two characters whose only apparent reason for inclusion is to make the joke that the scene contains. In the staging directions, the abbreviation LS stands for Long Shot, b.g. for background, f.g. for foreground, R. and L. for Right and Left, MCU for Medium Close Up, and so on.

LS yard and front of house. Zeke standing right b.g. Spunk standing L. b.g. at corner of house. Pappy comes from inside of house and stops on top of steps with gun in hand. Henry enters scene from R. and walks to L. Adam and Eve enter scene from f.g. L., followed by children. Walk to foot of steps, stop.

PAPPY: Hello, Adam and Eve — what you doin', 'round here?

MLS outside cabin. Pappy at top of stairs. Rose standing back of him. Henry, Spunk, Adam and Eve and Children facing Pappy. Pappy points at children.

ADAM: Well, we jes come down to see if you had time to marry us.

EVE: That's right.

PAPPY: To marry you?

ADAM: Yes.

PAPPY: Ain't these eleven chilrun yours?

MCU Adam and Eve looking at Children. Zeke standing at b.g.R. They all look off scene to L. and Eve bows over.

ADAM: Dat's r ght, and we thought it was about time for us to make it more permanent.

EVE: Dat's right. Ha.

MLS Ext. Cabin. Pappy and Rose standing at top of stairs at door. Henry and Spunk standing at foot of stairs. Adam and children standing along side Eve who is bowing over. Eve stands erect.

PAPPY: Seems like you made it mighty late gettin' 'round to get married — de damage is done.

MCU Eve, Adam and children; part figure of Zeke R.b.g.

ADAM: Sure is, but could you fix it up for us anyhow?

.... [Staging directions] ....

PAPPY: Well, it's never too late to do de will of de Lawd.

EVE: Dat's right.

MAMMY: Well, chilrun, I'se mighty glad dat you all done made up your mind to do de right thing.

EVE: Well, thank you. 'Cause you know I've always been a respectable woman and I don't want that to come up agains my charac-ter.

MAMMY: Look here, am ain't what you was, it's what you is today. You ain't got on no weddin' veil. Missy Rose, go git the weddin' veil.

MS of Rose int. Cabin walking from f.g. to window. Takes curtain and starts walking rapidly towards center f.g. . . .

SPUNK: The weddin's all over—they're married. Come on out and kiss the bride.

. . . . [Staging directions] . . . .

MLS in yard showing Spunk and Henry, Adam and Eve and Children. They all walk to L. and CAMERA PANS. Henry sits in chair playing banjo. Adam and Eve dancing to b.g. CAMERA PANS back, showing Henry and Spunk playing, Adam and Eve dancing back and forth. Mammy and Pappy dance into scene and scene FADES OUT. . . .[24]

The black American was the butt of ridicule in countless jokes, vaudeville sketches, and cartoons through the decade of the 1920s.[25] The following example is from the "official organ of the Brotherhood of Dining Car Conductors," a white union.

KNOW YOUR PULLMAN PORTER!

The Pullman Company thinks porters should be called by their right names. For the public to address all Pullman porters as "George" when they may be named Abraham Lincoln Brown, Thomas Jefferson Smith and Aristotle Xerxes Hannibal Jenks is considered unfair, and a campaign to end the practice will be launched.

The Pullman Company will place the name of each porter in the corridor of each car. For example:

The Porter on This
Pullman is
Grover Cleveland Swidge

There will be no excuse then for a passenger to address the porter as "I say, George," or "Listen, Sam." Unless, of course, the tip is sufficiently high to offset it. For 50 cents you can call a Pullman porter most anything.

The Pullman Company card may be satisfactory from the standpoint of the company, but what guaranty will the public have that the porter is really Grover Cleveland Swidge? It will always be possible for a card to state that the porter is Grover Cleveland Swidge when, as a matter of fact, his name is Napoleon Bonaparte Wiggins. It is of paramount importance, therefore, that the Pullman people take a leaf from the book of the taxicab campanies and place a photograph of the porter on the card thus:

The Porter on This
Pullman Is
Grover Cleveland Swidge
(Picture of Mr. Swidge in this space)

If you locate the porter and he is not the man shown in this photograph, stop the train the minute you pass a police station and call a cop at once.

Much as passengers will be pleased by the opportunity to know the porter personally, there is bound to be a feeling that the identification cards should go into detail, giving a more intimate sketch of the man, and making it possible for a passenger to know what topics of conversation will prove of interest. Something like this:

The Porter on This
Pullman Is
Julius Caesar Weems
He is 36 years old, married, and has a big family
to support.
He is well versed in matters of philosophy, art
and religion, and his hobbies are horse
racing, lotteries and fraternal orders.
His forlorn expression doesn't mean anything, as
he is really of a cheerful disposition and
very willing.
He can sing spirituals. Also clogs well.
Carries corkscrew.
Has no small change.

A card like that would really mean something. It is respectfully referred to Mr. and Mrs. Pullman for action.[26]

White attitudes toward blacks of course ran the gamut
from extreme hostility to genuine understanding and support. When the Chicago Commission on Race Relations
published its report on the race situation in Chicago in 1922,
it included a section on public opinion and sought to obtain
"a fair sample of sentiment" by learning the attitudes of a
small group of randomly selected business and professional,
white men and women. Despite the claims to objectivity
made by this rather well-educated group, one can readily
note the presence of the virus of prejudice.

A——: I have rather definite opinions of Negroes. As a class they
cannot be depended upon. They are shiftless and really must be
treated like children. I make allowance for the fact that they have
not the years of education back of them.

My opinions are based on visits made to the South and on information obtained from relatives who live in the South as well as
from the colored help we have had. As a child my contact with
Negroes began with our Negro house servants, and my first consciousness of a racial difference came while visiting relatives in
the South. I know but two persons who might speak with authority
on the race question. . . . It is very seldom that I inquire for information on this subject. People whom I know are not interested in the
problem.

The only Negroes whom I know are my present colored help and
those who have worked for me. I don't know whom to consider
leaders among the colored people either in Chicago or in the
United States. Concerning the Negro periodicals, I have occasionally read copies of one of their newspapers which bore out my
opinion of their simple minds. Discussion of domestic help and of
newspaper articles about Negroes and sociological conditions
most frequently lead to the discussion of the Negro in my circle. If
it were in my power to do so, I would segregate Negroes as to living
quarters and do all possible to help them educate and help themselves.

. . . I agree that if you educate Negroes, you increase their demands, but I also believe that as they become educated, greater
demands will arise in their own groups.

In my opinion prejudice has its principal basis in the fact that
one can't depend upon Negroes.

B —— : I have more or less definite opinions about Negroes. I believe that as a race they are entitled to more leniency and consideration than we would give to adult whites because as a race they are not as mature as whites. I think it is unfortunate that we have such a race question to deal with, but we ought to meet it squarely and insist that under the law Negroes are entitled to equal protection and equal consideration. I do not believe in any attempt at social equality because the antipathy between whites and Negroes is so acute that such attempt would not only break down itself but it would lead to serious race difficulties. I think the Negro race has as much right to protect its race purity as the white race. I believe Negro women are entitled to the same protection from white men that we demand on behalf of white women against black men. I believe Negroes should have decent housing conditions, proper social outlets and opportunities to earn a living at the same wages paid white men for the same class and character of work. They should share equally in the benefits of government, with particular reference to schools, bathing-beaches, playgrounds, parks, etc. They should be protected against exploitation by employers, property owners, merchants, etc.

I do think Negroes possess distinguishing traits of both mentality and character. For many years now I have come into more or less personal contact with Negroes. I have been in contact with them in public schools, in colleges, in politics and in civic work. I cannot say that any particular incidents or experiences stand out in my memory.

My opinions are based upon my personal observation, personal contacts with Negroes and discussions with other white persons having independent contacts. . . .

I used to think that the Negro question might be best solved if the Negroes would be colonized in some favorable spot in Africa under an American protectorate until they were capable of self-government. I realize, however, that no such scheme ought to be attempted if the Negroes obstinately objected, and in that event I would see to it, if I had the power, that they were protected from exploitation, were given a square deal and had the equal protection of the laws. They should have schools adequate to their needs and average living conditions.

I believe the Negro race should be educated, but I believe at the same time that the most solid foundation for the race is education in accordance with the ideas of the late Booker T. Washington as I understand those ideas. While I think this type of education will mean more for the race in the long run I believe at the same time that individual Negroes should have an opportunity fully to develop individual capacities.

I think there is an element of fear in the prejudice of Negroes, but I don't think this is the chief element. I think the real basis for this prejudice is a racial antipathy that is instinctive and fundamental in the white race. I imagine that in individual cases where this prejudice does not exist it is not because it was not there originally, but because it has been overcome by reason and education. It isn't unlikely that this prejudice is in the main grounded upon an instinct in the white race to keep its strain pure and strong. . . .

A minority of the population will not get complete justice at the hands of an overwhelming majority. But this is true of all minorities, whether racial, political, or religious. All we can do is to keep working for an approximation to ideal justice. A minority has the right to demand, and a majority should be willing to grant, substantial justice and that is all that can be expected in the present state of civilization.

D——: I assume that it is a fact recognized by science that Negroes are so different from whites that the two races cannot be amalgamated. This fact interposes a barrier to social relationships. I share in the general dislike of Negroes as neighbors or traveling companions on the street cars. The white race is responsible for the existence of the Negro problem in America, and must submit patiently to the penalty for many years to come. Lincoln's second inaugural is the best expression of this thought. The Negro race is extraordinarily docile and easy to handle. If surrounded by good living conditions and given a proper education they would be good citizens. The progress of their race since slavery, considering their many handicaps, has been very creditable. The prejudice against them is probably the most deep-seated of all American prejudices, and must be reckoned with as one of the great factors in the problem.

In my opinion they are characterized by distinctly inferior mentality, deficient moral sense, shiftlessness, good nature, and a happy disposition. I have in mind no special facts, authorities or sources of information on which I base my opinions. I do, however, recognize the bearing of Christianity on the problem, and find it impossible to formulate a viewpoint which I can reconcile with the demands of Christianity. . . .

I do not know that I can cite any friends, acquaintances, favorite authors or scholars well fitted to speak with authority on the question. Lincoln's views always seemed true to me, while I have not been so favorably impressed by southern writers. Every southerner I have ever met, no matter how reasonable on other subjects, seemed to be incapable of looking at this question with an open mind. His confidence that he knew all about the Negro and the problem seemed absolute, and therefore he was not in position to learn. I occasionally inquire for information on this subject.

I feel that Negroes would be happier if segregated in neighborhoods which allowed contact with the dominant race. I feel that they are as unhappy to be isolated among whites as the whites would be to be isolated among Negroes. I feel they should have the right to live under decent conditions, with those things which make life livable and enjoyable. Probably part of my unwillingness to have them for neighbors lies in the fear of undesirable neighbors (bad citizens), in the fear of property depreciation which would follow, and because of the lack of interests in common that make for neighborly intercourse. I suppose I am as inconsistent as others in this, for in my heart I have no prejudice of which I am aware, yet I believe I am infected with the universal indefinite prejudice, if I could but analyze it thoroughly. . . .

It is probably true that prejudice is based on fear, a result of the abuse of female slaves by the whites in slavery time, and the resultant desire on the part of a few Negroes engendered during the reconstruction period by the carpet-baggers, to have social equality. I have discussed this subject of "social equality" with intelligent, fine Negroes, and believe they meant what they said when they assured me that among decent Negroes there is no more desire for this than there is among the white people. I feel that it is a bugaboo, useful in increasing fear and prejudice against the Negro. . . .

Even a minority has the right to expect and demand justice in opportunity to develop industrial, social and spiritual growth. I recognize that education of both whites and blacks is necessary to overcome fear and prejudice and make this possible.[27]

Chicago newspapers expressed the same uncertainty as the educated man-in-the-street. On the one hand, there was awareness of the need to recognize the essential humanity of black Americans, but on the other hand—not so fast. The first of the two following selections from the *Chicago Daily Tribune* appeared prior to the midsummer riot of 1919 that began with the stoning of a Negro boy who was swimming in a "white" section of Lake Michigan and ultimately caused the death of thirty-six persons and injury to hundreds; the second selection, an editorial, appeared shortly after the riot.

NEGRO'S MENTAL GROWTH IS ISSUE IN RACE PROBLEM
ANALYST FINDS CHANGING CHARACTERS MUST BE CONSIDERED
—By Eye Witness

III *The New Negro Psychology*

An essential fact in the Negro situation as it confronts Chicago is that the white man has got to deal with a new type of black man. That type, like the old, not only breeds fast and strong, but it also is developing a distinct social consciousness, and with the growth of that consciousness come questionings and, inevitably, resentments.

The new type works hard, grows steadily prosperous, and, simultaneously with the realization of the worth of its labor, is irked by patronage, by those jokes about the razzor [*sic*] which some of us still think are droll, and by that lofty petting which some of us still believe colored men from 17 to 70 must like. They do not.

You may not like the new type as well as you liked the obsequious, chuckling "nigger boy" of the barber shops, and certainly you will not find him as easy to deal with, but here he is with his head full of book learning and his heart stirring with ambitions and resentments and questions; not content any more to be the pet and the butt of the white barbers. . . .

All this new Negro psychology and new Negro consciousness is as surely a fact and a factor in the local situation as is the increasing number of Negroes in our midst. It cannot be left out of the problem if the problem is to be approached rationally and humanely. It may seem like writing all around the subject and not getting into it to harp on this theme of growing social consciousness of the Negroes as a race and the growing sense of his personal dignity manifested by the Negro as an individual—a sense not the less real because it often manifests itself in surliness and rudeness.

But insistence upon the new note is not mere harping and word spinning. Leave the new fact and the new factor out of your calculations and you instantly obliterate the most effective points of economic and community contact which must be established if the two races are to get into conference and cooperation for the solution of their mutual problem.

Evidence Is Everywhere

You see manifestations of the new note everywhere. A public man receiving, not long ago, a delegation of colored people desirous of enlisting his support in a good cause, showed a disposition to deal curtly with them, although they had come at his suggestion. "I don't think," he said at one point in the discussion, "that I have time to go into that phase of the subject now." He was somewhat abruptly brought to realize that he was dealing with a new type of "cullod person" when the leader of the delegation crisply replied: "We have no more time to waste on platitudes than you have to listen to them." Then the conference got down to business.

The new sense of personal dignity often comes out in unexpected ways even among colored people of humble station. At an intimate dinner where a colored woman served, an actor, ever an honored guest in the house, but long absent from it, glanced at the old servant as she drew back his chair and said: "Good evening, Mammy."

He meant it kindly, and his greeting was civilly received, but the startled look in the woman's eyes and the tightening of her lips showed to one observer at least that the pleasantry was not relished. There was no responsive chuckle, no obsequious "Yes, sir." The colored folks up north have got by the "mammy" and "uncle" stage.

For several decades the enfranchised Negro sought patronage and liked it. Then he came to distrust and resent it. And now the clear headed representatives of the race take it with equanimity and as it is meant—take it kindly when it is meant kindly, but they don't like it the better for that. When men of large affairs wax patronizing in their sympathetic assurances to a colored man like Alexander Jackson, [28] one of the clearest brained men, white or black, in this community, he says, "Yes, you must guide us. We must look to you." He has tact.

Mayor Thompson is not generally believed to represent a very spacious ideal of either statesmanship or tactfulness, but few men so thoroughly appreciate this new sensitiveness of the northern Negroes as he does. That is why he holds them to him in such numbers. He doesn't talk down to them, but with them, and when he bends forward over the platform and says in his friendly roar, "Mr. Chairman and my good friends, I am glad to be here this afternoon to discuss with you certain problems of interest to you, your homes and your community" — then every colored man and woman in the audience experiences, rightly or wrongly, an access of community feeling that results in something constructive. (Constructive for Big Bill, but that is beside the point we are making.)

The returning colored soldiers are a big factor in, and big contributors to, this new Negro consciousness. They return with heads up, with a more acute sense of the hard conditions to which they were born, and with a fresh determination, since they rightly enough have been made much of, to make something of themselves. They have been under discipline and the effect of discipline is dual. It both tames and makes a man, and it has done both for thousands of these once irresponsible lads.

Dr. Gary says that many of them have told him that they tire and sicken of the banquets and dances given them upon their return, and that they seek "something lasting, something worth while."

The phrase epitomizes the new aspiration of the new Negro. "Something lasting, something worth while."[29]

CRITICISM FROM THE SOUTH

Southern newspapers have not failed to upbraid Chicago on the score of the recent riots, and unless we mistake the tenor of their utterances they find a particular satisfaction in the fact that this outbreak has occurred in the city in which THE TRIBUNE is published.

It is a theory that is a little difficult to comprehend. It could only have a rational foundation if THE TRIBUNE was accustomed to denounce the south for depriving the Negroes of the power to exercise political or social control; if, in fact we had ever proposed that the white population should surrender its position of dominance. But, on the contrary, it has been stated over and over again in these columns that we recognize the south has a peculiar problem — a problem which cannot possibly be solved by sentimental considerations of the brotherhood of man [and] of the equality of all peoples.

But this is quite a different thing from condoning mob "justice." We do not condone it here in Chicago. We believe that there will be an accounting; we believe the community will insist that our public officials exert every effort to bring the instigators of these crimes to justice and that the severest penalties be inflicted.

The indictments returned by the grand jury are at least an indication that due process of law and not mob justice is going to be invoked in Chicago to deal with these offenders.

But if the community should show a disposition to treat them tenderly, to condemn them in public and give them aid and comfort in private, then Chicago will deserve just as much harsh criticism as has been applied to the south.

It is the privilege of the south to watch developments in Chicago to ascertain whether the people of this city are merely giving lip service to the support of law and order or whether they are fundamentally opposed to violence and murder as a means of settling any problem, racial or otherwise.[30]

VIEWS ON RACE: FROM THE LEFT

Not all whites were hesitant about advocating support for racial justice in the United States. Frequently such expressions came from groups motivated by a sense of brotherhood rooted in religious faith, from groups motivated by political and economic radicalism, and from those that were heir to the progressive reformist tradition that has had so pronounced an influence in the nation.

For the most part, organized religion had little to say in regard to race relations during the 1920s. This is hardly surprising in light of the fact that most blacks were Protestant and most Protestant churches were segregated and segregating institutions.[31] Nevertheless, several denominations did issue brief pronouncements opposing lynching and/or calling for more equitable treatment for black Americans.[32] The Federal Council of the Churches of Christ in America sponsored an interracial conference in 1925 that concerned itself with mutual airing of opinions and with emphasizing the belief that "racial antagonism arises fundamentally from social conditions, and that as such it is remediable through changes in those conditions, which will lead to revised social attitudes."[33] The following selection is from the organ of the Methodist Episcopal Church in New England, a group more than ordinarily concerned about the race problem in the

United States. It was written in response to the Chicago Commission on Race Relations report, *The Negro in Chicago*.

The report constitutes a frank recognition of the glaring injustices that the American Negro has been called upon to endure since he was given his so-called freedom at the time of the Civil War. The fact that the investigation was of an official character and scientifically conducted gives added weight to the findings. In the light of "The Negro in Chicago," cheap prejudice against the black man and the pooh-poohing of stories relative to persecutions of Negroes will no longer have the weight that heretofore has been accorded them in some quarters. The report has revealed gross discrimination against the colored race in recreational centers, and conditions of such congestion in areas where the Negro has been forced to live as tended to breed vice, crime and disease. There has also been a shameful neglect of sanitary provisions in Chicago's Negro sections. Inadequate schooling advantages and a lack of institutional care for dependent Negro children likewise receive attention in the report of the Chicago Commission. Among other abuses noted by the investigators are the prevalence of the low vice resorts of the whites in the colored residential districts, and the practise of property-owners in arbitrarily advancing rents merely because Negroes become tenants.

The situation thus honestly uncovered in Chicago will, we believe, create a new and irresistible public opinion that will give the black man a chance such as he has never had since Abraham Lincoln died.

The Chicago Commission on Race Relations, fortunately, went deeper into the Negro problem than simply to take cognizance of bad environment and the numerous abuses involving destructive physical consequences to the colored race. These investigators saw that it was possible to kill the soul of a man while leaving his body intact. It is a fact that the white race, with all too few exceptions, since the emancipation has been busy taking the heart out of the Negro by denying his rights as a man, by a galling condescension, by discounting his achievement, by withholding opportunity, by studied neglect. "The Negro in Chicago" carries a frank admission of our sins against the colored man and reaches some very pertinent conclusions respecting the attitude of white persons toward Negroes. . . .

What is the duty of the Christian Church and its individual mem-

bers toward the colored race, now that we have such a thorough-
going scientific report of the race situation in the second largest
city in the country to take the place of a mass of guesses, hearsay
opinions, prejudices, and expressions of petty enmity on the subject of the American Negro? There can be but one answer to the
question. If we are to be true to Jesus Christ, we simply must be
found in the very fore-front of those seeking to blaze the way to still
larger freedom and opportunity for the black man. It is inconceiv-
able, in the light of gospel teaching, how any Christian white man,
no matter how annoyed he may be over the ignorance, limitations,
and even sins of individual Negroes, can bring himself to withhold
in the least measure a fair chance from a race struggling out of the
slavery of body and soul to the heights of intellectual and spiritual
attainment. It strikes us that the wrong of closing the doors of opportunity in the face of the Negro, either through a positive aversion
to him or through indifference and neglect, comes very near to the
sin against the Holy Ghost.

Let there be no more of that facile dismissal of the whole problem
represented by such trite, outworn, and irrelevant expressions
as "Would you want your daughter to marry a Negro?" "The Negro
is naturally lazy," and "If you had ever lived in the South, you
would change your mind about the Negro." As Christian men and
women, we are under obligation to cultivate a certain breadth of
mind, if we do not already possess it. Certainly we ought to develop
largeness of soul—any one can reach at least that goal through the
power of the living Christ. When the love of God is shed abroad in
our hearts, and the intellect is raised above petty provincialisms,
there is some chance for the gospel of the brotherhood of man. Let
us give the Negro a new and enlarged chance.[34]

As was true of most religious denominations, major political groups in the United States were notably reluctant to
speak forcefully on the question of race relations. Both an
unwillingness to alienate significant numbers of white voters
and a failure to perceive the matter as requiring immediate
attention contributed to this silence. Even the platform of
Robert M. La Follette, the Progressive candidate for president in 1924, made no reference to the problems of minorities. Radical political parties with relatively small national
appeal saw the cultivation of support among dispossessed

minorities as an opportunity to gain strength. The Communists and Socialists spoke directly to black Americans and urged them to join in common enterprise to do away with both capitalism and racism.

WORKERS' (COMMUNIST) PARTY NATIONAL PLATFORM, 1928

XII. Oppression of the Negroes — (Demands)

1. Abolition of the whole system of race discrimination. Full racial, political, and social equality for the Negro race.

2. Abolition of all laws which result in segregation of Negroes. Abolition of all Jim Crow laws. The law shall forbid all discrimination against Negroes in selling or renting houses.

3. Abolition of all laws which disfranchise the Negroes.

4. Abolition of laws forbidding intermarriage of persons of different races.

5. Abolition of all laws and public administration measures which prohibit, or in practice prevent, Negro children or youth from attending general public schools or universities.

6. Full and equal admittance of Negroes to all railway station waiting rooms, restaurants, hotels, and theatres.

7. Federal law against lynching and the protection of the Negro masses in their right of self-defense.

8. Abolition of discriminatory practices in courts against Negroes. No discrimination in jury service.

9. Abolition of the convict lease system and of the chain gang.

10. Abolition of all Jim Crow distinctions in the army, navy, and civil service.

11. Immediate removal of all restrictions in all trade unions against the membership of Negro workers.

12. Equal opportunity for employment, wages, hours, and working conditions for Negro and white workers. Equal pay for equal work for Negro and white workers. [35]

Eugene V. Debs, Socialist leader, spoke for another group of politico-economic radicals, but his views on race were similar.

MR. DEBS: Friends and Comrades and Fellow-workers — I feel especially complimented by the invitation which has made it possible for me to stand in this inspiring presence to-night. I must first of all thank you and each of you in all sincerity for this very cordial greeting—this hearty manifestation of your sympathy and goodwill for the cause for which I am to speak to you to-night, and for the all too generous introduction of my young Comrade, the Chairman of the occasion, which touches me too deeply for words. I return my thanks to the dear little children whose floral offerings so enrich and reward me for the little that I have been able to do in the service of this great cause. The one regret of my life is that I have so little to give in return for all that is given me.

This great movement which I have been trying to serve; this movement in the interest of a higher social order, a nobler humanity, a diviner civilization that has given me my principles and my ideals and the right to live and to serve—I am only sorry that it is in my power to give so little in return.

I am more than glad to see the colored people represented here to-night. From the beginning of my life my heart has been with them. I never could understand why they were denied any right or any privilege or liberty that the white man had a right to enjoy. I never knew of any distinction on account of the color of the flesh of a human being. Indeed, when I think of what the colored people have been made to suffer at the hands of their supposedly superior race, every time I look a colored brother in the face I blush for the crimes that my race has committed against his race. (Great applause.)

I do not speak to my colored friends to-night in any patronizing sense; I meet them upon a common basis of equality; they are my brothers and my sisters, and I want nothing that is denied them, and if there is one of them who will shine my shoes and I am not willing to shine his, he is my moral superior. (Applause.) One reason why I became a Socialist was because I was opposed to this cruel discrimination against human beings on account of the color of their skin. I never could understand it. When I travelled over the Southern States thirty-five years ago organizing the workers, oh, what a desolate, unpromising situation it was! I made my appeal to them wherever I went, to open their doors to the colored workers upon equal terms with the white workers, but they refused. Poor as most of them were, they still felt themselves superior to the colored people.

It is one of the surest indications of their own ignorance and their own inferiority (applause); but, of course, they are not conscious of it. There is what they call a race prejudice, that is simply another name for ignorance (applause), and you can trace it to that and that alone. It is comparatively easy to forgive a man who has wronged you, but it is a very difficult thing to forgive the man that you have wronged. And this is the attitude in which we find our colored brother who has been the victim of this so-called civilization during the last two centuries; and if there is any man who has read the history of the institution of chattel slavery on American soil from its beginning—from its inception through all of its frightful stages, and who does not blush for himself and for his Anglo-Saxon race, it is because he is something less than a real human being. (Applause.)

Stolen from their native land, torn from their families ruthlessly by the brutal hand of conquest, and then thrown aboard vessels and herded like animals, half of them perishing on the way over from starvation or disease or ill-treatment, and the rest put upon auction blocks and sold to the highest or lowest bidders, and then through the years that followed designedly kept in ignorance and then despised, persecuted and punished because of their alleged inferiority!

The colored man has just as much in him that is potential and capable of development as the white man (great applause); and all he needs is a chance, that is all; he has never had that chance. (Renewed applause.)

I am sometimes surprised to think of the claims that are made in the name of religion and the much-vaunted Christian civilization that has everything in it but Christianity. (Applause.) Even in the great Christian Church the colored people have got to sit aloft— (A Voice: "Next to Heaven." Laughter.)—and I have had many a heated argument down in the Southern States and sometimes narrowly avoided trouble, making the contention that the colored man was a human being and had some rights that the white man ought to respect. (Applause.) . . .

I have a word to you workers—you colored workers—about your duty in this campaign—your duty to yourselves, your families, your class and to humanity. I am not here asking for anything for myself. If I were seeking office, you know, I would not be in the Socialist Party. (Applause and laughter.) I want to speak to you very plainly to-night, especially you colored people, and have you understand that it is not in my power to do anything for you but to take my place side by side with you. That is all I can do. (Applause.) But while I can do nothing for you there is nothing that you cannot do for yourselves. (Applause.) There is one thing that I want to impress upon your minds to-night; it is self-respect. You can compel the respect of others only when you respect yourselves. (Applause.) As long as you are willing to be the menials and servants and slaves of the white people, that is what you will be. (Applause.) You have to realize that there are 12,000,000 of you in this nation, and that if you will unite and stand together and be true to each other, you will develop a power that will command respect. (Applause.) As long as you are unorganized — as long as you are indifferent, as long as you are satisfied to remain in ignorance you will invite contempt and receive it, but when you rise in the majesty of your manhood and womanhood, close up the ranks and stand together, you will command respect and consideration and you will receive it. (Thunderous applause.) It is the only way you ever will receive it. Everything depends upon your education. You have a brain; you can develop your capacity for clear-thinking. That is a duty owing to yourselves and your class, to your race and to humanity. (Applause.) That is the appeal I am making to you to-night. . . .

I am speaking for the workers to-night. It does not make any difference to me where they were born or what the color of their skin may be, or what their religion is, or their creed, or anything of that kind. I ask no question as to that; they are all of the working class, the lower class, the class that does all of society's useful work, that produces all its wealth, and makes all the sacrifices of health and limb, and life through all the hours of the day and night; the class without which the whole social fabric would collapse in an instant. It is this class regardless of color that creates and supports all civilization; this class that in all the ages of the past, throughout history, in every nation on earth has been the lower class; for the badge of labor has always been the symbol of servitude and upon the brow of Labor there has always been the brand of social inferiority. . . .

Give a colored man the same chance, the same opportunity that you give a white man, and he will register as high upon the mental and moral thermometer of civilization. (Great applause.) Give him a chance! and that is what the Socialist Party is going to do. (Applause.) We admit colored members to our Party upon equal terms with the rest. We sit side by side with them in our Party councils. They are welcomed gladly to all our conferences and conventions. We treat them in no patronizing sense. We are not doing them any favor. They are our comrades and our equals, and we want them to have every right and privilege we enjoy. . . .

I appeal directly to you colored workers. You have got to build up your own press; you have got to develop your own power; you will never count until you do. Unite with all other workers in the unions; unite with them in the Socialist Party; develop your industrial power and your political power. Most of you are inclined to buy the capitalist newspapers and support the capitalist press and every time there is a strike you know what side they are on. You will never hear the truth until you hear it through your own press. . . .[36]

Among the white Americans who called for racial justice were those who gave of their time, money, and ability to such organizations as the National Association for the Advancement of Colored People and the National Urban League. Founded at the end of the first decade of the century, these two organizations received substantial help from Caucasians whose sense of justice was offended by the oppression of black people. These liberal reformers included such men as Moorfield Storey, Joel and Arthur Spingarn, and Oswald Garrison Villard. The following selection exemplifies the feelings of the white reformers.

OSWALD GARRISON VILLARD
ISSUES 20TH ANNIVERSARY N.A.A.C.P. CALL

Celebrating the twentieth anniversary of the original Lincoln's Birthday Call, which resulted in the formation of the National Association for the Advancement of Colored People, Oswald Garrison Villard, who as editor of the New York Evening Post wrote the first call, has this year, as editor of the Nation, written a second call after an interval of twenty years. The call is as follows:

"Born on the one hundredth anniversary of the birth of Abraham Lincoln, the National Association for the Advancement of Colored People was formed by men and women of both races who felt that that hour called for a rededication of the country to the work begun by the Emancipator when he signed the Emancipation Proclamation.

"They were determined that prejudice, superstition and lawlessness should not make a mockery of the one solid achievement of the Civil War. They beheld forces at work which had even induced the Supreme Court to lay down the doctrine that any state might legally forbid the assembling in market places of Negroes and whites. They saw millions of law-abiding and industrious Americans deprived of every attribute of citizenship solely because of their color.

"They believed that the American Republic could no more exist half slave and half free in 1909 than it could in 1863. They were aware that no republic had continued long to exist in which there were two classes of citizens. Out of this knowledge and out of their ardent desire to right flaming wrongs, and at the same time to benefit the entire country, came the National Association for the Advancement of Colored People.

" 'You are crazy,' people said. 'It can't be done. There is not interest enough among either the whites or the blacks.' They were wrong, those faint hearts. No one can fight for liberty and not rally many to his standard. There came a year when there were 100,000 members banded together to see even-handed justice done to the colored man and woman, drawn to the association by its simple platform of making colored people 'physically free from peonage, mentally free from ignorance, politically free from disfranchisement, and socially free from insult.'

"Within a few years the N.A.A.C.P. had branches in 44 states and the District of Columbia, with gross expenditures in 1926 of no less than $78,834. From the beginning it fought the horrible crime of lynching. Its campaign carried the Dyer Anti-Lynching Bill to passage by the House of Representatives, being blocked only by a filibuster of Southern Senators in the Senate.

"During the 20 years of the association's service, lynchings have decreased in America from 89 in 1908 to eleven in 1928.

"Against the Ku Klux Klan the association flung itself from the very beginning, accepting the challenge of this un-American organization.

"Into the courts the N.A.A.C.P. has gone whenever it had opportunity and money. Five decisive victories have been won before the United States Supreme Court establishing decisions against residential segregation (Louisville and Louisiana cases); against the disfranchisements of colored people by 'grandfather clauses'; against exclusion of colored people from 'white primaries' in the South; and, in the famous Arkansas peonage cases, establishing that a trial dominated by a mob is not due process of law.

"Wherever a discriminatory law has shown itself; wherever there has been illegal segregation, in motion picture theatres, theatres, schools, restaurants, railways and other places of public accommodation, the association has fought for true Americanism. On legal cases alone, including the five victories before the U.S. Supreme Court, the N.A.A.C.P. spent in the years from 1910 to September 30, 1928, the sum of $80,080.21, a trifling expenditure in view of the results achieved, the smallness of it being due to the public spirit and the generosity of prominent lawyers, among them Moorfield Storey, Arthur B. Spingarn and Clarence Darrow. The N.A.A.C.P. has even reached out beyond the United States, for its exposure of conditions in the American Occupation of Haiti resulted in Congressional inquiry and an abatement of the worst excesses.

"More than this the association has championed the individual victims of injustice. It has opened the doors of jail after jail for those unjustly confined because of their race. It has stood between innocent men and the scaffold—yes, time after time. It has defended the unjustly accused and prevented their conviction even when the law machinery and the police of a great city were determined to have them found guilty. Above all, perhaps, it has penetrated the very marrow of American public sentiment. It has changed that sentiment, slowly, persistently, and the change has been profound.

"There it has stood, the National Association for the Advancement of Colored People, for twenty years a tower of light, its rays thrown into dark places, illuminating the skies of hope, a beacon for all in distress because of their race to turn to for aid. Who can estimate what its mere existence has meant for the courage, the faith, the loyalty of twelve millions of Americans?

"And now this association turns to the public and asks a beggarly $200,000, ten thousand dollars a year for each year of its patriotic service. It needs an endowment not only because of the added strength which ten thousand dollars a year will bring, but because of the assurance this small endowment fund will give to colored people everywhere that the chief champion of their liberties is here to stay; that it is receiving the support that its extraordinary achievements merit.

"A million dollars is what it should have, and if it had it every cent could be spent wisely and well in its battle for the fundamental principles of American life. Two hundred thousand dollars is what it asks and what it expects. To every American who believes in fair play, . . . the enjoyment of life, liberty and the pursuit of happiness, we make this appeal."[37]

5

View Across the Color Line: Black

Hope for ultimate achievement by black Americans of full equality in American life existed as a spur to the efforts of many of the leaders of the race. As Americans, they were outraged at the shabby, unjust treatment so often given to the black citizens of the republic. As blacks, they were spurred on by the resilience demonstrated over decades of oppression. So long as some whites remained ready to lend assistance and support for the goal of equality, it seemed clear that others might be won over. Lofty national precepts and the fundamental sense of justice that lay at the heart of the American creed demanded no less.

Not all black leaders, of course, were in agreement regarding the best course to follow in the drive for racial justice. Many of the most conservative were heirs to the accommodationist policy of Booker T. Washington, which stressed the idea of acquiring property and learning trades and professions. By being law abiding, frugal, hard working, clean, and wholesome, blacks would earn, according to this mode of thought, acceptance as legal equals. Conservative spokesmen sometimes made the best of a bad thing by pointing out that "whatever political power the negro exerts is derived from segregation" in the large northern cities and that residential segregation had given rise to considerable acquisition of urban property by black Americans.[1]

The stress on individual achievement led Robert R. Moton, Washington's successor as principal at Tuskegee Institute, to declare that "a demonstration of equality in actual achievement will go further toward eliminating prejudice all round than any amount of legal protection in an atmosphere already prejudiced."[2]

At the other extreme in racial opinion were a number of radical groups representing several points of view. Some, like A. Philip Randolph and Chandler Owen, editors of the *Messenger*, combined economic radicalism during the early years of their magazine with demands for social equality between the races. Such demands were being made at a time when racial conservatives were hoping merely for a lifting of legal barriers.

Just as radical, but moving in a different direction and in a class by itself, was the Universal Negro Improvement Association led by Marcus A. Garvey. Garvey's recognition of the difficulty of ever achieving for black people a position of equality in a society dominated by whites led him to stress race pride and the importance of a Negro nation in Africa. Garvey's ability to tap the frustration of blacks, particularly of the lower class, who felt that they could not reach full stature in a white-dominated society, made the Universal Negro Improvement Association an agency of great importance despite its relatively short period of ascendency. Although the membership of the UNIA cannot be known with any certainty, estimates range between 9,703 and 4 million.[3] Perhaps even more important than numbers was the kind of comment made by the pastor of New York's Abyssinian Baptist Church. "I am not writing a brief for Marcus Garvey," he said, "but it is recording the truth . . . to say that he is the only man that ever made Negroes who are not black ashamed of their color."[4]

Between the black radicals and the conservatives was a large middle ground of racial opinion of such variety as to defy easy categorization. The National Association for the Advancement of Colored People, for example, pursued the policy indicated by the organization's name through public protest over major atrocities such as lynching and minor atrocities involving discrimination. In addition, the NAACP sought legal redress in the courts and improved understanding of black Americans on the part of government officials and the public generally. The National Urban League, more conservative than the NAACP, concentrated on problems of housing and employment while carrying on a fairly extensive program of social research.

Black churches played an enormously important role among black Americans. In addition to ministering to spiritual needs, the churches served as centers of community action and as islands of freedom and release from worldly problems. Particularly was this true for the members of the masses who were not directly involved in the activities of such middle-class organizations as the NAACP, but who were able to find opportunity for acceptance and self-expression in the all-black churches.[5] Some churches served also as focal points for community efforts in education, for cultural activities, and for community action groups.[6] In addition, there were members of black organizations, some affiliated with churches and some independent, devoted to special causes such as health, interracial cooperation, and professional advancement among black people.[7]

Many independent voices contributed to discussion of the racial situation in the United States. The commission investigating the Chicago riot of 1919 sought out black citizens to ask their opinions.[8] Journals like the *Crisis* and *Opportunity* frequently offered statements by writers unaffiliated with their respective sponsors, the NAACP and the Urban League. Magazines like *Survey* and the *American Mercury* made their pages available to black writers. Indeed, the growing numbers of talented black journalists, poets, novelists, and other artists reached such importance that the term "Negro Renaissance" came into common usage. These writers often cried out bitterly against racial conditions throughout the nation; other frequent themes were pride in black beauty and black heritage.

There has always been a tension between protest and accommodation in the thought of black Americans. This tension was certainly present in the years following the Great Migration, but the emphasis on fighting for democracy that existed during World War I, the increasingly large black population living in the relative freedom of the North, and the continued strivings of the black population shifted the balance ever more toward protest and away from accommodation.

ACCOMMODATION

By the 1920s Dean Kelly Miller of Howard University was a well-known spokesman on race issues. Earlier in the century, when Booker T. Washington and W. E. B. DuBois were in contention over the proper course of action to advance the Negro, Miller was unable to agree with the vigorous course proposed by DuBois and the NAACP in seeking racial justice. Just how far Miller moved toward vigorous protest may be seen in the selection below.[9] Even more impressive is the change in the Tuskegee position as stated by Robert R. Moton, Washington's successor at that institution. Although both men remained conservative on the race issue, conservatism was no longer a hat-in-hand position.

[1] KELLY MILLER SAYS

The month of August marks a decade since the beginning of the World War and the completion of the first year of President Coolidge's administration.

The last ten years has been the most remarkable decennial in the history of the human race. The press all over the world is indulging in appraisement of the momentous events of this period which change the trend of human history. Mine is the minor task of pointing out the significance of these transformations as they bear upon the fortune and the future of the Negro race.

During the past ten years there has been a radical change in the government of every great nation of the globe except the United States. The party of LaFollette, the tribune of the people, may presage a change in our government, such as that which has taken place in England, during the next twelve years.

In such an event the Negro will experience the far reaching effect of the new governmental policy. The world is fast falling under the rulership of the ten-fingered workers. The Negro works with the ten fingers of both hands, and cannot be incurious concerning the growing demands of the toilers of the world.

Four hundred thousand Negro youth participated in the World War. They entered upon the struggle with great expectation and high hopes. I recall vividly having called upon Secretary [of War] Baker along with a delegation of colored men to urge upon him the wisdom of the establishment of a colored officers' training camp. . . .

I addressed twelve hundred colored cadets at this camp. I never before had witnessed a group of Negro youth who were so buoyant and expectant of big things. The next week they were to be awarded shoulder straps. . . .

A sudden change of plans was announced. The period of training was extended for three weeks. The cadets were commissioned with lower ranks than was at first intended. The career of the Negro officer was doomed. . . .

It was declared that the Negro makes a good soldier, but a poor officer. This was the proposition that the Army wanted to prove. They proved it, to their own satisfaction, but not to ours.

A race of followers of alien command without the capacity for self leadership is exactly the kind of race that the white man wants to prove the Negro to be. This is, alas, the kind of race that many Negroes are disposed to accept as their ordained lot. But I believe that any people in the world, under proper environment and tutelage, will produce their own best and wisest leadership in every field of endeavor. If I am in error in this conceit, it is a delusion which I cherish with sweet delight. Though the dry land turn to sea, it will not make any change in me.

Our four hundred thousand soldier boys, after fighting to free the old world from the shackles of the ages came back home to find themselves a disappointed lot.

They were frankly told that they need not expect to share in that democracy which their prowess had helped to bring to white men. New barriers were to be faced that did not exist before. The rising tide of color, the intensification of the white race conscience-ness [sic], the recrudescence of the Ku Klux Klan, all focussed on the purpose to keep the Negro in his subordinate place. And yet he faces the situation with fortitude, resolution and hope.

The war killed off millions of the best equipped talent of the human race. It created a vacuum in the labor market. Negroes rush-ed by thousands into the mills and factories of the North, from which they had previously been excluded on account of race and color.

Nobody willed this movement; nobody planned or directed it. When bricks must be made, the brick makers will be forth coming. It is needless to speculate or moralize about this Negro migration. High wages is the one great incentive to human movement. The Negro came to the North, is coming now, and will continue to come as long as the higher payroll proves attractive.

This is the one outstanding compensative benefit which the war brought the Colored race. He is thus brought into close and inti-mate touch with the higher efficiency and industrial method of the North. The permanence of this advantage will depend upon the skill and readiness with which he absorbs this higher secret and method. This the South could never teach him; for it hasn't it to impart. The war intensified race consciousness.

This in turn led to limitation of immigration on the selective basis of racial preference. Here again the Negro became the benefi-ciary. He is likely to retain his place in the industrial life of the North as long as he demonstrates his efficiency and worth. The political education as well as economic consequences of this north-ern movement are big with possibilities for the future. So that what we lost in one respect, we may gain in another.

Internally the race has profited very little from the experiences of the last ten years. It has gained nothing in political prospects, except the incidental consequences of the northern migration. Our schools and colleges have been strengthened from a concrete and material standpoint; but some how there is lacking the correspond-ing upreaching of the spirit. . . .

The civil life of the race has experienced little stimulation. Alone of backward and suppressed groups, the Afro-American has re-mained almost unmoved by the experience of the world war in so far as his civil status is concerned.

Although the war was expressly fought for the self-determination of minor races and suppressed groups, the American Negro finds his lot not less oppressive than before. Not a single disability has been removed. . . .[10]

Two years later, Kelly Miller wrote the following:

[2] KELLY MILLER SAYS

President Coolidge has been in office thirty-six months. He has thirty more months to serve. The character and attitude of his administration on all great public questions have been determined. His achievements are declared to be satisfactory by his political supporters, and otherwise by his political adversaries.

President Coolidge is a man of solid character and fixed purpose. He does not shift his mood to suit the winds of shifting exigencies. His policy for the remaining two and a half years will be but a continuance of those already set in operation. Nothing but some unforeseen foreign involvement or domestic disturbance will radically alter the even tenor of the administration's way.

Something less than two years ago in the midst of the presidential campaign, I wrote a release entitled "President Coolidge in Account with the Negro." I also wrote several articles on his prospective treatment of the race question in case of his reelection.

On reviewing these contributions I am almost amazed at the accuracy of my own predictions. . . .

I clearly recall in October, 1924, . . . a symposium on the presidential candidates and issues. . . .

I was called upon for a few remarks. I began by expressing amusement at intelligent colored men lashing themselves into political fury over what white man should occupy the White House for the ensuing four years, as if it made any vital difference which of the three bore off the palm. Any one of them would have made a very good white man's president.

The status and treatment of the Negro would be but feebly affected by which ever of the three might be chosen. I wish now to extend that prophecy to cover the next quadrennium beginning in 1929.

The partisan advocates claimed that President Coolidge, who at that time had been in the White House for more than a year, was restrained by the policies of his predecessor, but if elected and given office in his own right he would then show the Negro great political favor.

I asked the question which was of a purely mathematical char-

acter: "If Mr. Coolidge appointed no colored man to office in fourteen months, how many would he appoint in forty-eight months?"
The ratio has been maintained with all but mathematical accuracy.

Aside from a replacement appointment, no colored man has yet
yet received a confirmatory office at the hands of the president. I
then maintained that the moment the President took the oath of
office he was as much president in his own right and power as he
ever could be under the constitution.

Deference to the policy of his predecessor was merely a matter
of courtesy. The Negro is the victim of the policy of his party, and
not of whoever for the moment happens to be its political dispenser.

This brings me to the main point and purpose of this release. The
race need no longer look to existing parties for political salvation.
What the Grand Old Party has done is of record. The past at least is
secure. The Negro's only chance is to use parties as instruments to
effect his welfare as best he may. Wise affiliation depends upon
time, place, and circumstances.

No party is going to espouse his cause by reason of the inherent
righteousness of his plea. It is wholly a matter of manoeuvering for
advantage. There is little hope for affirmative legislation and not
much more for appointive office; it matters not what party is in
charge of the machinery of government. . . .

It is useless to condemn President Coolidge or the Republican
party. Politics is a game of force. Complaint is as impotent as the
bleating of the ewe against the wolf. It is power and power alone
that gets results in the game of politics.

The fall campaign is now approaching. Let us hope that we shall
never again be forced to listen to the same old out-worn political
dope that has soothed the Negro's simple soul for two generations.
President Coolidge is too honest a man to deceive the Negro. The
race has no earthly reason to be disappointed in him. He promised
nothing and has faithfully kept his promise.[11]

The principal of Tuskegee Institute did not disagree with
Miller.

In effect the Negro is segregated in public thought as well as
in public carriers. The active hostility of an original few has induced a very general and almost complete ignorance of what the
Negro does face in this good land of "equal opportunity." The hostility, except for an occasional sporadic upheaval, is on the decline;

but the ignorance remains, as does also its effect. All over our country, in every section and every state, the Negro faces handicaps,
suffers discriminations, is meted injustices which make of the race
the most underprivileged group in American life. The extent to
which this is true is known only to those who labour under its disadvantages. In spite of them the race has forged ahead. But with
this advance the sense of inequality and injustice has deepened.
Along with it, however, goes to-day the conviction that not all of
his disadvantages are the result of malicious intent so much as of
ignorance and indifference. He, furthermore, believes that the inborn sense of fairness which in general characterizes American
life, will, when the facts are revealed, assert itself in removing the
inequalities and opening the way for the unhampered development
of its Negro citizenship in their constructive and original contribution to American life. The persistent voicing of his grievances
and his obvious separation from the rest of his fellow citizens, along
with the continual appeal for assistance in the enterprises that make
for the development of his race, have stimulated an increasing desire to know the facts concerning the Negro's life and activities as
a part of our national existence. A younger generation in all sections, along with fair-minded men and women of an older generation, are interested to learn what lies at the bottom of the Negro's
unrest and dissatisfaction, and what, if any, occasion exists for the
anomaly of the black man's segregation in the midst of a professedly
democratic situation. . . .

Properly to interpret the Negro one should understand at the out-
set that the psychology of the Negro is protective. The Negro everywhere has a steadfast purpose of survival: the race must be very
old, for that is its ingrained habit. It has long been subject to adversity: this has made the race cautious. It has had a long history
of slavery, long before American slavery: this has made it secretive
in the presence of manifestly preponderant power and general
animosity. The race still survives, for it has learned the discretion
that is the better part of valour. In this last trait the Negro stands in
distinct contrast to the North American Indian. The Indian also is
cautious and secretive, proverbially so; but he will stand and fight
a regiment of artillery with no other weapon than a bow and arrow.
To him survival does not enter into consideration at all; his is
probably the most spirited race among mankind. It paid the price
of its valour with the risk of entire extinction. In the same situation
the Negro would waive the challenge to hostilities, come volun-

tarily into the enemies' camp, and by ingratiating usefulness and discretion soon win his way to command of the very weapons designed for use against him.

In this the careful observer will discover another characteristic of Negro psychology—his quick perception of physical disadvantage and his equally quick adjustment to secure the moral advantage. In all the agitation concerning the Negro's status in America, the moral advantage has always been on his side, and with that as a lever he has steadily effected progress in spite of material disadvantages. In this he has surprised both friends and foes. Somehow there has been an element of the white race in America that has constantly expected the Negro to resort to violence for the satisfaction of his grievances. This apprehension existed in a large degree immediately after his emancipation and was a strong factor in the developments of "reconstruction." It presented itself again after the World War.

There were those who feared that the experiences of the black man on the soil of France would make him bitter and vengeful on his return to America. With this thought in mind many communities, especially in the South, prepared themselves for physical encounters with returning Negro soldiers. Sheriffs in some instances went so far as to supply themselves with machine guns and took other measures to protect the community against possible violence. But in this there was a surprising and general, though agreeable, disappointment. These boys did return with a deeper sense of the injustices of their position in America. Those who remained at home, both men and women, were more sensible than ever of their wrongs. But their indignation took the form of stern resolve to wield the moral weapons of their incongruous position to their utmost effect in securing what in the fervour of war was their admitted right as American citizens. This was the attitude of the Negro then and is his attitude now, and has been his attitude throughout his long contact with the white man in America.

All this registers a keen sense of the inconsistencies of the practice of democracy as applied to the Negro. He sees quite clearly just where the white man's professions of Christianity and his practice of the code in his relations with his darker brother in Christ do not harmonize. Beneath his guileless, pleasant exterior there is a deep-seated concern. He has no intention of deceiving with his smile. It is his saving grace; it is primarily for his own benefit; it salves the wounds of adversity.

In this mood the Negro has taken on a fresh interest in his fellow Americans. He is thinking, and it is always interesting when people begin to think. It is in answer to this interest that the attempt is here made to make some revelation of the experiences of the Negro which produce the irritations of racial contacts, the thoughts they stimulate, and in addition some of the feelings that rise in his breast as he reflects upon the ways of the white man. Some things here recorded may surprise a great many white people, but that is only because the Negro has always been quite chary of disclosing all his thoughts to the white man. He seldom tells all the truth about such matters: a great deal of it may not find its way into this volume; but what is here set forth may be confirmed almost any time, anywhere; not, indeed, by asking the individual Negro a direct question on the subject, but by changing places with him — which nobody in America wants to do, not even his most devoted and sympathetic friends — and living for a brief period among the uncertainties, perplexities, and inconsistencies which are the daily experience in greater or less degree of every Negro in these United States.

The hope is that this candid revelation will tend to convince all classes that the Negro has just cause for dissatisfaction with his present condition in American life; that the things complained of are not necessary to safeguard the welfare and prosperity of any group of American citizens; that most of these abuses could be corrected through the application of courage, conscientiousness, and consistency; and that the Negro himself is equipped and qualified as well as ready to do his share, and more if necessary, to make the adjustments that would bring harmony, good will, contentment, prosperity, and safety to all.[12]

RADICALISM

Although support for economic radicalism was never widespread among black Americans, expression of such radicalism is highly significant as an indicator of racial protest. In the case of the *Messenger*, a magazine published after 1917 by a group headed by A. Philip Randolph and Chandler Owen, racial protest was an essential ingredient in its editorial position. In its earlier years this magazine, calling itself a journal of "scientific radicalism," argued that private enterprise and competition made race prejudice profitable to the capitalist class and were incentives to race conflict.[13]

By 1923, however, the *Messenger* had changed its views sufficiently to devote an entire issue to the praise of black capitalism.[14] That issue contained, among other things, an enthusiastic account of black business ventures,[15] an account of the career of Robert S. Abbott, publisher of the *Chicago Defender*, in the best Horatio Alger style,[16] and a considerable quantity of advertising for black insurance firms, banks, hotels, and real estate brokers. The *Messenger*'s point of view, which developed in a context of increasing political and economic conservatism in the United States after World War I, remained one of vigorous race pride and protest against second-class citizenship.

In 1919 the *Messenger* devoted considerable space to outlining a program of demands for Negro rights—political, social, civil, and industrial. Many of the demands were concerned with some of the worst outrages perpetrated in the South, but others applied with equal force throughout the nation.

INTRODUCTION

In America there are several groups of classes and races. Each has, to a certain extent, special problems, while all are affected by certain general problems.

Among the variegated reasons for divisions in the respective groups (the extreme physical oppositeness and the late emancipation from chattel slavery) which have resulted in widespread poverty and ignorance—present a sharp line of demarcation as respects the Negro.

The reconstruction program for the Negro must involve the introduction of the new social order—a democratic order in which human rights are recognized above property rights. We recognize, in sketching, in broad outline, this new order, that there cannot be any separate and distinct principles for the social, political and economic emancipation of the Negro which are not applicable to all other people.

The reason why we present a special program for the Negro is that heretofore, in the United States, programs referring to "all persons," "all people," "all men," have meant all white men. And, consequently, this has become a part of the public psychology. Hence, this brief explanation for our reconstruction program for the Negro. . . .

POLITICAL PROGRAM

5. Industrial Control

The private domination of industry for private gain has brought such disastrous consequences both among and within the nations of the world as to make public ownership for public service the first necessity in any forward-looking plan of reconstruction both for the nation and the Negro.

We, therefore, demand that all public utilities and basic industries of the United States be taken over by the people and that this process shall be undertaken as speedily as is consistent with public order and security, and allowing for the utmost possible degree of local autonomy.

We demand the full and permanent nationalization of the railroads and other means of transportation such as canals, waterways, etc., steamships and steamship lines, telegraph and telephone lines, power, such as coal mines, oil wells and water power; also large scale industry such as stock yards, grain elevators, flour mills and lumber lands.

This means a reduced cost of food, clothing and fuel, as well as of telephone and telegraph messages, all of which the Negro must use daily and frequently. It will operate to increase the wages of Negro employees, both actually and relatively, because the government pays a larger money income, while the lower price paid for goods and services will increase the purchasing power of the dollar. The government can do this because it pays no profits to private individuals, but runs these utilities for service of the public. . . .

8. Taxation

In 1876 [*sic*] it was alleged that taxation without representation is tyranny, and that it produced the Revolutionary War. We in 1919 reaffirm that taxation without representation is tyranny. We hereby demand that in no political division of the U.S. shall an individual be taxed without receiving representation, whatever his color, race or nationality.

We advocate a radical revision of our system and methods of taxation to the end that all indirect taxes on consumers' goods shall be abolished. Taxes should be placed upon those most able to bear them.

We therefore favor:

1. A progressive income tax, aiming at the abolition of all incomes, above the needs of a comfortable and secure livelihood.

2. A progressive inheritance tax, rising to 100% in large estates.

3. Taxation of the unearned increment of land; all lands held out of use to be taxed at full rental value.

4. A more adequate corporations tax.

These taxes will be of special benefit to the Negro because he buys almost exclusively consumers' goods, as do the large majority of working white people. He buys little or no producers' goods, since there are but few Negro capitalists, manufacturers or large bonanza agriculturists.

9. Woman Suffrage

We favor the adoption of the Susan B. Anthony amendment to the Constitution, granting suffrage to women—both white and colored.

10. We favor proportional representation as being the most democratic basis of representation.

11. We favor the initiative referendum and recall.

SOCIAL PROGRAM

Education

The object of true education is two-fold: one, the popular dissemination of useful information; two, the stimulation of invention and discovery.

We, therefore, favor the adoption of the following measures:

(1) A system of universal and compulsory education. Every child up to the age of eighteen years should be compelled to go through an approved system of technical and scientific courses.

(2) The extension of high school facilities and the increase in the number of common schools.

(3) A complete revision and change in curricula by a commission of able educational experts. We recommend the teaching of a thorough course in the physical sciences, sociology, economics, and history in the high schools; the subordination of the dead languages, such as Latin and Greek, the Bible and many of the valueless English classics.

(4) We favor a definite increase in the pay of teachers and condemn any variation in the pay, based upon race, color, or nationality. They should also be permitted to organize, collectively bargain and strike for more pay, shorter hours and better working conditions.

(5) The school terms in the rural districts in the South should be extended to eight months in every year.

(6) We demand that equal appropriations be made for white and black children alike.

(7) The school buildings should be uniform in numbers in proportion to population, and equipment, and should be used for all community interests. There should be no bar to the use of the school by any organization whose program does not include the physical destruction of the school plant.

Public Education

(8) A systematic course of public lectures on all subjects should be carried on in the school auditorium for the general education of the community. These lectures should be especially devoted to political, social and economic problems.

(9) All political parties should have access to the school, free of charge, during and after political campaigns. No trick should be used to prevent the use of the school by requiring parties to secure a certain enrolled vote, or vote cast for them, as a condition to qualifying.

(10) Public libraries owned and controlled in toto by the municipality should be established. No censorship should be exercised in the selection of books beyond a reasonable demand for literary form and freedom from obscenity and indecency.

No private contributions should be accepted by the municipality or state for the use of these libraries, but such monies as are needed for their equipment, maintenance and development should be applied from the funds raised through taxation. . . .

CIVIL RIGHTS

Social Equality

We favor "Social equality" in every sense of the phrase. We demand a new order based upon a society of equals. Evasions, pretexts and excuses cannot explain away the fact that no genuine brotherhood can exist so long as the issue of social equality is not squarely met. Democracy cannot exist upon a foundation of caste.

We cannot work side by side in factory, field and office and then maintain that we cannot sit side by side in restaurant, theatre, and public conveyance.

How may social equality be achieved? History shows that the growth of equality—political, social and economic—has grown out of the two cardinal and corollary principles of *identity of treatment and free interchangeability.* . . .

We now approach the American bugaboo—the question upon which Negroes and whites alike evade, equivocate, compromise and set up false theories in flagrant violation and defiance of the most fundamental principles of social evolution. We refer to inter-marriage between the whites and Negroes. We favor the inter-marriage between any sane, grown persons who desire to marry— whatever their race or color. We favor the intermarriage of white men with colored women as well as colored men with white women. . . .

We therefore demand the repeal of all laws against intermarriage as being inimical to the interests of both races. We further call attention to the fact that there is no desire to check the associations of white men with colored women, colored women with white men, nor to serve any interests of Negro men. And inasmuch as no law requires any woman under any circumstances to marry a man whom she does not will or want to marry, these laws narrow themselves down to the prevention of white women marrying colored men whom they desire to marry.

Moreoever, social history in the South records in the ineradicable faces of four million mullatoes that there is "social equality galore after dark" when the blackness of night enables the human desires to take their free, unhindered, natural and proper course.

We repudiate and condemn any pretense at opposition to Jim Crowism, segregation and all forms of discrimination which does not accept the principle of social equality, since it is upon the fallacious theory of inequality and racial inferiority that all these evils are established and continued. We do not accept the doctrine of old, reactionary Negroes that the Negro is satisfied to be himself. We desire as much contact and intercourse—social, economic and political—as is possible between the races. This is not because of our belief in the inferiority or superiority of either race, but be-cause of our recognition that the principle of social equality is the only sure guarantee of social progress—the inevitable trend of evolution.

CIVIL LIBERTIES

Civil liberty in the United States is dead. Any true reconstruction program must deal with its resuscitation and its reintroduction
into American life. Civil Liberty for the Negro, however, was dead
even before the war [First World War], killed by a combination of
an hypocritical North and an unregenerate South who colluded to
sweep from the Negro his last vestige of liberty. . . .[17]

PROPAGANDA, PROTEST AND WELFARE ORGANIZATIONS

In the years before World War I both the National Association for the Advancement of Colored People and the National Urban League had assumed the task of improving the
condition of the race. This meant, for the NAACP, an emphasis on protest, agitation, and political action. Begun in
1909, the Association had members in 325 branches in forty-
four states by 1929.[18] Established through the combined efforts of black leaders like W. E. B. DuBois and white Pro-
gressives like Oswald Garrison Villard, the NAACP investigated lynchings and made strong protests, undertook the
legal defense of the victims of race riots in 1917 and 1919,
and sought to prevent miscarriages of justice against blacks,
as in the defense of Dr. Ossian Sweet and his family. Almost
from the start, the Association undertook legal action to secure the enforcement of the Fourteenth and Fifteenth
Amendments. In 1915 it succeeded in having the Supreme
Court deny the constitutionality of the grandfather clause [19]
and in 1917 the Court outlawed residential segregation imposed by municipal ordinance.[20]

Court battles in defense of the right of black people to vote
and to reside in a home of their own choosing continued to
be a major activity of the Association.[21] At the same time it
publicized its work and its philosophy through its official
organ, the *Crisis,* edited by DuBois, and engaged in other
important activities such as lobbying for the Dyer Anti-
Lynching bill in 1921 and successfully opposing the appoint-

ment of Judge John J. Parker, considered to be a racist, to the Supreme Court in 1930.[22]

Although the NAACP was concerned about the problem of job discrimination, it generally left the major work in that area to the National Urban League. Founded in 1910, the League was also an interracial organization and, like the Association, was at first dominated by white reformers. The League attempted to convince employers of the value of hiring black workers and labor unions of the shortsightedness of viewing blacks as economic rivals. In this latter quest the League was generally unsuccessful. This failure, together with the middle-class background of most of its officials, may account for much of the Urban League's anti-union attitude. The League also undertook investigation of conditions in many urban centers around the country and published some of the results of the work of its Research Department in its official organ, *Opportunity*. Whatever success the League had in advancing the cause of the black worker was, unfortunately, severely impaired by the depression after the 1920s.

Ironically, both the Urban League and the NAACP were not especially successful in enlisting the support of the black masses. Basically middle class in orientation, the two organizations were unable adequately to reach across class lines in black society. To some extent this was true also of black churches, the larger ones tending to appeal to the middle class. In the case of churches and fraternal societies, both of tremendous importance as sources of racial solidarity, there were such numbers of them, and so many small ones, that their meeting places provided a haven for almost anyone who cared to come.

An excerpt from a typical NAACP report follows.

SCHOOLS

Let us pursue a little farther the Association's campaign against the segregation principle. The year 1927 showed one victory over residential segregation and one over the segregated vote. Another point of attack has been the schools. It has long been realized that to implant the idea of race antagonism in young people is to lay the seeds of race dissension among adults. For this reason the N.A.A.C.P. has tirelessly opposed the extension of the segregated school principle in the North. One such attempt occurred in Toms River, New Jersey, last spring and attracted the attention of the entire country. The N.A.A.C.P. was informed that colored children were being excluded from the public school there and were being herded in a building which was not only separate from the whites, but unfit for use as a school being dark and unsanitary. The N.A.A.C.P., realizing that this was a case which not only deserved to be fought on its merits, but which might serve as a precedent in the Northern states if allowed to pass uncontested, retained an attorney, Mr. Eugene R. Hayne, of Asbury Park. A hearing of protest was arranged before the Governor of New Jersey at which national officers of the N.A.A.C.P. were in attendance as well as representatives from most of the New Jersey branches. The case was carried both into the courts and before New Jersey's Education Commission. The case was won decisively and the Commissioner of Education ordered that the colored children be restored to the school from which they had been illegally excluded. The case was given the widest publicity in the press and it was made known to the country that colored people were opposed to the extension of the segregation principle in the schools; and what is more that they were prepared to fight it to a conclusive show-down. This was again made clear in Gary, Indiana, where the white students of the Emerson High School, inspired no doubt by the Klan spirit which is rife in that state, went on "strike" against the continued presence in their schools of upwards of a score of colored pupils. The city council, capitulating to this expression of mob spirit, voted $15,000 for the erection of a "temporary" segregated high school to house these colored students. Again the N.A.A.C.P., both through its ably led and well-organized Gary branch and through the National Office, took this case to court. The expenditure of the $15,000 Gary city funds, which were derived from the taxes paid by both colored and white citizens, for a segregated high school was enjoined. And the Mayor of Gary finally realized that the position the city had taken was untenable. The city council rescinded their appropriation. The injunction against the segregated institution was made permanent. And, as a price for the discontinuance of further court procedure, the city of Gary paid the cost of the legal proceedings which had been brought by the N.A.A.C.P.

Every one of the four cases thus far listed as part of the victorious achievement of the N.A.A.C.P. for the year 1927, has helped to establish and to strengthen a general principle. It is the principle that it is contrary to the American idea that human beings shall be deprived of any citizenship privileges, whether of right or residence, of voting, or of public schooling among their fellows because of the accident of race or color. Virtually every case fought by the N.A.A.C.P. depends upon the affirmation of this principle in one form or another. If a keystone of the Association's work were sought, it might be found in this consistent and persistent opposition to the segregation or "Jim Crow" spirit.[23]

An address by an Urban League official described that organization's role.

It would not be amiss . . . to tell just a few of the types of work that this movement does and of some of the outstanding achievements. The city of Detroit with 6,000 Negro population in a total population of 250,000, suddenly begins to realize that its Negro population is increasing to unheard of proportions. In fact, it increased within a period of four to five years from 6,000 to 40,000 in a population of a million souls. There are not sufficient churches and houses and employment service to take care of this rapidly increasing Negro group, most of whom are coming from the small towns and rural districts of the south. The white charitable agencies are not equipped to cope with the situation and in many instances are not willing to assume the responsibilities that accompany such a sudden change in the complexion of its population.

The Detroit Urban League is formed. An employment bureau is established through this agency. Contacts are made with the largest industrial plants; jobs are found fitted to the men and men are found fitted to the jobs. Recreational facilities are provided for the leisure time of the workers and for the members of their families who are beginning to arrive in large numbers. New homes are found with rents suitable to the income of the newcomers. Those unsocial and handicapped members of the group who find themselves in misery and despair are brought in contact with those social agencies which are especially equipped for handling such cases. Order is developed out of chaos and we find . . . within a period of two years, leading social magazines and social workers throughout our country pointing to Detroit as a place where thousands of Negro newcomers have been brought into a community and absorbed with hardly a vibration in the social structure. . . .

Similar activities are now seen in practically all of the largest industrial communities in America. Pittsburgh, Chicago, Columbus, St. Louis and Kansas City as industrial centers; St. Paul and Minneapolis in the far north; Richmond, Atlanta, and Tampa in the far south; Boston, New York, Newark and Philadelphia on the seaboard and Los Angeles on the Pacific Coast in addition to other cities which I could mention are enjoying the fruits of this service. Baltimore, the latest of the cities organizing with an executive secretary, can testify to the untiring efforts of the members of the national movement to bring to communities which are in need of this service this organization's aid in the solution of one of America's baffling problems.

The New York School of Social Work, the first school to offer fellowships for the training of Urban League appointees, has been followed by the Chicago University Graduate School of Social Administration; the University of Pittsburgh; the Pennsylvania School of Social and Health Work and the School of Social Work of Simmons College, Boston, Mass., which are offering from year to year the same opportunities. And there are other institutions which now have indicated their willingness to cooperate in the same manner. The total number of students who have received this training thus far is 28. These "Fellows" become Urban League executives, probation and parole officers, family case workers, girls' and boys' club supervisors, specialists in mental hygiene, directors of recreational activities in connection with play-grounds for public schools and secretaries for the Y.M.C.A. and Y.W.C.A.

The League has been instrumental in securing some very significant openings for colored people such as internes in Bellevue Hospital, in New York City. It was responsible for the establishment of the policy of employing Negro representatives in the United States Department of Labor; the employment of Negro personnel workers in many of the large industrial plants; the employment of clerks—male and female—in important business houses; the securing of positions of chemists and general foremen and highly skilled artisans in some of the great industries.

The League has been responsible for inaugurating the systems of vocational guidance and visiting teachers in several public school systems after first testing the practicability of the scheme. It has organized probation and Big Sister and Big Brother work in connection with its general activities. It has been responsible for the establishment of institutions for wayward girls, community houses and recreational centers and it has published "OPPOR-TUNITY" a magazine which is rapidly becoming recognized as one of the outstanding journals of Negro life, discussing in a dispassionate and highly scientific manner the problems growing out of race conditions. This magazine is now being used in classes in Sociology in over forty of our leading white universities north and south. More than 200 school and city libraries receive it regularly and every day it seems that we are adding to this list and receiving requests for the full volumes covering the two years during which it has been published.

We have developed a Department of Research and Investigations which makes special studies of social conditions in our large cities, publishes them for the good it will do those cities as well as other cities of similar character and supplies information for debates, lectures, and writings to many of the leading students of inter-racial problems. . . .

The League has made a very definite and conscious effort to develop more confidence in the Negro on the part of white persons —those in positions of responsibility such as the employing class and those who are of the rank and file. Yet, we have not lost sight of the fact that after all is said and done one cannot gain very surely the love of those who are about him without first commanding their respect and this we have emphasized, urging Negroes to measure up in every way to the requirements of our modern civilization and to command the respect of those who deign to sit in judgment on their capacity and their worth. . . .

The material things involved in our work are important. They certainly are things that people can most easily see, but above all, we value the spirit of good will and confidence in mankind which through our endeavors, we are privileged to encourage.[24]

George E. Haynes, one of the founders of the National Urban League and secretary to the Commission on Race Relations of the Federal Council of the Churches of Christ in America, comments on the establishment of black churches, particularly in the cities.

So recently have men of all races come to dwell in cities that their churches often have the organization and equipment typical of the small town and rural district. This is especially the case with the Negro church because only in the past sixty years have its constituents been moving with the population stream from the rural districts to urban centers. Only within the last twenty years have the numbers assumed large proportions in most of the communities that have grown up around the industrial plants of the Northern cities. As Negroes moved North they have brought their church with them. Individuals and groups, mainly of Baptists and Methodists, have transferred their relationships from the little churches of their Southern communities to the "watch-care" or to full membership of churches of the "same faith and order" in Northern communities. In a few cases whole congregations from Southern communities have moved North together and brought their pastors with them. In other cases Negro churches in Northern cities, which before the heavy migration of the last ten years had small struggling congregations, have increased their membership to large numbers and have become powerful in resources. Many of them have able ministers who, like the physicians, lawyers, editors, and business men who followed in the wake of the wage-earners, have come from the South to answer the Northern call. . . .

Besides the large self-supporting congregations with well-appointed buildings, there are nearly a score of "house-front" and "mission" churches. The "mission" churches are those that receive a part of their support from denominational missionary or extension societies which are stirred to action by the teeming unchurched masses of the district. These societies subsidize salaries of ministers, assist in the purchase of buildings or in other ways help to extend their denominational effort to evangelize and serve the people of this region. The "house-front" churches are started usually when some individual who has felt the call to the ministry has gathered about himself a little flock, or when several persons join together and ask a minister to lead them. The purchase of an equity in a private house is usually made. The double parlors on the first floor are used for church purposes while the upper floors serve as a residence for the minister or for other tenants.

The organization, support and operation of Negro churches have become increasingly independent of white people. Negroes have thus had valuable experience and group training in standing upon their own legs and in going forward to achieve ends mapped out by themselves. The Negro churches are almost exclusively racial both in their membership and in their administration. Even congregations that belong to denominations made up of a majority of white communicants, such as the Protestant Episcopal, Methodist Episcopal and the Congregational Churches, are for all practical purposes autonomous, exercising great independence in government and being controlled only to a nominal extent by the general organization. . . .

In the independent Negro denominations there are more than 35,000 churches with over four million members enrolled and church property valued at over seventy million dollars. In the mixed religious bodies there are over 6,000 Negro churches, nearly three quarter million Negro members enrolled and over seventeen millions in church property.[25]

There is a strong racial tie between Negro churches, both of the independent group and of mixed denominations. Recently churches of the several denominations of Harlem joined forces in a league, affiliated with the New York Church Federation and employed an executive secretary. Denominational differences are no problem with these churches as there are frequent visits of delegations from one congregation to another and frequent ministerial fellowship and exchange of pulpits. . . .

The spirit of the Negro people is shown in the fleeting hours of their amusement and play, in the furtive expression of their appreciation of things beautiful, and in outpourings of personality and emotion as they gather in their places of worship, and as they render the many personal services the one to the other in the routine of daily life. Free self-expression in these directions is often limited in America by economic and social discriminations. Emotional experience and the personal experience of service, however, find large objective opportunity through the Negro church. . . .[26]

A Detroit survey reports on the psycho-social role of black churches.

THE PROGRAM OF THE NEGRO CHURCH: SOCIAL

The Negro Church as a Social Center in the Community.

The church is the most frequented institution in the social life of the Negro population of Detroit. It is to the church the Negro can go with the greatest assurance of being courteously received. He

has been humiliated in so many public and privately owned institutions and amusement places that he has resorted to the church
as a place in which he can be sure of peacefully spending his leisure time. To a large extent it takes the place of the theatre, the
dance halls, and similar amusement places and fills the vacancy
created by the failure of the public and commercial places of recreation and amusement to give him a cordial welcome. Consequently, the average Negro church in Detroit keeps its doors open
constantly for the use of the community. Numerous suppers, lectures, recitals, debates, plays and the like are given by clubs and
individuals from within and without the congregation. In order to
serve his congregation most efficiently, therefore, the Negro minister must be a community worker as well as a moral teacher. The
family schedules which were taken to the heads of one thousand
families show that with the exception of the "movies," church
entertainments are the principal form of recreation. This wider use
of the church is forcing many of the more old fashioned churches
to acquire a broader vision of providing facilities for wholesome
leisure time activities for the community.

Notwithstanding the fact that there are no set and fast social
classes among Negro churches, yet there is a tendency on the part
of those who fancy themselves to [be] the intelligentsia and of the
better paid workmen and business men to seek membership in the
larger Protestant Episcopal churches, while the masses of the laboring classes make up almost the entire membership of the smaller
Baptist and Methodist churches. The membership of the so-called
"hysteria" churches is also made up entirely of the unskilled laboring classes. The flocking of the masses of Negro migrants to these
smaller and less efficient churches has been due largely to the belief that many of the large churches have given them "the cold
shoulder" instead of the warm welcome which is supposed to be
due every applicant for membership irrespective of his social
standing. It is this belief which has largely helped to create the
numerous little churches that are found in the various Negro areas
of Detroit, and the fact should be carefully weighed before criticiz-
ing them too severely.

The Negro Church as a Force for Community Betterment.

The Negro churches of Detroit are beginning to have a vision of
social betterment. The old type of church that appealed only to the
spiritual side of the individual is being replaced by the type which

is striving for both the spiritual and the social improvement of the community. A great deal of the social work conducted in Negro churches has been unscientific and consequently there has been much overlapping of effort, in each case largely due to the employment of workers who have not the proper educational background.

The large influx of Negro migrants to Detroit has probably given greater impetus to community betterment work among Negro churches than any other force. Many of these migrants needed aid and a number of the larger churches developed social welfare departments to meet their needs. In most cases, the work was turned over to untrained laymen and in other cases pastors, little qualified themselves, attempted to conduct this phase of the church activities.

The introduction of such untrained and unqualified workers into social welfare work was a handicap in the development of a program that would be of help to the newcomers. These untrained laymen were handicapped both by their own inexperience and by a lack of the necessary facilities for the efficient carrying on of a welfare program. They endeavored to find employment for the newcomers, to find houses, and in general to do everything within their power to adjust the migrants to urban life. Although these activities were carried on in an extremely unscientific manner, yet the motive behind them was one of real helpfulness and service.

Today several of the larger churches maintain trained social workers to minister to the social needs of the Negro community. There is need for more trained workers who will coordinate their efforts in such a way as to prevent duplication. If the welfare departments of the various churches are not carefully welded together, many undeserving families and individuals will take advantage of the lack of coordination and receive help from several churches at the same time.

The welfare departments of some of the larger colored churches provide for such activities as sewing, cooking, millinery, music, the securing of employment for men and women, and such leisure time forms of play as baseball, basketball, tennis and volleyball. The recreational phase of welfare work, however, has been sadly neglected by the majority of churches because of lack of equipment. The only real gymnasium among Negro churches is located at Bethel A.M.E. though plans are on foot at Second Baptist and several other churches for the construction of gymnasiums to meet the recreational needs of the community.[27]

GARVEYISM

In 1914 Marcus Garvey established in his native Jamaica the Universal Negro Improvement Association which, among its major aims, sought "to establish a Universal Confraternity among the race [and] to promote the spirit of race pride and love."[28] Throughout his career Garvey devoted himself to these goals and to the liberation of all black people on every continent. Within a few years after Garvey arrived in the United States in 1916, the UNIA had established branches in many American cities and several foreign countries. Believing that "prejudice we shall always have between black and white, so long as the latter believes that the former is intruding upon their right," and that the "Negro needs a nation and a country of his own, where he can best show evidence of his own ability in the art of human progress,"[29] Garvey held out as a utopian ideal the wholesale migration of American Negroes to Africa. Until this ideal could be achieved, Garvey urged black people to support Negro businesses; the UNIA itself organized a number of stores and factories. It was the UNIA's poor management of the Black Star Steamship Line that Garvey's enemies seized upon, however. Here Garvey was vulnerable, and in 1923 he was convicted of mail fraud and given a vindictively heavy sentence.

It was not Marcus Garvey's concern for Africa alone that makes his role an important one, however. Pan-Africanism was hardly a new phenomenon. In 1900, H. Sylvester-Williams, a black West Indian practicing law in London, had issued a call for a Pan-African Congress, and in 1912 an international conference was held at Tuskegee Institute to investigate the possibility of applying Tuskegee methods to assist black people in Africa, the West Indies, and South America.[30] During the 1920s W. E. B. DuBois was actively engaged in promoting a series of Pan-African conferences, hoping to create among black people everywhere improved status and a sense of community.[31] Garvey's contribution lay in his ability to stir the black masses, to develop race pride where only frustration had existed, and to convey to his tens of thousands of followers a sense of the power that was theirs if they could work together.

THE TRUE SOLUTION OF THE NEGRO PROBLEM — 1922

As far as Negroes are concerned, in America we have the problem of lynching, peonage and dis-franchisement.

In the West Indies, South and Central America we have the problem of peonage, serfdom, industrial and political governmental inequality.

In Africa we have, not only peonage and serfdom, but outright slavery, racial exploitation and alien political monopoly.

We cannot allow a continuation of these crimes against our race. As four hundred million men, women and children, worthy of the existence given us by the Divine Creator, we are determined to solve our own problem, by redeeming our Motherland Africa from the hands of alien exploiters and found there a government, a nation of our own, strong enough to lend protection to the members of our race scattered all over the world, and to compel the respect of the nations and races of the earth.

Do they lynch Englishmen, Frenchmen, Germans, or Japanese? No. And why? Because these people are represented by great governments, mighty nations and empires, strongly organized. Yes, and ever ready to shed the last drop of blood and spend the last penny in the national treasury to protect the honor and integrity of a citizen outraged anywhere.

Until the Negro reaches this point of national independence, all he does as a race will count for naught, because the prejudice that will stand out against him even with his ballot in his hand, with his industrial progress to show, will be of such an overwhelming nature as to perpetuate mob violence and mob rule, from which he will suffer, and which he will not be able to stop with his industrial wealth and with his ballot.

You may argue that he can use his industrial wealth and his ballot to force the government to recognize him, but he must understand that the government is the people. That the majority of the people dictate the policy of governments, and if the majority are against a measure, a thing, or a race, then the government is impotent to protect that measure, thing or race.

If the Negro were to live in this Western Hemisphere for another five hundred years he would still be outnumbered by other races who are prejudiced against him. He cannot resort to the government for protection for government will be in the hands of the majority of the people who are prejudiced against him, hence for the Negro to depend on the ballot and his industrial progress alone, will be hopeless as it does not help him when he is lynched, burned, jim-crowed and segregated. The future of the Negro therefore, outside of Africa, spells ruin and disaster.[32]

The following speech carries some of the flavor of Garvey's powerful oratory.

SPEECH DELIVERED AT LIBERTY HALL N.Y.C. DURING SECOND
INTERNATIONAL CONVENTION OF NEGROES
AUGUST 1921

Four years ago, realizing the oppression and the hardships from which we suffered, we organized ourselves into an organization for the purpose of bettering our condition, and founding a government of our own. The four years of organization have brought good results, in that from an obscure, despised race we have grown into a mighty power, a mighty force whose influence is being felt throughout the length and breadth of the world. The Universal Negro Improvement Association existed but in name four years ago, today it is known as the greatest moving force among Negroes. We have accomplished this through unity of effort and unity of purpose, it is a fair demonstration of what we will be able to accomplish in the very near future, when the millions who are outside the pale of the Universal Negro Improvement Association will have linked themselves up with us.

By our success of the last four years we will be able to estimate the grander success of a free and redeemed Africa. In climbing the heights to where we are today, we have had to surmount difficulties, we have had to climb over obstacles, but the obstacles were stepping stones to the future greatness of this Cause we represent. Day by day we are writing a new history, recording new deeds of valor performed by this race of ours. It is true that the world has not yet valued us at our true worth but we are climbing its attitude toward us. Wheresoever you turn your eyes today you will find the moving influence of the Universal Negro Improvement Association among Negroes from all corners of the globe. We hear among

Negroes the cry of "Africa for the Africans." This cry has become a positive, determined one. It is a cry that is raised simultaneously the world over because of the universal oppression that affects the Negro. You who are congregated here tonight as Delegates representing the hundreds of branches of the Universal Negro Improvement Association in different parts of the world will realize that we in New York are positive in this great desire of a free and redeemed Africa. We have established this Liberty Hall as the centre from which we send out the sparks of liberty to the four corners of the globe, and if you have caught the spark in your section, we want you to keep it a-burning for the great Cause we represent.

There is a mad rush among races everywhere towards national independence. Everywhere we hear the cry of liberty, of freedom, and a demand for democracy. In our corner of the world we are raising the cry for liberty, freedom and democracy. Men who have raised the cry for freedom and liberty in ages past have always made up their minds to die for the realization of the dream. We who are assembled in this Convention as Delegates representing the Negroes of the world give out the same spirit that the fathers of liberty in this country gave out over one hundred years ago. We give out a spirit that knows no compromise, a spirit that refuses to turn back, a spirit that says "Liberty or Death," and in prosecution of this great ideal—the ideal of a free and redeemed Africa, men may scorn, men may spurn us, and may say that we are on the wrong side of life, but let me tell you that way in which you are travelling is just the way all peoples who are free have travelled in the past. If you want Liberty you yourselves must strike the blow. If you must be free you must become so through your own effort, through your own initiative. Those who have discouraged you in the past are those who have enslaved you for centuries and it is not expected that they will admit that you have a right to strike out at this late hour for freedom, liberty and democracy.

At no time in the history of the world, for the last five hundred years, was there ever a serious attempt made to free Negroes.

We have been camouflaged into believing that we were made free by Abraham Lincoln. That we were made free by Victoria of England, but up to now we are still slaves, we are industrial slaves, we are social slaves, we are political slaves, and the new Negro desires a freedom that has no boundary, no limit. We desire a freedom that will lift us to the common standard of all men, whether they be white men of Europe or yellow men of Asia, therefore, in our desire to lift ourselves to that standard we shall stop at nothing until there is a free and redeemed Africa.

I understand that just at this time while we are endeavoring to create public opinion and public sentiment in favor of a free Africa, that others of our race are being subsidized to turn the attention of the world toward a different desire on the part of Negroes, but let me tell you that we who make up this Organization know no turning back, we have pledged ourselves even unto the last drop of our sacred blood that Africa must be free. The enemy may argue with you to show you the impossibility of a free and redeemed Africa, but I want you to take as your argument the thirteen colonies of America, that once owed their sovereignty to Great Britain, that sovereignity has been destroyed to make a United States of America. George Washington was not God Almighty. He was a man like any Negro in this building, and if he and his associates were able to make a free America, we too can make a free Africa. Hampden, Gladstone, Pitt and Disraeli were not the representatives of God in the person of Jesus Christ. They were but men, but in their time they worked for the expansion of the British Empire, and today they boast of a British Empire upon which "the sun never sets." As Pitt and Gladstone were able to work for the expansion of the British Empire, so you and I can work for the expansion of a great African Empire. Voltaire and Mirabeau were not Jesus Christs, they were but men like ourselves. They worked and overturned the French Monarchy. They worked for the Democracy which France now enjoys, and if they were able to do that, we are able to work for a democracy in Africa. Lenine and Trotzky were not Jesus Christs, but they were able to overthrow the despotism of Russia, and today they have given to the world a Social Republic, the first of its kind. If Lenine and Trotzky were able to do that for Russia, you and I can do that for Africa. Therefore, let no man, let no power on earth, turn you from this sacred cause of liberty. I prefer to die at this moment rather than not to work for the freedom of Africa. If liberty is good for certain sets of humanity it is good for all. Black men, Colored men, Negroes have as much right to be free as any other race that God Almighty ever created, and we desire freedom that is unfettered, freedom that is unlimited, freedom that will give us a chance and opportunity to rise to the fullest of our ambition and that we cannot get in countries where other men rule and dominate.

We have reached the time when every minute, every second must count for something done, something achieved in the cause of Africa. We need the freedom of Africa now, therefore, we desire the kind of leadership that will give it to us as quickly as possible. You will realize that not only individuals, but governments are using their influence against us. But what do we care about the unrighteous influence of any government? Our cause is based upon righteousness. And anything that is not righteous we have no repect for, because God Almighty is our leader and Jesus Christ our standard bearer. We rely on them for that kind of leadership that will make us free, for it is the same God who inspired the Psalmist to write "Princes shall come out of Egypt and Ethiopia shall stretch out her hands unto God." At this moment methinks I see the Angel of God taking up the standard of the Red, the Black and the Green [the U.N.I.A. colors], and saying "Men of the Negro Race, Men of Ethiopia, follow me." Tonight we are following. We are following 400,000,000 strong. We are following with a determination that we must be free before the wreck of matter, before the crash of worlds.

It falls to our lot to tear off the shackles that bind Mother Africa. Can you do it? You did it in the Revolutionary War. You did it in the Civil War; You did it at the Battles of the Marne and Verdun; You did it in Mesopotamia. You can do it marching up the battle heights of Africa. Let the world know that 400,000,000 Negroes are prepared to die or live as free men. Despise us as much as you care. Ignore us as much as you care. We are coming 400,000,000 strong. We are coming with our woes behind us, with the memory of suffering behind us — woes and suffering of three hundred years — they shall be our inspiration. My bulwark of strength in the conflict for freedom in Africa, will be the three hundred years of persecution and hardship left behind in this Western Hemisphere. The more I remember the suffering of my fore-fathers, the more I remember the lynchings and burnings in the Southern States of America, the more I will fight on even though the battle seems doubtful. Tell me that I must turn back, and I laugh you to scorn. Go on! Go on! Climb ye the heights of liberty and cease not in well doing until you have planted the banner of the Red, the Black and the Green on the hilltops of Africa.[33]

A contemporary black sociologist, E. Franklin Frazier, commented on the Garvey movement.

What has distinguished the Garvey Movement is its appeal to the masses. While Negroes have found a degree of self-magnification in fraternal orders and the church, these organizations have not given the support to their ego-consciousness that whites find in the Kiwanis and especially the Klan. Garvey re-introduced the idea of a Moses, who was incarnate in himself, and with his masterly technic for dealing with crowds, he welded Negroes into a mass movement.

Before considering Garvey and his work, something should be said of the people he had to work with. The social status of the Negro in America should make them fertile soil for a mass movement to spring up in. They are repressed and shut out from all serious participation in American life. Not only does the Negro intellectual feel this repression, but the average Negro, like all mediocre people whose personalities must be supported by empty fictions, must find something to give meaning to his life and worth to his personality. One has simply to note how the superficial matter of color raises the most insignificant white man in the South to a place of paramount importance, in order to appreciate how much support a fiction gives to one's personality. Yet American Negroes have been relatively free from mass movements. This fact should not be regarded as a further testimony to the Negro's reputation for a policy of expediency in his present situation. There have been other factors to take the place of mass movements.

Many American Negroes have belittled the Garvey Movement on the ground that he is a West Indian and has attracted only the support of West Indians. But this very fact made it possible for him to contribute a new phase to the life of the American Negro. The West Indian Negroes have been ruled by a small white minority. In Jamaica, the Negro majority has often revolted and some recognition has been given to the mulattoes. This was responsible for Garvey's attempt, when he first came to this country, to incite the blacks against those of mixed blood. He soon found that there was no such easily discernible social cleavage recognized by the whites in this country. Yet his attempt to draw such a line has not failed to leave its effect. The fact that the West Indian has not been dominated by a white majority is probably responsible for a more secular view of life. The Garvey Movement would find the same response among the Negroes of the South as among the West Indians were it not for the dominating position of the preacher, whose peculiar position is symtomatic [*sic*] of an other-worldly outlook among the masses. Even in the face of this situation foreign Negroes have successfully converted hard-shelled Baptists to the Movement in spite of the opposition of their ministers. This secular influence in the life of the Negro attains its true significance when viewed in relation to the part that preparation for death plays in the life of the black masses.

The Garvey Movement afforded an asylum, as all mass movements, for those who were dissatisfied with life for many reasons, which could in this case be attributed to their status as Negroes. Although most of his followers were ignorant, we find among them intellectuals who had not found the places in the world that their education entitled them to. Instead of blaming themselves—and they were not always individually responsible—they took refuge in the belief that in an autonomous black Africa they would find their proper place. The black rabble that could not see its own poverty, ignorance, and weakness vented its hatred upon obscure "traitors" and "enemies," who generally turned out to be Negro intellectuals who had achieved some distinction in American life. There is good reason to believe that Garvey constantly directed the animosity of his followers against the intellectuals because of his own lack of formal education.

We have noted how the Garvey Movement turned the Negro's attention to this world. This was accomplished not only by promising the Negro a paradise in the future in Africa; but through the invention of social distinctions and honors, the Negro was made somebody in his present environment. The humblest follower was one of the "Fellowmen of the Negro Race," while the more distinguished supporters were "Knights" and "Sirs." The women were organized into the Black Cross Nurses and the men into the Great African Army. "A uniformed member of a Negro lodge paled in significance beside a soldier of the Army of Africa. A Negro might be a porter during the day, taking his orders from white men, but he was an officer in the Black Army when it assembled at night in Liberty Hall. Many a Negro went about his work singing in his heart that he was a member of the great army marching to 'heights of achievements.' " Yet these extravagant claims were based upon the deep but unexpressed conviction in the minds of most Negroes that the white man has set certain limits to their rise in this country. . . .

Many people are at a loss to understand how Garvey was able to attract supporters to a scheme which was manifestly infeasible and has been discredited by continued exposes of corruption and bickering within the organization. But such tests of reasonableness can not be applied to schemes that attract crowds. Crowds, it has been said, never learn by experience. The reason is clear, for the crowd satisfies its vanity and longings in the beliefs it cherishes. Not only because of their longing for something to give meaning to their lives, but because of the scepticism about them, Negroes do not find the satisfaction that their fathers found in the promise of heavenly abode to compensate for the woes of this world. They therefore offer a fine field for charlatans and fakirs of every description. This Movement has attracted many such men who give the black crowds the escape they are seeking. The work carried on by the National Association for the Advancement of Colored People, which has been the subject of so many attacks by Garvey, has never attracted the crowd because it does not give the crowd an opportunity to show off in colors, parades, and self-glorification. The Association appeals to intelligent persons who are trying to attain tangible goals through cooperation. The same could be said of the Urban League. Dean Kelly Miller, it is said, once made the shrewd observation that the Negro pays for what he wants and begs for what he needs. This applies here as elsewhere. Those who support this Movement pay for it because it gives them what they want— the identification with something that makes them feel like somebody among white people who have said they were nobody.

Before concluding this brief interpretive sketch, we must add a few observations. Doubtless the World War with its shibboleths and stirrings of subject minorities offered a volume of suggestion that facilitated the Garvey Movement. Another factor that helped the Movement was the urbanization of the Negro that took place about that time. It is in the cities that mass movements are initiated. When the Negro lived in a rural environment he was not subject to mass suggestion except at the camp meeting and revival.

One of the most picturesque phases of the Movement has been the glorification of blackness which has been made an attribute of the celestial hierarchy. To most observers this last fact has been simply a source of merriment. But Garvey showed a knowledge of social psychology when he invoked a black god to guide the destiny of the Negro. The God of Israel served the same purpose. Those whites who said they would rather go to hell than to a heaven presided over by a black god, show what relation the average man's god must bear to him. The intellectual can laugh, if he will; but let him not forget the pragmatic value of such a symbol among the type of people Garvey was dealing with. . . .[34]

CITY LIFE

Much that has already been said about the lives of black Americans in the cities of the North need not be repeated here—the inadequate housing, poor health conditions, job discrimination. What is still lacking is a sense of the city as made up of diverse elements for blacks as well as whites. For the black part of the city was the scene of night clubs, jazz music and rent parties, of quiet strolling in the sunlight, of vigorous business enterprise and the quiet apathy of hopeless frustration. It was the scene of cosmopolitan literary soirees and refugees fresh from the rural South. The black areas of Northern cities were as diverse as cities usually are, a diversity that can only be suggested here.

If we were to offer a symbol of what Harlem has come to mean in the short span of twenty years it would be another statue of liberty on the landward side of New York. It stands for a folk-movement which in human significance can be compared only with the pushing back of the western frontier in the first half of the last century, or the waves of immigration which have swept in from overseas in the last half. Numerically far smaller than either of these movements, the volume of migration is such none the less that Harlem has become the greatest Negro community the world has known—without counterpart in the South or in Africa. But beyond this, Harlem represents the Negro's latest thrust towards Democracy.

The special significance that today stamps it as the sign and center of the renaissance of a people lies, however, layers deep under the Harlem that many know but few have begun to understand. Physically Harlem is little more than a note of sharper color in the kaleidoscope of New York. The Metropolis pays little heed to the shifting crystallization of its own heterogeneous millions. Never having experienced permanence, it has watched, without emotion or even curiosity, Irish, Jew, Italian, Negro, a score of other races drift in and out of the same colorless tenements.

So Harlem has come into being and grasped its destiny with little heed from New York. And to the herded thousands who shoot beneath it twice a day on the subway, or the comparatively few whose daily travel takes them within sight of its fringes or down its main arteries, it is a black belt and nothing more. The pattern of delicatessen store and cigar shop and restaurant and undertaker's shop which repeats itself a thousand times on each of New York's long avenues is unbroken through Harlem. Its apartments, churches and storefronts antedated the Negroes and, for all New York knows, may outlast them there. For most of New York, Harlem is merely a rough rectangle of commonplace city blocks, lying between and to east and west of Lenox and Seventh Avenues, stretching nearly a mile north and south — and unaccountably full of Negroes.

Another Harlem is savored by the few — A Harlem of racy music and racier dancing, of cabarets famous or notorious according to their kind, of amusement in which abandon and sophistication are cheek by jowl — a Harlem which draws the connoisseur in diversion as well as the undiscriminating sightseer. This Harlem is the fertile source of the "shufflin' " and "rollin' " and "runnin' wild" revues that establish themselves season after season in "downtown" theaters. It is part of the exotic fringe of the metropolis.

Beneath this lies again the Harlem of the newspapers — a Harlem of monster parades and political flummery, a Harlem swept by revolutionary oratory or draped about the mysterious figures of Negro "millionaires," a Harlem preoccupied with native adjustments to a white world — a Harlem, in short, grotesque with the distortions of journalism.

Yet in final analysis, Harlem is neither slum, ghetto, resort or colony, though it is in part all of them. It is — or promises at least to be — a race capital. Europe seething in a dozen centers with emergent nationalities, Palestine full of a renascent Judaism — these are no more alive with the spirit of a racial awakening than Harlem; culturally and spiritually it focuses a people. Negro life is not only founding new centers, but finding a new soul. The tide of Negro migration, northward and cityward, is not to be fully explained as a blind flood started by the demands of war industry coupled with the shutting off of foreign migration, or by the pressure of poor crops coupled with increased social terrorism in certain sections of the South and Southwest. Neither labor demand, the bollweevil nor the Ku Klux Klan is a basic factor, however contributory any or all of them may have been. The wash and rush of this human tide on the beach line of the northern city centers is to be explained primarily in terms of a new vision of opportunity, of social and economic freedom, of a spirit to seize, even in the face of an extortionate and heavy toll, a chance for the improvement of conditions. With each successive wave of it, the movement of the Negro migrant becomes more and more like that of the European waves at their crests, a mass movement toward the larger and the more democratic chance—in the Negro's case a deliberate flight not only from countryside to city, but from medieaval [sic] America to modern.

The secret lies close to what distinguishes Harlem from the ghettos with which it is sometimes compared. The ghetto picture is that of a slowly dissolving mass, bound by ties of custom and culture and association, in the midst of a freer and more varied society. From the racial standpoint, our Harlems are themselves crucibles. Here in Manhattan is not merely the largest Negro community in the world, but the first concentration in history of so many diverse elements of Negro life. It has attracted the African, the West Indian, the Negro American; has brought together the Negro of the North and the Negro of the South; the man from the city and the man from the town and village; the peasant, the student, the businessman, the professional man, artist, poet, musician, adventurer and worker, preacher and criminal, exploiter and social outcast. Each group has come with its own separate motives and for its own special ends, but their greatest experience has been the finding of one another. Proscription and prejudice have thrown these dissimilar elements into a common area of contact and inter-action. Within this area, race sympathy and unity have determined a further fusing of sentiment and experience. So what began in terms of segregation becomes more and more, as its elements mix and react, the laboratory of a great race-welding. Hitherto, it must be admitted that American Negroes have been a race more in name than in fact, or to be exact, more in sentiment than in experience. The chief bond between them has been that of a common condition rather than a common consciousness; a problem in common rather than a life in common. In Harlem, Negro life is seizing upon its first chances for group expression and self-determination. That is why our comparison is taken with those nascent centers of folk-expression and self-determination which are playing a creative part in the world today. Without pretense to their political signifi-cance Harlem has the same role to play for the New Negro as Dublin has had for the New Ireland or Prague for the New Czechoslovakia.

It is true the formidable centers of our race life, educational, industrial, financial, are not in Harlem, yet here, nevertheless, are the forces that make a group known and felt in the world. The reformers, the fighting advocates, the inner spokesmen, the poets, artists and social prophets are here, and pouring in toward them are the fluid ambitious youth and pressing in upon them the migrant masses. The professional observers, and the enveloping communities as well, are conscious of the physics of this stir and movement, of the cruder and more obvious facts of a ferment and a migration. But they are as yet largely unaware of the psychology of it, of the galvanizing shocks and reactions, which mark the social awakening and internal reorganization which are making a race out of its own disunited elements.

A railroad ticket and a suitcase, like a Bagdad carpet, transport the Negro peasant from the cotton-field and farm to the heart of the most complex urban civilization. Here, in the mass, he must and does survive a jump of two generations in social economy and of a century and more in civilization. Meanwhile the Negro poet, student, artist, thinker, by the very move that normally would take him off at a tangent from the masses, finds himself in their midst, in a situation concentrating the racial side of his experience and heightening his race-consciousness. These moving, half-awakened newcomers provide an exceptional seedbed for the germinating contacts of the enlightened minority. And that is why statistics are out of joint with fact in Harlem, and will be for a generation or so. . . .[35]

James Weldon Johnson, teacher, poet, novelist, and NAACP leader, wrote of the leisure-time activities of ordinary Harlemites.

Within the past ten years Harlem has acquired a worldwide reputation. It has gained a place in the list of famous sections of great cities. It is known in Europe and the Orient, and it is talked about by natives in the interior of Africa. It is farthest known as being exotic, colourful, and sensuous; a place of laughing, singing, and dancing; a place where life wakes up at night. This phase of Harlem's fame is most widely known because, in addition to being spread by ordinary agencies, it has been proclaimed in story and song. And certainly this is Harlem's most striking and fascinating aspect. New Yorkers and people visiting New York from the world over go to the night-clubs of Harlem and dance to such jazz music as can be heard nowhere else; and they get an exhilaration impossible to duplicate. Some of these seekers after new sensations go beyond the gay night-clubs; they peep in under the more seamy side of things; they nose down into lower strata of life. A visit to Harlem at night—the principal streets never deserted, gay crowds skipping from one place of amusement to another, lines of taxicabs and limousines standing under the sparkling lights of the entrances to the famous night-clubs, the subway kiosks swallowing and disgorging crowds all night long—gives the impression that Harlem never sleeps and that the inhabitants thereof jazz through existence. But, of course, no one can seriously think that the two hundred thousand and more Negroes in Harlem spend their nights on any such pleasance. Of a necessity the vast majority of them are ordinary, hardworking people, who spend their time in just about the same way that other ordinary, hard-working people do. Most of them have never seen the inside of a night-club. The great bulk of them are confronted with the stern necessity of making a living, of making both ends meet, of finding money to pay the rent and keep the children fed and clothed neatly enough to attend school; their waking hours are almost entirely consumed in this unromantic task. And it is a task in which they cannot escape running up against a barrier erected especially for them, a barrier which pens them off on the morass—no, the quicksands—of economic insecurity. Fewer jobs are open to them than to any other group; and in such jobs as they get, they are subjected to the old rule, which still obtains, "the last to be hired and the first to be fired."

Notwithstanding all that, gaiety is peculiarly characteristic of Harlem. The people who live there are by nature a pleasure-loving people; and though most of them must take their pleasures in a less expensive manner than in nightly visits to clubs, they nevertheless, as far as they can afford—and often much farther—do satisfy their hunger for enjoyment. And since they are constituted as they are, enjoyment being almost as essential to them as food, perhaps really a compensation which enables them to persist, it is well that they are able to extract pleasure easily and cheaply. An average group of Negroes can in dancing to a good jazz band achieve a delightful state of intoxication that for others would require nothing short of a certain per capita inbibition of synthetic gin. The masses of Harlem get a good deal of pleasure out of things far too simple for most other folks. In the evenings of summer and on Sundays they get lots of enjoyment out of strolling. Strolling is almost a lost art in New York; at least, in the manner in which it is so generally practised in Harlem. Strolling in Harlem does not mean merely walking along Lenox or upper Seventh Avenue or One Hundred and Thirty-fifth Street; it means that those streets are places for socializing. One puts on one's best clothes and fares forth to pass the time pleasantly with the friends and acquaintances and, most important of all, the strangers he is sure of meeting. One saunters along, he hails this one, exchanges a word or two with that one, stops for a short chat with the other one. He comes up to a laughing, chattering group, in which he may have only one friend or acquaintance, but that gives him the privilege of joining in. He does join in and takes part in the joking, the small talk and gossip, and makes new acquaintances. He passes on and arrives in front of one of the theatres, studies the bill for a while, undecided about going in. He finally moves on a few steps farther and joins another group and is introduced to two or three pretty girls who have just come to Harlem, perhaps only for a visit; and finds a reason to be glad that he postponed going into the theatre. The hours of a summer evening run by rapidly. This is not simply going out for a walk; it is more like going out for an adventure. . . .

Harlem is also a parade ground. During the warmer months of the year no Sunday passes without several parades. There are brass bands, marchers in resplendent regalia, and high dignitaries with gorgeous insignia riding in automobiles. Almost any excuse for parading is sufficient—the funeral of a member of the lodge, the laying of a cornerstone, the annual sermon to the order, or just a general desire to "turn out." Parades are not limited to Sundays; for when the funeral of a lodge member falls on a weekday, it is quite the usual thing to hold the exercises at night, so that members of the order and friends who are at work during the day may attend. Frequently after nightfall a slow procession may be seen wending its way along and a band playing a dirge that takes on a deeply sepulchral tone. But generally these parades are lively and add greatly to the movement, colour, and gaiety of Harlem. A brilliant parade with very good bands is participated in not only by the marchers in line, but also by the marchers on the sidewalks. For it is not a universal custom of Harlem to stand idly and watch a parade go by; a good part of the crowd always marches, keeping step to the music.

Now, it would be entirely misleading to create the impression that all Harlem indulges in none other than these Arcadian-like pleasures. There is a large element of educated, well-to-do metropolitans among the Negroes of Harlem who view with indulgence, often with something less, the responses of the masses to these artless amusements. There is the solid, respectable, bourgeois class, of the average proportion, whose counterpart is to be found in every Southern city. There are strictly social sets that go in for bridge parties, breakfast parties, cocktail parties, for high-powered cars, week-ends, and exclusive dances. Occasionally an exclusive dance is held in one of the ballrooms of a big downtown hotel. Harlem has its sophisticated, fast sets, initiates in all the wisdom of worldliness. And Harlem has, too, its underworld, its world of pimps and prostitutes, of gamblers and thieves, of illicit love and illicit liquor, of red sins and dark crimes. In a word, Harlem possesses in some degree all of the elements of a cosmopolitan centre. And by that same word, striking an average, we find that the overwhelming majority of its people are people whose counterparts may be found in any American community. Yet as a whole community it possesses a sense of humor and a love of gaiety that are distinctly characteristic. . . .[36]

Although Harlem may have been the Negro "capital," black Chicago was not far behind.

Ever since Harlem won the reputation for being the Mecca of the New Negro, the Negro Community in Chicago has been very conscious of its place in Negro life. Lately because of this quickened consciousness the leaders among Chicago Negroes have bestirred themselves to make the American public cognizant of their contributions to, and place in, Negro life in America. The feeling of rivalry between Harlem and Chicago has caused each to cast uncomplimentary epithets at the other. New York has charged Chicago Negroes with being a group of money getters, without any sense for the finer things of life; while Chicago has retorted that the "homeless ones" of New York float in the clouds of spirit without any sound economic basis for their culture. While Chicago has produced no poets to sing in her cabarets and novelists to celebrate her night life, she has extended one of her most successful businesses, the Victory Life Insurance Company, within the territory of her rival. Moreover, Chicago held a Negro in Art Week, in order to show her cultured rival what her artists could do. Finally, to assure her superiority to her rival in deeds, Chicago now boasts of sending the first Negro to Congress after a lapse of over a quarter of a century.

Because Chicago has not attained the cosmopolitan character of New York and has not lost many of the features of smaller cities, she represents more nearly the pattern of Negro life at large in America. Chicago has drawn on the plantations of the lower South for her population more than New York whereas the latter has in her population a larger proportion of the eastern Seaboard. A trip on a local elevated train from the Chicago Loop will not only make visible in the types of houses along the route the different strata of the population, but those who get off at the stations are living documents of the different sections of the population they represent. Yet within this diversity there is a certain unity expressed in a community consciousness that is lacking in the cosmopolitan life of New York. . . .

The distribution of the Negro community in the city of Chicago gives some evidence of its solidarity. Like most American cities the Negro group is not completely segregated from the white community although about ninety per cent of the population is found in a rather well defined area which is known as the Black Belt. Besides small communities of Negroes on the Near West Side, the Near North Side, Morgan Park, Englewood, and Woodlawn, there are isolated families widely scattered over the city. When the Negro community began to expand during the heavy migrations from the South there were constant conflicts on the fringe of the Negro community which culminated in the riot of 1919. Contrasted with the violence attending the expansion of the Negro area at that time is the pacific penetration which is slowly taking place today as barber shops, lunch rooms and drug stores reflect the change in clientele. The so-called "invasions" by the Negro groups have been no exception to the processes taking place in the growth of the city at large. Many of the so-called fine residences taken over by Negroes were really being deserted as the city expanded, and the Negro group being a migrant group without many children was economically and culturally suited to take over these houses and fill them up with roomers. White immigrant groups with hosts of children could have filled the houses but could not have paid the rents. It is the whirl of life that goes on in the "Black Belt" that one thinks of when he talks of the Negro community.

Although the *Chicago Defender* in the manner of the proverbial ostrich would bury the name Negro, it is, nevertheless, the visible spokesman along with the *Bee* and the *Whip* of a race conscious community. These papers are read because they carry news about people who are conscious of their relations to other people of the same group or race. They are indices of the public opinion which the Negro group is building up concerning matters of importance to its welfare. . . .

It is within this little community that we find reproduced all the stages of culture and various aspects of Negro life at large. The different stages of culture of the Negro population are accentuated in the religious life of the Negro community in Chicago. In a trip through the Black Belt one can find Negroes enjoying their religion in the primitive form in which they enjoyed it in the South. This type of religious experience appeals to those who have not broken away from the Southern way of life. In the numerous "store-front" churches which are found along State Street, an effort is made to keep up the primary relationships that existed in the South. One recent migrant to Chicago complains that she left the big church because the pastor did not know her, whereas back home when she was absent from church her pastor was at her house to find out why "Sister Jones" was not in her seat on Sunday. The mass of working class Negroes are to be found in the orthodox churches, principally Baptist and Methodist, where they enjoy a service which is free for the most part from the primitive forms of worship. Some of the older members perpetuate the older forms of worship, whereas the emancipated younger generation is inclined to the ceremonial and ritual of the high churches. A small group is to be found in the Lutheran, Episcopal and Catholic Churches. . . .

In presenting a cross-section picture of Negro life, Chicago includes in her achievements a conspicuous development of business enterprises. In the field of life insurance where the Negro has probably made the greatest strides in well-founded large enterprises, Chicago has two companies to her credit, the Liberty Life Insurance Company and the Victory Life Insurance Company. Moreover, in the field of banking there are the Binga State Bank and the Douglass National Bank which are pioneer achievements. The Thirty-fifth Street Arcade nearing completion represents the unabated enterprise of Jesse Binga. In Chicago the Negro has proved himself a pioneer in many other economic undertakings. The Parker House Sausage Company which has a large wholesale trade represents the initiative of a young man. The Universal Therapeutic Lamp Company, another achievement in a field usually thought outside of the Negro's economic sphere, is due to the enterprise of Paul Johnson. The Overton Hygienic Company is an earlier achievement of Anthony Overton, whose business ability was later responsible for the Douglass National Bank and the Victory Life Insurance Company. The *Chicago Defender* is not only the largest Negro newspaper in the country, but it is a business enterprise of tremendous economic significance to the group. Once the South was regarded as the only field in which Negro business could attain any significant development, but Chicago with one of the largest Negro communities in the world has shown the possibilities of the North.

Even in regard to its laboring population Chicago exhibits the possibilities of the Negro as an industrial worker as no other city. The number of men employed in manufacturing and mechanical pursuits according to the United States census was one-third more than the number in domestic and personal services which generally ranks first. Among the women the same situation does not exist but nearly one-fourth of the women employed were in manufacturing and mechanical occupations. Nearly two-thirds of the women were classified under domestic and personal services. A large number of Negroes in manufacturing and mechanical pursuits is in the Stockyards. A large variety of relations to the industrial world are maintained by the Negro laboring group. In the case of some industries they are shut out completely; and in other cases the entire laboring force is colored. One box factory employs only "light" colored girls. In some industrial plants whites and Negroes work side by side in all occupations. In other industries there is segregation as to work and recreation. In still others separation exists either as to recreation or as to work. The unions in their relations to the Negro worker offer every possible form of adjustment with rationalizations to suit each situation. Nevertheless, the place which the Negro has secured in the industrial life of Chicago is indicative of the Negro's future in industry.

The center of the life of the Black Belt has shifted southward as the community has expanded. Once Thirty-fifth and State was the corner where Negroes from many parts of the country met each other. At the present time the center of life representing the average culture of the Chicago Negro is at Forty-seventh and Grand Boulevard, called South Parkway since the "invasion" of Negroes. On this corner stands one of the Walgreen Chain drug stores manned chiefly by Negroes. Next door is the South Center Department Store with Negroes forming about fifty per cent of its working force in all departments. When it was proposed that Negro clerks should be employed the same old arguments about the impossibility of whites and Negroes working together and the undesirability of having Negroes wait on whites were urged. But the aroused consciousness of the Negro community was insistent in its demand that Negroes be employed as clerks. Not only were these demands listened to but Negroes insisted upon the employment of colored people who were dark enough for their racial identity, to be unmistakable. The strategic economic position of the Negro in relation to these stores was more potent than any abstract principles of justice and interracial goodwill. The unit on this corner includes the Regal Theatre which offers the conventional movie and vaudeville entertainment of the playhouses in the Loop. Although a few white entertainers who appear downtown help on the programs, Negro actors are in the majority on the programs. Because of the restricted demand in the different cities for Negro actors the Negro theatre-goer must endure the same faces who appear too frequently. The Savoy Ballroom next to the Regal Theatre occupies in the Negro community about the same position as the large dance halls among the whites. Both in the theatre and the dance hall because of the restricted group which they depend upon for patronage there is an attempt to overcome the anonymity of the large white places of amusement, by introducing a community interest.

The political consciousness of the Negro community on the whole is the same as the white community. Chicago has long been known as the political paradise of the Negro. His political leaders have been part of the machine that has controlled the city. The Negro's political power has given him jobs which have helped in his economic emancipation. At the same time his political strength has been used to benefit those who receive contributions from the underworld. White people have constantly decried the political morality of the Black Belt. When there was considerable agitation about cleaning up the vice on the South Side the greatest emphasis was placed upon the mingling of whites, especially white women, with Negroes in places of amusement. But since Negroes have quite naturally preferred living in hell as equals than living in a Jim Crow heaven supervised by white folk, the so-called reformers have not found much comfort among Negroes. The so-called debased elements among the political powers offered the Negroes something concrete in the way of jobs and protection. The mass of Negroes have not been inspired by nobler aims of political action, but they are nearer reality than the white people who expect Negroes to be bloodless saints casting their votes altruistically for a purified city that left them to feed upon their idealism. When there was a split in the Republican ranks during a recent party fight, Negroes were found supporting the reform element when real cooperation was established.

Since the Black Belt is an area of communal life it has developed its social distinctions and class divisions. The members of the Old Settlers Society which is made up of the oldest residents in Chicago and their children, are very conscious of their place in the Negro community. At one time they occupied the foremost place in the community and have not viewed with indifference the incoming of succeeding waves of Negro migrants from the South. All the older residents have seen that the increase in the Negro population meant increasing racial discrimination. Many of them fled the southern migrants who represented a lower cultural level. They scarcely regarded themselves as members of the same race. The race riot in 1919 helped to consolidate all the elements of the Negro population into a race conscious community. At the same time the older residents were not only brought face to face with a group on a lower cultural level that threatened their status in the white community, but they had to face a group of educated professional and business men who challenged their place in the Negro community. The older residents had acquired their status because of their cultural and economic superiority to the masses; but now they had to compete with a group who had education and initiative. The new element in the population had followed the masses whom they were to serve. It was the old problem of the old established families against the *nouveau riche*.

The phenomenal increase in the Negro population as the result of the migrations created by the demands for labor effected a fundamental change in the organization of the Negro community. The old equilibrium was destroyed. The growth in business enterprise has come as one of the results of this change. The newcomers who came to Chicago created a voluminous demand for different kinds of services. In the South they had been served by their own institutions and when they came to Chicago they created their own organizations. Many of them transferred their saving from the South and sought, besides homes, opportunities for investments. Often the leaders of the Negro community in the South followed their constituents. In order to serve the newly created as well as the old wants of the Negro population a large group of professional and business men and women were attracted to the city. This group has become large enough to comprise a new leadership as well as a distinct class in the community. Some of the older residents are identified with this class because they too have a functional relationship to the mass. This new class of professional and business men is setting the standards of behavior for the rest of the community. . . .[37]

VOICES

Some of the "voices" recorded here are those of the Negro Renaissance of the 1920s, an explosion of black artistic talent quite without precedent. Not that blacks had not been professional singers before tenor Roland Hayes, against incredible odds, became the first black concert artist widely accepted as such; not that blacks had not been writing professionally before the poetry and prose of Countee Cullen, Langston Hughes, and Claude McKay were published for America. Quite the contrary. The roots of the Renaissance, both as artistic movement and as racial outlook, go back to the social and intellectual developments taking place around the beginning of the century,[38] and possibly to the black bohemian life of the 1880s in New York described by James Weldon Johnson.[39] "The Negro today wishes to be known for what he is," wrote Alain Locke in 1925. "He resents being spoken for as a social ward or minor, even by his own, and . . . regarded [as] a chronic patient for the sociological clinic."[40] The relative freedom of northern cities, underscored by promises of democracy at the time of World War I, was revealed as incomplete by the realities of northern riots and discrimination. The situation seemed almost to demand racial expression. And this expression was cultivated by the sudden interest of whites in the black minority, an interest related to the concern for cultural pluralism widespread among liberals in the 1920s and aided by the general prosperity of the time.

Nevertheless, as Langston Hughes had said, "ordinary Negroes hadn't heard of the Negro Renaissance. And if they had, it hadn't raised their wages any."[41] Two of the "voices" included here are an unnamed black student and W.E.B. DuBois, whose reputation as scholar and essayist long antedates the 1920s[42] and whose effort as propagandist and leader of protest[43] make him one of the most significant figures of the age.

The emphasis upon African heritage, the evidence of race pride, the sense of group solidarity that runs through much of the writing of black Americans in the 1920s had its nonliterary analogue in the Garvey movement. The cultivation of racial identity and the desire to be admitted fully into American life would seem to be in paradoxical relationship to each other. But the New Negro accepted himself; without that there could be no acceptance by the larger society.

Pride

TO A DARK GIRL

I love you for your brownness,
And the rounded darkness of your heart;
I love you for the breaking sadness in your voice
And shadows where your wayward eyelids rest.

Something of old forgotten queens
Lurks in the lithe abandon of your walk,
And something of the shackled slave
Sobs in the rhythm of your talk.

Oh, little brown girl, born for sorrow's mate,
Keep all you have of queenliness,
Forgetting that you once were slave,
And let your full lips laugh at Fate![44]

NO IMAGES

She does not know
Her beauty,
She thinks her brown body
Has no glory.

If she could dance
Naked,
Under palm trees
And see her image in the river
She would know.

But there are no palm trees
On the street,
And dish water gives back no images. [45]

Bitterness

LAUGHERS

Dream singers,
Story tellers,
Dancers,
Loud laughers in the hands of fate—
    My people.
Dish-washers,
Elevator-boys,
Ladies' maids,
Crap-shooters,
Cooks,
Waiters,
Jazzers,
Nurses of babies,
Loaders of ships,
Rounders,
Number writers,
Comedians in vaudeville
And band-men in circuses—
Dream-singers all,—
    My people.
Story-tellers all,—

My people.
Dancers—
God! What dancers!
Singers and dancers.
Dancers and laughers.
  Laughers?
Yes, laughers . . . laughers . . . laughers—
Loud-mouthed laughers in the hands
Of Fate.[46]

Black men did not necessarily face discriminatory practices every day, but as W.E.B. DuBois points out, the ever-
present possibility was a constant burden.

My friend who is pale and positive, said to me yesterday, as the
tired sun was nodding:
"You are too sensitive." . . .
"Why don't you stop all this?" . . .
"There you go, again. You know that I—"
Wait! I answer. Wait!
I arise at seven. The milkman has neglected me. He pays little
attention to colored districts. My white neighbor glares elaborately.
I walk softly, lest I disturb him. The children jeer as I pass to work.
The women in the street car withdraw their skirts or perfer to stand.
The policeman is truculent. The elevator man hates to serve Ne-
groes. My job is insecure because the white union wants it and does
not want me. I try to lunch, but no place near will serve me. I go
forty blocks to Marshall's, but the Committee of Fourteen closes
Marshall's; they say white women frequent it.
"Do all eating places discriminate?"
No, but how shall I know which do not—except—
I hurry home through crowds. They mutter or get angry. I go to
a mass-meeting. They stare. I go to a church. "We don't admit
niggers!"
Or perhaps I leave the beaten track. I seek new work. "Our
employees would not work with you; our customers would object."
I ask to help in social uplift.
"Why—er—we will write you."
I enter the free field of science. Every laboratory door is closed
and no endowments are available.
I seek the universal mistress, Art; the studio door is locked.

I write literature. "We cannot publish stories of colored folks of that type." It's the only type I know.

This is my life. It makes me idiotic. It gives me artificial problems. I hesitate, I rush, I waver. In fine, — I am sensitive!

My pale friend looks at me with disbelief and curling tongue.

"Do you mean to sit there and tell me that this is what happens to you each day?"

Certainly not, I answer low.

"Then you only fear it will happen?"

I fear!

"Well, haven't you the courage to rise above a — almost a craven fear?"

Quite — quite craven is my fear, I admit; but the terrible thing is — these things do happen!

"But you just said — "

They do happen. Not all each day, — surely not. But now and then — now seldom, now, sudden; now after a week, now in a chain of awful minutes; not everywhere, but anywhere — in Boston, in Atlanta. That's the hell of it. Imagine spending your life looking for insults or for hiding places from them — shrinking (instinctively and despite desperate bolsterings of courage) from blows that are not always but ever; not each day, but each week, each month, each year. Just, perhaps, as you have choked back the craven fear and cried, "I am and will be the master of my — "

"No more tickets downstairs; here's one to the smoking gallery."

You hesitate. You beat back your suspicions. After all, a cigarette with Charlie Chaplin — then a white man pushes by —

"Three in the orchestra."

"Yes, sir." And in he goes.

Suddenly your heart chills. You turn yourself away toward the golden twinkle of the purple night and hesitate again. What's the use? Why not always yield — always take what's offered, — always bow to force, whether of cannon or dislike? Then the great fear surges in your soul, the real fear — the fear beside which other fears are vain imagining; the fear lest right there and then you are losing your own soul; that you are losing your own soul and the soul of a people; that millions of unborn children, black and gold and mauve, are being there and then despoiled by you because you are a coward and dare not fight!

Suddenly that silly orchestra seat and the cavorting of a comedian with funny feet become matters of life, death, and immortality; you grasp the pillars of the universe and strain as you sway back to that befrilled ticket girl. You grip your soul for riot and murder. You choke and sputter, and she seeing that you are about to make a "fuss" obeys her orders and throws the ticket at you in contempt. Then you slink to your seat and crouch in the darkness before the film, with every tissue burning! The miserable wave of reaction engulfs you. To think of compelling puppies to take your hard-earned money; fattening hogs to hate you and yours; forcing your way among cheap and tawdry idiots — God! What a night of pleasure![47]

Satire

The ability of blacks to laugh took the form of self-mocking, of robust joking, of gentle irony, as well as of defiance. The following selection, from a novel by Rudolph Fisher, is a scene laid at the Annual Ball of the General Improvement Association, an interracial organization devoted to advancing the race.

Meanwhile Miss Agatha Cramp sat quite overwhelmed at the strangeness of her situation. This was her introduction to the people she planned to uplift. True to her word she had personally investigated the G.I.A. and been welcomed with open arms. Certain members of the executive board knew her and her past works — one or two had been associated with her in other projects — and her experience, resources, and devotion to service were unanimously acclaimed assets. And nobody minded her excessively corrective attitude — all new board members started out revising things. Furthermore, the Costume Ball was at hand and that would be enough to upset anybody's ideas of revision.

Never had Miss Cramp seen so many Negroes in one place at one time. Moreover, never had she dreamed that so many of her own people would for any reason imaginable have descended to mingle with these Negroes. She had prided herself on her own liberality in joining this company to-night. And so it shocked and outraged her to see that most of these fair-skinned visitors were unmistakably enjoying themselves, instead of maintaining the aloof, kindly dignity proper to those who must sacrifice to serve. And of course little did she suspect how many of the fair-skinned ones were not visitors at all but natives.

When she met Nora Byle, for instance, she was first struck with the beauty of her "Latin type." To save her soul she could not help a momentary stiffening when Buckram Byle, who was a jaundice-brown, was presented as Nora's husband: Intermarriage! She recovered. No. The girl was one of those mulattoes, of course; a conclusion that brought but temporary relief, for the next moment the debonair Tony Nayle had gone off with the "mulatto," both of them flirting disgracefully.

It was all in all a situation which robbed Miss Cramp of words; but she smiled bravely through her distress and found no little relief in sitting beside Fred Merrit, whose perfect manner, cherubic smile and fair skin were highly comforting. She had not yet noticed the significant texture of his hair.

"Well, what do you think of it?" Merrit eventually asked.

"I don't know what to think, really. What do you think?"

"I? Why—it's all too familiar now for me to have thoughts about. I take it for granted."

"Oh—you have worked among Negroes a great deal, then?"

Merrit grinned. "All my life."

"How do you find them?"

That Merrit did not resist temptation and admit his complete identity at this point is easier to explain than to excuse. There was first his admitted joy in discomfiting members of the dominant race. Further, however, there was a special complex of reasons closer at hand.

Merrit was far more outraged by the flirtation between Nora Byle and Tony Nayle than had been even Miss Cramp herself, and with greater cause. His own race prejudice was a bitterer, more deep-seated emotion than was hers, and out of it came an attitude that caused him to look with great suspicion and distrust upon all visitors who came to Harlem "socially." He insisted that the least blameworthy motive that brought them was curiosity, and held that he, for one, was not on exhibition. As for the men who came oftener than once, he felt that they all had but one motive, the pursuit of Harlem women; that their cultivation of Harlem men was a blind and an instrument in achieving this end, and that the end itself was always illicit and therefore reprehensible.

It was with him a terribly serious matter, of which he could see but one side. . . .

And so beneath his pleasant manner, there was a disordered spirit which at this moment almost gleefully accepted the chance to vent itself on Miss Agatha Cramp's ignorance. To admit his identity would have wholly lost him this chance. And as for the fact that she was a woman, that only made the compensation all the more complete, gave it a quality of actual retaliation, of parallel all the more satisfying.

"How do I find Negroes? I like them very much. Ever so much better than white people."

"Oh Mr. Merrit! Really?"

"You see, they have so much more color."

"Yes, I can see that." She gazed upon the mob. "How primitive these people are," she murmured. "So primeval. So unspoiled by civilization."

"Beautiful savages," suggested Merrit.

"Exactly. Just what I was thinking. What abandonment—what unrestraint—"

"Almost as bad as a Yale-Harvard football game, isn't it?" Merrit's eyes twinkled.

"Well," Miss Cramp demurred, "that's really quite a different thing, you know."

"Of course. This unrestraint is the kind that is hostile to society, hostile to civilization. This is the sort of thing that you and I as sociologists must contend with, must wipe out."

"Yes indeed. Quite so. This sort of thing is, as you say, quite unfortunate. We must educate these people out of it. There is so much to be done."

"Listen to that music. Savage too, don't you think?"

"Just what had occurred to me. That music is like the beating of—what do they call 'em?—dum-dums, isn't it?"

"I was just trying to think what it recalled," mused Merrit with great seriousness. "Tom-toms! that's it—of course. How stupid of me. Tom-toms. And the shuffle of feet—"

"Rain," breathed Miss Cramp, who, since her new interest, had deemed it her duty to read some of Langdon's poetry. "Rain falling in a jungle."

"Rain?"

"Rain falling on banana leaves," said the lady. And the gentleman assented, "I know how it is. I once fell on a banana peel myself."

"So primitive." Miss Cramp turned to Mrs. Dunn, who sat behind and above her. "The throb of the jungle," she remarked.

"Marvelous!" exhaled Mrs. Dunn.

"These people—we can do so much for them—we must educate them out of such unrestraint.". . .

"Furthermore," expounded J. Pennington Potter, "there is a tendency among Negro organizations to incorporate too many words in a single designation with the result that what is intended as mere appellation becomes a detailed description. Take for example the N.O.U.S.E. and the I.N.I.A.W. There can be no excuse for entitlements of such prolixity. They endeavor to encompass a society's past, present and future, embracing as well a description of motive and instrument. There is no call you will agree, no excuse, no justification for delineation, history and prophecy in a single title.". . .

"Miss Cramp said in a low voice to Merrit: "Isn't he a wonderful person?"

"Who?" wondered Merrit.

"Mr. Potter. He talks so beautifully and seems so intelligent."

"He is intelligent, isn't he?" said Merrit, as if the discovery surprised him.

"He must have an awfully good head."

"Unexcelled for certain purposes."

"I had no idea they were ever so cultured. How simple our task would be if they were all like that."

"Like Potter? Heaven forbid!"

"Oh, Mr. Merrit. Really you mustn't let your prejudices prevail. Negroes deserve at least a few leaders like that."

"I don't know what they've ever done to deserve them," he said.

Unable to win him over to her broader viewpoint, she changed the subject.

"Mrs. Byle is very pretty, isn't she?"

"Yes."

"She is so light in complexion for a Negress."

"A what?"

"A Negress. She is a Negress, isn't she?"

"Well, I suppose you'd call her that."

"It is hard to appreciate, isn't it? It makes one wonder, really. Mrs. Byle is almost as fair as I am, while—well, look at that girl down there. Absolutely black. Yet both—"

"Are Negresses."

"Exactly what I was thinking. I was just thinking—Now how long have there been Negroes in our country, Mr. Merrit?"

"Longer than most one hundred percent Americans, I believe."

"Really?"

"Since around 1500, I understand. And in numbers since 1619."

"How well informed you are, Mr. Merrit. Imagine knowing dates like that—Why that's between three and four hundred years ago, isn't it? But of course four hundred years isn't such a long time if you believe in evolution. I consider evolution very important, don't you?"

"Profoundly so."

"But I was just thinking. These people have been out of their native element only three or four hundred years, and just see what it has done to their complexions! It's hard to believe that just three hundred years in our country has brought about such a great variety in the color of the black race."

"Environment is a powerful influence, Miss Cramp," murmured Merrit.

"Yes, of course. Chiefly the climate, I should judge. "Don't you think?"

Merrit blinked, then nodded gravely, "Climate undoubtedly. Climate. Changed conditions of heat and moisture and so on."

"Yes, exactly. Remarkable isn't it? Now just consider, Mr. Merrit. The northern peoples are very fair—the Scandinavians, for example. The tropic peoples, on the other hand are very dark—often black like the Negroes in their own country. Isn't that true?"

"Undeniably."

"Now if these very same people here to-night had originally gone to Scandinavia—three or four hundred years ago, you understand—some of them would by now be as fair as the Scandinavians! Why they'd even have blue eyes and yellow hair!"

"No doubt about that," Merrit agreed meditatively. "Oh yes. They'd have them without question."

"Just imagine!" marveled Miss Cramp. "A Negro with skin as fair as your own!"

"M-m. Yes. Just imagine," said he without smiling.[48]

Fear

Following is an account by a black university student of five and a half hours spent escaping from a white mob in Chicago in September 1920. He had ridden a streetcar into a hostile neighborhood where, unknown to him, a racial clash was taking place. A group of about twenty whites yelling "There's a nigger! Let's get him!" started for the car on which he was riding.

The motorman opened the door, and before they knew it I jumped out and ran up Fifty-first Street as fast as my feet could carry me. Gaining about thirty yards on them was a decided advantage, for one of them saw me and with the shout "There he goes!" the gang started after me. One, two, three, blocks went past in rapid succession. They came on shouting, "Stop him! Stop him!" I ran on the sidewalk and someone tried to trip me, but fortunately I anticipated his intentions and jumped into the road. As I neared the next street intersection, a husky, fair-haired fellow weighing about 180 pounds came lunging at me. I have never thought so quickly in all my life as then, I believe. Three things flashed into my mind—to stop suddenly and let him pass me and then go on; to try to trip him by dropping in front of him; or to keep running and give him a good football straight arm. The first two I figured would stop me, and the gang would be that much nearer, so I decided to rely on the last. These thoughts flashed through my mind as I ran about ten steps. As we came together, I left my feet, and putting all my weight and strength into a lunge, shot my right hand at his chin. It landed squarely and by a halfturn the fair-haired would-be tackler went flying to the road on his face.

That was some satisfaction, but it took a lot of my strength, for by this time I was beginning to feel weak. But determination kept me at it, and I ran on. Then I came to a corner where a drug-store was open and a woman standing outside. I slowed down and asked her to let me go in there, that a gang was chasing me; but she said I would not be safe there, so I turned off Fifty-first Street and ran down the side street. Here the road had been freshly oiled and I nearly took a "header" as I stepped in the first pool, but fortunately no accident happened. My strength was fast failing; the suggestion came into my mind to stop and give up or try to fight it out with the two or three who were still chasing me, but this would never do, as the odds were too great, so I kept on. My legs began to wobble, my breath came harder, and my heart seemed to be pounding like a big pump, while the man nearest me began to creep up on me. It was then that an old athletic maxim came into my mind—"He's feeling as tired as you." Besides, I thought, perhaps he smokes and boozes and his wind is worse than mine. Often in the last hundred yards of a quarter-mile that thought of my opponent's condition had brought forth the last efforts necessary for the final spurt. There was more than a medal at stake this time, so I stuck, and in a few strides more they gave up the chase. One block further on, when I had made sure that no one was following me on the other side of the street, I slowed down to walk and regained my breath. Soon I found myself on Forty-sixth Street just west of Halsted where the street is blind, so I climbed up on the railroad tracks and walked along them. But I imagined that in crossing a lighted street I could be seen from below and got down off the tracks, intending to cross a field and take a chance on the street. But this had to be abandoned, for as I looked over the prospect from the shadow of a fence I saw an automobile held up at the point of a revolver in the hands of one member of a gang while they searched the car apparently looking for colored men.

There is no place for a minister's son, I thought, and crept back behind a fence and lay down among some weeds. Lying there as quietly as could be I reflected on how close I had come to a severe beating or the possible loss of my life. Fear, which had caused me to run, now gave place to anger, and a desire to fight, if I could fight with a square deal. I remembered that as I looked the gang over at Fifty-first and Ashland I figured I could handle any of them individually with the possible exception of two, but the whole gang of blood-thirsty hoodlums was too much. Anger gave place to hatred and a desire for revenge, and I thought if ever I caught a green-buttoned "Ragen's Colt" [49] on the South Side east of State that one of us would get a licking. But reason showed me such would be folly and would only lead to reprisals and some other innocent individual getting a licking on my account. I knew all "Ragen's" were not rowdies, for I had met some who were pretty decent fellows, but some others—ye gods!

My problem was to get home and to avoid meeting hostile elements. Temporarily I was safe in hiding, but I could not stay there after daybreak. So I decided to wait a couple of hours and then try to pass through "No Man's Land"—Halsted to Wentworth. I figured the time to be about 11:30 and so decided to wait until 1:30 or 2:00 a.m., before coming out of cover. Shots rang out intermittently; the sky became illumined; the fire bells rang, and I imagined riot and arson held sway as of the previous year. It is remarkable how the imagination runs wild under such conditions.

Then the injustice of the whole thing overwhelmed me—emotions ran riot. Had the ten months I spent in France been all in vain? Were those little white crosses over the dead bodies of those dark-skinned boys lying in Flanders fields for naught? Was democracy merely a hollow sentiment? What had I done to deserve such treatment? I lay there experiencing all the emotions I imagined the innocent victim of a southern mob must feel when being hunted for some supposed crime. Was this what I had given up my Canadian citizenship for, to become an American citizen and soldier? Was the risk of life in a country where such hatred existed worth while? Must a Negro always suffer merely because of the color of his skin? "There's a Nigger: let's get him!" Those words rang in my ears—I shall never forget them.

Psychologists claim that it is in the face of overwhelming forces that man is prone to turn to the Supreme Being. I was no longer afraid, only filled with righteous indignation and a desire to get out of danger. But mingled emotions shook me, and a flood of tears burst forth. In the midst of it I found myself praying fervently to God against the injustice of it all, for strength and help to go through safely, and thanks for my deliverance from the gang which had chased me. Then relief came from all these pent-up feelings with the determination to get up and try to go through—and to fight, if necessary. I began to speculate on means. A freight train came along, and the impulse came to jump on it and ride out of town until the trouble was over, but the knowledge of only 15 cents carfare in my pocket compelled the rejection of this idea. I thought of phoning to a friend to come and get me in his car, but this was futile for where could I find a phone and be safe in that neighborhood? Some clothes on a line in a yard across the field offered a disguise, but even dressed as a woman I'd need a hat, and that idea had to be abandoned. With resources at an end I picked up four rocks for ammunition and started out.

For four blocks I glided from shadow to shadow, through alleys. A couple of dogs nearly "spilled the beans" when they barked just as an automobile came down the street. I dove for cover until the car had disappeared and then emerged. At Forty-ninth Street and Union Avenue I climbed up on the railroad tracks and cautiously walked along them in the darkness. All of a sudden a block ahead appeared what seemed to be about ten men standing on the tracks, so I dropped to the ground and made a pair of binoculars out of my hands. For what seemed like five minutes I watched these forms then decided they were uprights on a bridge and went on. Imagination and fear can play tricks, and this was one of them.

Finally I found myself at Thirty-seventh and Stewart Streets, having been walking northeast instead of east as I thought. I climbed down to the street and walked through back lanes until I saw the

Sox ball park. All was quiet, so I came out and crossed Wentworth Avenue. At State and Thirty-seventh I saw two colored fellows waiting for a car and ran up to them. Putting my hands on their shoulders I said, "Gee! I'm glad to see a dark skin." Then I related my experience. They assured me the "fun" was all over, and I was thankful. It was twenty-five minutes to four, just five and a half hours after I had started for home from work. A white man came along, and my first impulse was to jump on him and beat him up. But again reason told me he was not responsible for the actions of a gang of rowdies, and he was as innocent as I had been when set upon.[50]

Determination

IF WE MUST DIE

If we must die, let it not be like hogs
Hunted and penned in an inglorious spot,
While round us bark the mad and hungry dogs,
Making their mock at our accursed lot.
If we must die, O let us nobly die,
So that our precious blood may not be shed
In vain; then even the monsters we defy
Shall be constrained to honor us though dead!
O kinsmen! we must meet the common foe!
Though far outnumbered let us show us brave,
And for their thousand blows deal one death-blow!
What though before us lies the open grave?
Like men we'll face the murderous, cowardly pack,
Pressed to the wall, dying, but fighting back![51]

Afterword

As we look back on the 1920s from the last third of the twentieth century, the plight of the black American in those far-off days seems miserable indeed. Since that time, the number of blacks living in the nation's northern urban centers has increased enormously. During the Depression of the 1930s, the exodus of black people from the South slowed. It increased rapidly during World War II, and in the quarter-century following that war the proportion of black Americans living in the South declined from more than three-fourths to about one-half. Altogether, over 4.5 million blacks left the South between 1940 and 1970.[1] By 1960, 73.2 percent of America's black population lived in urban areas, as compared to 70 percent of the total population[2]; by 1970, 74 percent of America's black population lived in metropolitan areas, including 58 percent in the central cities. At the same time, 68 percent of the white population lived in metropolitan areas, including 28 percent who lived in the central cities.[3] Those Negroes who remained in the South also tended to settle in the cities.

In 1960, of the twenty-one American cities with populations of at least 500,000, only Boston, Buffalo (New York),

Milwaukee, San Antonio, San Diego, and Seattle had fewer than 100,000 black inhabitants. [4] In 1970 blacks made up more than half the central city population of Atlanta and Washington, D.C., as well as the two northern cities of Newark, New Jersey, and Gary, Indiana, and several smaller cities.[5]

Black people are found in increasing numbers in executive positions in the nation's major business concerns. Black actors and actresses have appeared more and more frequently in plays, movies, and television shows that no longer treat Negroes as objects of ridicule. Performing artists like Leontyne Price, Shirley Verrett, and Arthur Mitchell have made unequivocally clear the capacity of black people for opera and ballet. The world of sports has seen prodigious achievements by black athletes. Black men now sit in the councils of government here and there across the land.

The Supreme Court has made its pronouncements on equality in education, on the use of transportation facilities, on the right to vote, and in a multitude of other areas. City and state governments have enacted legislation designed to protect the rights of black citizens seeking housing and employment.

All these improvements in the racial situation in the United States have come about through the efforts of black Americans striving for full and complete recognition as men and women and as citizens of the Republic. Often, what gains have been made have come about with the assistance of whites sharing the same ideal of equality for all Americans. Each victory has been hard won, the result of intensive efforts by such older organizations as the NAACP and the National Urban League, and by more recent organizations such as the Congress of Racial Equality, the Southern Christian Leadership Conference, the Student Non-Violent Coordinating Committee, the Black Panthers, and a host of local organizations. More and more frequently the advocates of racial justice have relied on pressure tactics to move antipathetic whites to action—on the threat or the actuality of economic boycott and on the ballot box.

Still, events did not move fast enough. The steady pressure and extraordinary patience, characteristic during the 1920s of the racial organizations formed earlier in the century, gave way in public attention to demonstrations and urban riots. Continued concern about urban violence evidenced in the nation's newspapers long after the last of the major riots of the 1960s suggests the degree to which racial tension persists. Militant groups such as the Black Panthers have little sympathy for the black tradition of patience, resilience, and continued efforts for change. They, and many in sympathy with them, want change now, change immediate and sweeping. A multitude of black organizations with no rhetoric of violence is seeking rapid economic and social progress as well.

Why the need for continued change? Have not the laws of the land been adjusted in favor of equality for all men? Is it not true that many corporations are actively seeking black executives, that colleges and universities are actively looking for promising or even potentially promising black undergraduates? To be sure. But entrenched privilege yields slowly and social disorganization caused by several centuries of slavery and racial discrimination does not disappear with the passage of a law or the handing down of a court decision. For the ordinary black citizen, the circumstances of life have been less favorable in recent years than is ordinarily supposed, and considerably less favorable than many would like to believe. In 1962, for example, the chances of a Negro baby being born in a hospital were 87 in 100, while for a Caucasian baby they were 99 in 100.[6] In 1960 the mortality rate for nonwhite infants under eleven months was 43.3 per 1,000 live births, a bit less than double that for white infants. By 1968 the nonwhite rate had declined to 34.6 per 1,000 live births, still 13.4 greater than that for white infants. And in 1968 the maternal mortality rate per 1,000 live births for nonwhites was still triple that for whites.[7] In 1962 the Negro tuberculosis death rate of 11.5 per 100,000 was over twice the white rate of 4.2.[8] In 1964 life expectancy at birth for blacks was 64.1 years, while for whites it was 71 years.[9] In

1964, a year of general prosperity, the unemployment rate for black males was 9.1 percent, a figure one and a half times as large as that for whites during any of the preceding recession years since World War II.[10] In 1970 the rates for black and white unemployed were 8.2 and 4.5 percent respectively, while for blacks aged sixteen to nineteen the rate was a staggering 29.1 percent as compared to 13.5 percent for white youth of the same age.[11]

In 1969 the median black family income was $5,999, only 61 percent of that for whites. The income of the average black family with three earners is not significantly different from the income of the average white family with only one earner.[12] While the proportion of both blacks and whites below the poverty level decreased between 1959 and 1969, the decline was greater for whites than for blacks.

The poverty level, set according to a complex formula by the federal government, was $3,743 for a nonfarm family of four in 1969 and $2,973 for a similar family in 1959. In 1969 approximately 10 percent of whites and about 32 percent of blacks were below the poverty level. The number of whites below the poverty level had dropped 41 percent during the preceding decade while for blacks there was only a 27 percent reduction.[13] The situation is undoubtedly due in part to the difference in educational attainment between blacks and whites, but even with comparable schooling black incomes are far inferior to white. In 1963 Negro families in which the head of household had completed high school had a median income of $4,530. White families in the same situation had a median income of $6,997 — almost 55 percent more.[14] And in 1969, white males with an eighth grade education obtained a median income of $7,018, 12 percent *more* than the black male high school graduate.[15]

Clearly, racial discrimination has not disappeared from the United States; it remains to affect the black citizen in ways that really matter. Not only are the health and welfare of the black citizen at stake, but his self-respect is still frequently assaulted by racial slurs and subtle discrimination. As the Report of the National Advisory Commission on

Civil Disorders pointed out in discussing the causes of urban riots, one of "the most bitter fruits of white racial attitudes" is the "continuing exclusion of great numbers of Negroes from the benefits of economic progress through discrimination in employment and education, and their enforced containment in segregated housing and schools."[16]

The movement of black Americans to the cities that began in earnest during World War I was but one great step toward full involvement in American life. The changes in the racial scene have been enormous. The black peasantry has become a black proletariat; the legal restrictions of the earlier time have largely been removed. In terms of power relationships, however, change is far less noticeable. It is white America that permits change to take place, not as a matter of right, but as a concession. It is white America that determines what black America may have. Until concession is replaced with a recognition of right, the struggle goes on.

Notes

Introduction

1. Frederick Lewis Allen, *Only Yesterday: An Informal History of the Nineteen-Twenties* (New York: Harper and Brothers, Publishers, 1931), pp. 94-95.

2. Winthrop D. Jordan, *White Over Black: American Attitudes Toward the Negro, 1550-1812* (Baltimore: Penguin Books, Inc., 1969), passim. See especially pp. 252-59.

3. August Meier and Elliott M. Rudwick, *From Plantation to Ghetto: An Interpretive History of American Negroes* (New York: Hill and Wang, 1966), p. 75.

4. Leon F. Litwack, *North of Slavery: The Negro in the Free States, 1790-1860* (Chicago: University of Chicago Press, 1961), pp. 24-26.

5. These arguments are suggested by Horace Mann Bond, "Main Currents in the Educational Crisis Affecting Afro-Americans," *Freedomways*, VIII (Fall, 1968), pp. 303-4.

6. W. E. B. DuBois, *Darkwater: The Twentieth Century Completion of "Uncle Tom's Cabin"* (Washington, D.C.: Austin Jenkins Co., 1920), p. 8.

7. W. E. B. DuBois, *Dusk of Dawn: An Essay Toward an Autobiography of a Race Concept* (New York: Schocken Books, 1968), p. 100.

8. Quoted in Bond, "Main Currents," p. 304.

9. See, for example, *Chicago Defender*, February 10, 1917, p.1.

10. See, for example, Claude McKay, *Harlem: Negro Metropolis* (New York: E. P. Dutton and Company, 1940).

11. Marcus Garvey, *Philosophy and Opinions of Marcus Garvey*, ed. by Amy Jacques-Garvey (New York: Atheneum, 1969), II, p. 78.

12. *Chicago Defender*, editorial, "With A Capital 'N,' " January 22, 1916, p. 9.

13. The story is told in Bennie Butler, "The Significance and Story Behind the Fight to Have 'Negro' Spelled with Capital 'N,' " WPA Writing Program, Negroes of New York Papers, Schomburg Collection, New York Public Library.

14. Langston Hughes, *The Big Sea* (New York: Hill and Wang, 1963), pp. 103-4.

15. Alphonso Pinkney, *Black Americans* (Englewood Cliffs, N.J.: Prentice-Hall, Inc., 1968), pp. xiii-xiv. This is not strictly the case since the word is English. Although not in common use in polite conversation in recent memory, it was not uncommon in the eighteenth century and before.

16. *New York Times*, April 23, 1969, p. 29.

17. Southern Commission on the Study of Lynchings, *Lynchings and What They Mean* (Atlanta: Southern Commission on the Study of Lynchings, 1931), pp. 8-10.

18. 163 U.S. 537.

19. Buchanan v. Warley, 245 U.S. 60 (1917).

20. Strauder v. West Virginia, 100 U.S. 303 (1880).

21. See Ray Stannard Baker, *Following the Color Line: American Negro Citizenship in the Progressive Era* (New York: Harper and Row, 1964), p. 50.

22. August Meier, *Negro Thought in America 1880-1915: Racial Ideologies in the Age of Booker T. Washington* (Ann Arbor: University of Michigan Press, 1963), p. 163; Baker, *Following the Color Line*, pp. 117-29.

23. Lorenzo J. Greene and Carter G. Woodson, *The Negro Wage Earner* (Washington, D.C.: Association for the Study of Negro Life in History, Inc., 1930), pp. 89-99.

24. Sterling D. Spero and Abram L. Harris, *The Black Worker: The Negro and the Labor Movement* (New York: Atheneum, 1968), pp. 87 ff.; Baker, *Following the Color Line*, pp. 131-36.

25. Rayford W. Logan, *The Betrayal of the Negro from Rutherford B. Hayes to Woodrow Wilson* (New York: Collier Books, 1965),

p. 362. The order did not apply to females nor before 9:00 A.M.

26. Henry Fairfield Osborn, "The Evolution of Human Races," *Natural History*, XXVI (January, 1926), p. 5.

27. I. A. Newby, *Jim Crow's Defense: Anti-Negro Thought in America, 1900-1930* (Baton Rouge: Louisiana State University Press, 1965), pp. 28-29 ff. Newby enlarges considerably on this list.

28. William A. Dunning, *Reconstruction, Political and Economic, 1865-1877* (New York: Harper and Brothers, 1907), pp. 57-58, 213-14; James Ford Rhodes, *History of the United States from the Compromise of 1850* (New York: The Macmillan Company, 1904), V, pp. 555-59; John W. Burgess, *Reconstruction and the Constitution* (New York: Charles Scribner's Sons, 1902), pp. 44-45, 52-54; Walter L. Fleming, *The Sequel of Appomatox* (New Haven: Yale University Press, 1919), pp. 115-16; Ulrich B. Phillips, *American Negro Slavery* (New York: D. Appleton and Company, 1918), pp. 307-8.

29. Newby, *Jim Crow's Defense*, pp. 86-91.

30. Robert Moats Miller, *American Protestantism and Social Issues, 1919-1939* (Chapel Hill: University of North Carolina Press, 1958), pp. 131-36, 296-313; Frank S. Loescher, *The Protestant Church and the Negro* (New York: Association Press, 1948), pp. 29-89.

31. Thomas Nelson Page, *The Negro: The Southerner's Problem* (New York: Charles Scribner's Sons, 1904).

32. Collected in Thomas Nelson Page, *Bred in the Bone* (New York: Charles Scribner's Sons, 1904).

33. Thomas Dixon, *The Clansman, An Historical Romance of the Ku Klux Klan* (New York: Doubleday, Page and Company, 1905).

34. Quoted in Logan, *Betrayal of the Negro*, p. 383.

35. *Ibid.*, pp. 390-91.

36. Noel P. Gist, "The Negro in the Daily Press," *Social Forces*, X (March, 1932), pp. 405-11; George Eaton Simpson, *The Negro in the Philadelphia Press* (Philadelphia: University of Pennsylvania Press, 1936), pp. 89-100, 116.

37. For further discussion of Washington's role see August Meier, "Toward a Reinterpretation of Booker T. Washington," *Journal of Southern History*, XXIII (May, 1957), pp. 220-27; and Donald J. Calista, "Booker T. Washington: Another Look," *Journal of Negro History*, XLIX (October, 1964), pp. 240-55.

38. W. E. Burghardt DuBois, *The Souls of Black Folk: Essays and*

Sketches (Chicago: A. C. McClurg and Co., 1903). See especially chapter iii, "Of Mr. Booker T. Washington and Others."

39. *Niagara Movement Declaration of Principals,* pamphlet, 1905. Cited in Elliott M. Rudwick, *W. E. B. DuBois: Propagandist of the Negro Protest* (New York: Atheneum, 1968), pp. 96-97.

40. These were the Committee for Improving Industrial Conditions of Negroes in New York, the National League for the Protection of Colored Women, and a Coordinating Committee formed by the two organizations.

41. U.S., Department of Commerce, Bureau of the Census, *Negro Population 1790-1915* (Washington, D.C.: Government Printing Office, 1918), pp. 88, 94.

42. Among the studies of this aspect of racism are Mary Ellen Goodman, *Race Awareness in Young Children* (New York: Collier Books, rev. ed. 1964), especially pp. 50-88, and Abram Kardiner and Lionel Ovesey, *The Mark of Oppression: Explorations in the Personality of the American Negro* (Cleveland and New York: World Publishing Company, 1962), especially pp. 339-87.

Chapter One

1. Everett Lee, "The Turner Thesis Reexamined," *American Quarterly,* XIII (Spring, 1961), p. 78.

2. George W. Pierson, "The M-Factor in American History," *American Quarterly,* XIV, part 2 (Summer, 1962), pp. 275-89.

3. Louise Veneble Kennedy, *The Negro Peasant Turns Cityward: Effects of Recent Migrations to Northern Centers* (New York: Columbia University Press, 1930), p. 30.

4. U.S., Department of Commerce, Bureau of the Census, *Negroes in the United States, 1920-32* (Washington, D.C.: Government Printing Office, 1935), p. 3.

5. Charles S. Johnson, "How Much Is the Migration a Flight from Persecution?" *Opportunity,* I (September, 1923), p. 273.

6. Kennedy, *Negro Peasant Turns Cityward,* p. 30.

7. *New York Times,* May 7, 1915, p. 4; October 2, 1915, p. 17; February 17, 1916, p. 9; June 7, 1916, p. 11; July 8, 1916, p. 6; July 17, 1916, p. 18; July 18, 1916, p. 9; July 19, 1916, p. 17; August 14, 1916, p. 4.

8. *Ibid.,* October 19, 1918, p. 17; September 1, 1916, p. 17; December 12, 1916, p. 15.

9. U.S., Bureau of Immigration, *Annual Report of the Commissioner-General of Immigration* (Washington, D.C.: Government Printing Office, 1922), p. 108.

10. U.S., Bureau of the Census, *Historical Statistics of the United States, Colonial Times to 1957* (Washington, D.C.: Government Printing Office, 1960), p. 416.

11. See LaVerne Beales, "Negro Enumeration of 1920," *Scientific American*, XIV (April, 1922), pp. 352-60; Kelly Miller, "Enumeration Errors in Negro Population," *ibid.*, XIV (February, 1922), p. 168; and V. D. Johnston, "Negro Migration and the Census of 1920," *Opportunity*, I (June, 1923), pp. 235-38.

12. Chicago Commission on Race Relations, *The Negro in Chicago: A Study of Race Relations and a Race Riot* (Chicago: University of Chicago Press, 1922), p. 87.

13. *Chicago Defender*, September 2, 1916, p. 10; September 9, 1916, p. 9.

14. *Ibid.*, February 10, 1917, p. 5.

15. *Ibid.*, June 30, 1917, p. 9.

16. *Ibid.*, June 30, 1917, p. 9; July 7, 1917, p. 10; August 11, 1917, p. 9.

17. *Ibid.*, August 25, 1917, p. 9.

18. *Ibid.*, December 1, 1917, p. 10.

19. *Ibid.*, February 10, 1917, p. 3.

20. Matthew Henson was a member of the Peary expedition to the North Pole in 1908-09. He subsequently wrote *Negro Explorer at the North Pole* (New York: Fred A. Stokes and Company, 1912).

21. *Chicago Defender*, February 10, 1917, p. 7.

22. Emmet J. Scott, "Negro Migration During the War," *Preliminary Economic Studies of the War*, ed. David Kinley (New York: Oxford University Press, 1920), p. 17.

23. Clyde Vernon Kiser, *Sea Island to City: A Study of St. Helena Islanders in Harlem and Other Urban Centers* (New York: Columbia University Press, 1932), pp. 122-24.

24. *Ibid.*, p. 133.

25. Beloit, Wisconsin, *News*, editorial, August 25, 1916.

26. *New York Globe*, editorial, July 31, 1916.

27. *Philadelphia Christian Recorder*, editorial, February 1, 1917.

28. *Chicago Defender*, editorial, May 19, 1917.

29. See, for example, George J. Baldwin, "The Migration: A Southern View," *Opportunity*, II (June, 1924), p. 183; "Negro Migration as the South Sees It," *Survey*, XXXVIII (August 11, 1917),

p. 428; P. O. Davis, "The Negro Exodus and Southern Agriculture," *American Review of Reviews*, LXVIII (October, 1923), pp. 401-7; and "The South Calling Negroes Back," *Literary Digest*, LIV (June 23, 1917), p. 1914.

30. *The Commercial Appeal*, Memphis, editorial, October 5, 1916.
31. Scott, *Negro Migration During the War*, pp. 73, 78.
32. *Chicago Defender*, August 12, 1916, p. 3.
33. *Ibid.*
34. *Ibid.*, August 19, 1916, p. 2.
35. *Ibid.*
36. *Ibid.*, March 24, 1917, p. 1.
37. Langston Hughes, "Bound No'th Blues," *Selected Poems* (New York: Alfred A. Knopf, 1959). By permission of Alfred A. Knopf, Inc. An earlier version of the poem appeared in *Opportunity*, IV (October, 1926), p. 315.

Chapter Two

1. Thomas J. Woofter, *Negro Problems in Cities* (Garden City, N.Y.: Doubleday, Doran and Co., Inc., 1928), p. 22.
2. See, for example, Edith Abbott, *The Tenements of Chicago 1908-35* (Chicago: University of Chicago Press, 1936), *passim*. Abbott does report, however, that her survey revealed housing in the West Side Negro district of Chicago to be in a worse state of repair than in any other area except the Jewish quarter, *ibid.*, p. 123.
3. Woofter, *Negro Problems in Cities*, p. 153. Woofter found this to be the case in every one of the seven northern and nine southern cities he studied.
4. Detroit Bureau of Governmental Research, "The Negro in Detroit," Section V, "Housing," Detroit, 1926, pp. 127-28. (Mimeographed.)
5. A number of surveys of conditions among Negro city dwellers in the 1920s were published. They include Ira DeA. Reid, *Twenty-Four Hundred Negro Families in Harlem* (New York: New York Urban League, 1927); Reid, *Social Conditions of the Negro in the Hill District of Pittsburgh* (Pittsburgh: General Committee on the Hill Survey, 1930); Reid, "The Negro Population of Elizabeth, New Jersey: A Survey of Its Economic and Social Condition," National Urban League, Department of Research, for the Elizabeth Interracial Committee, 1930 (mimeographed); Mary Louise Mark,

Negroes in Columbus, Ohio State University Studies, Graduate School Series in Social Science No. 2 (Columbus: Ohio State University Press, 1928), and others. A lengthy excerpt from a report of the Philadelphia Armstrong Association (Urban League) begins on page 52.

6. Woofter, *Negro Problems in Cities,* p. 87.

7. Philadelphia Housing Association, *Housing in Philadelphia,* Annual Report (Philadelphia, 1925), p. 24.

8. A. L. Manly, "Where Negroes Live in Philadelphia," *Opportunity,* I (May, 1923), pp. 10-15. Reprinted with permission of the National Urban League, Inc.

9. Reid, "The Negro Population of Elizabeth, New Jersey," p. 19.

10. Detroit Bureau of Governmental Research, "The Negro in Detroit," Section V, "Housing," pp. 21-23.

11. *Ibid.,* Section IX, "Crime," p. 7.

12. U.S. Bureau of the Census, *Crime Conditions in the United States as Reflected in Census Statistics of Imprisoned Offenders* (Washington, D.C.: Government Printing Office, 1926), p. 59 of *Prisoners, 1923.* Quoted in Thorsten Sellin, "The Negro Criminal: A Statistical Note," *Annals of the American Academy of Political and Social Science,* CXL (November, 1928), p. 53. These figures include the South, but even in the North there is some reason to believe that race prejudice may be a factor in arrest and incarceration. See Sellin, "The Negro Criminal"; Anne J. Thompson, "A Survey of Crime Among Negroes in Philadelphia," *Opportunity,* IV (July, 1926), pp. 217-19, (August, 1926), pp. 251-54, and (September, 1926), pp. 285-86; and Chicago Commission on Race Relations, *The Negro in Chicago: A Study of Race Relations and a Race Riot* (Chicago: University of Chicago Press, 1922), pp. 350-55.

13. These factors are discussed in E. Franklin Frazier, "The Negro Family," *Annals of the American Academy of Political and Social Science,* CXL (November, 1928), pp. 44-51.

14. See, for example, Louis I. Dublin, "The Health of the Negro," *Annals of the American Academy of Political and Social Science,* CXL (November, 1928), pp. 77-85; H. M. R. Landis, "Tuberculosis and the Negro," *ibid.,* pp. 86-89; and H.L. Rockwood, "The Effect of Negro Migration on Community Health in Cleveland," *Proceedings of the National Conference of Social Work,* 1926 (Chicago: University of Chicago Press, 1926), pp. 239-44.

15. Winfred B. Nathan, *Health Conditions in North Harlem 1923-1927*, Social Research Series No. 2 (New York: National Tuberculosis Association, 1932), pp. 44-45.

16. Detroit Bureau of Government Research, "The Negro in Detroit," Section XII, "Welfare," pp. 17-20, 26-27.

17. Chicago Commission on Race Relations, *The Negro in Chicago*, p. 152.

18. *Ibid.*, pp. 170-72.

19. *Ibid.*, pp. 180-81.

20. *Ibid.*, p. 183.

21. Everett Johnson, "A Study of the Negro Families in the Pinewood Avenue District of Toledo, Ohio," *Opportunity*, VII (August, 1929), pp. 243-45.

22. Buchanan v. Warley, 245 U.S. 60.

23. Emma Lou Thornbrough, "Segregation in Indiana During the Klan Era of the 1920's," *Mississippi Valley Historical Review*, XLVII (March, 1961), p. 600.

24. Harmon v. Tyler, 273 U.S. 668.

25. Herman H. Long and Charles S. Johnson, *People vs. Property: Race Restrictive Covenants in Housing* (Nashville, Tennessee: Fisk University Press, 1947), p. 32.

26. This remained the situation until 1948, when the Supreme Court held that court enforcement of restrictive covenants was a denial of equal protection of the law guaranteed by the Fourteenth Amendment. Shelley v. Kraemer, 334 U.S. 1.

27. Parmalee et al. v. Morris, 218 Mich. 625.

28. *Property Owners' Journal*, February 15, 1920. Reprinted in Chicago Commission on Race Relations, *The Negro in Chicago*, pp. 121-22.

29. Jesse Binga was founder and president of the Binga State Bank, the first Negro bank in Chicago. Oscar De Priest, a black politician, served in the United States House of Representatives from 1928 until he was swept out, along with many other Republicans, in the elections of 1934.

30. *Property Owners' Journal*, February 15, 1920. Full names appear in the original.

31. Chicago Commission on Race Relations, *The Negro in Chicago*, p. 122.

32. Detroit Bureau of Governmental Research, "The Negro in Detroit," Section V, "Housing," p. 28; Arthur Garfield Hays, *Let Freedom Ring* (New York: Boni and Liveright, 1928), pp. 220-21;

other instances are cited in the President's Conference on Home Building and Home Ownership, *Negro Housing* (Washington, D.C.: President's Conference on Home Building and Home Ownership, 1932), pp. 46-47.

33. Estimates vary widely. See the *Detroit Free Press*, November 18, 1925, p. 3, and Thomas J. Fleming, "The Right to Self-Defense," *Crisis*, LXXVI (January, 1969), p. 14.

34. This is an error. The date was September 9 and is referred to as such on page 80.

35. Mr. Smith's existence had caused no comment because he was fair enough in complexion to escape detection.

36. *Detroit Free Press*, November 19, 1925, p. 3.

Chapter Three

1. Sterling D. Spero and Abram L. Harris, *The Black Worker: The Negro and the Labor Movement* (New York: Atheneum, 1968), p. 152.

2. In 1920, 66.2 percent of gainfully employed blacks worked in agriculture or in personal and domestic service; in 1930 the figure was 74.7 percent. The number in agriculture declined 8.1 percent, but the number in domestic service rose. U.S., Bureau of the Census, *Negroes in the United States, 1920-32* (Washington, D.C.: Government Printing Office, 1935), p. 290, Table 7.

3. Spero and Harris, *Black Worker*, p. 194.

4. Quoted in *Opportunity*, IV (February, 1926), p. 68. See page 88 for another instance in which an observer reports the existence of wage differentials.

5. Alma Herbst, *The Negro in the Slaughtering and Meat-Packing Industry in Chicago* (Boston: Houghton Mifflin Company, 1932), p. 70.

6. See "Workers' (Communist) Party National Platform, 1928 — XII, Oppression of the Negroes," *American Labor Yearbook, 1929* (New York: Rand School of Social Science, 1929), p. 163; and "Resolutions Adopted by the Socialist Convention — Resolution on the Negro Workers," *Socialist World*, V (August, 1924), p. 11.

7. Wilson Record, *The Negro and the Communist Party* (Chapel Hill: University of North Carolina Press, 1951). The failure of the Socialists and the International Workers of the World to gain major support is mentioned (pp. 11-12), but the book concentrates on the

Communist Party, whose lack of success is summed up in the last chapter, "Red and Black: Unblending Colors."

8. Thomas L. Dabney, "Negro Workers at the Crossroads," *Labor Age*, XVI (February, 1927), p. 9; Francis L. Broderick, *W. E. B. DuBois: Negro Leader in a Time of Crisis* (Stanford, Cal.: Stanford University Press, 1959), p. 141; Herbst, *Negro in the Slaughtering and Meat-Packing Industry*, pp. 63-65.

9. National Negro Business League, *Minutes of the "Silver Jubilee" and Twenty-fifth Annual Meeting* (Chicago, 1924), p. 62.

10. St. Clair Drake and Horace R. Cayton, *Black Metropolis: A Study of Negro Life in a Northern City* (New York: Harper and Row, Publishers, 1962), II, p. 465.

11. Edmund David Cronon, *Black Moses: The Story of Marcus Garvey and the Universal Negro Improvement Association* (Madison: University of Wisconsin Press, 1962), p. 60.

12. "Industrial Problems in Cities," *Opportunity*, IV (February, 1926), pp. 68-69, 71-72. Reprinted with permission of the National Urban League, Inc.

13. New York *World*, November 30, 1920, p. 19.

14. George S. Schuyler, "From Job to Job: A Personal Narrative," *World Tomorrow*, VI (May, 1923), pp. 147-48.

15. Abram L. Harris, "The Negro Worker," *Labor Age*, XIX (February, 1930), p. 5.

16. National Urban League, Department of Research and Investigations, *Negro Membership in American Labor Unions* (New York: The Alexander Press, 1930), p. 33.

17. Interestingly, Article 8, Section 29(b) of the 1953 Revision of the Constitution still contained the white only provision, with the additional clarification that "Mexicans or those of Spanish-Mexican extraction are not eligible."

18. As quoted in the *Proceedings of the Twenty-second Regular Convention* (Detroit, 1925), p. 194.

19. As quoted in Spero and Harris, *Black Worker*, pp. 62-63.

20. Niles Carpenter and Associates, *Nationality, Color, and Economic Opportunity in the City of Buffalo*, University of Buffalo Studies, V, 1926-1927 (Buffalo, N.Y.: University of Buffalo Press, 1927), p. 113.

21. U.S., Congress, Senate, Committee on the Judiciary, *Limiting Scope of Injunctions in Labor Disputes*, before a subcommittee of the Committee on the Judiciary, Senate, on S. 1482, 70th Cong., 1st sess., 1928, part IV, pp. 605-7. Personal identification omitted.

22. *Ibid.*, pp. 609-14.

23. Press release of the National Association for the Advancement of Colored People, July 3, 1924, reprinted in *Monthly Labor Review*, XIX (September, 1924), pp. 678-79.

24. See Brailsford R. Brazeal, *The Brotherhood of Sleeping Car Porters: Its Origin and Development* (New York: Harper and Brothers, 1946).

25. William Z. Foster, *The Great Steel Strike and Its Lessons* (New York: B. W. Huebsch, Inc., 1920), p. 207.

26. Spero and Harris, *Black Worker*, p. 263.

27. Claude McKay, *Home to Harlem* (New York: Harper and Brothers, 1929), pp. 43-49. McKay, born in Jamaica, came to the United States in 1912. After a short stint as a student in Kansas he turned to traveling in this country and Europe, working at a variety of jobs. His prose and particularly his poetry are highly regarded.

28. Carpenter, *Nationality, Color, and Economic Opportunity in the City of Buffalo*, p. 146.

29. Letter from Leroy A. Lincoln, vice-president, Metropolitan Life Insurance Company. Quoted in a report dated April 23, 1930, in Floyd G. Snelson, "Major Occupations from Which Negroes Are Barred," WPA Writers Program, Negroes of New York Papers, Schomburg Collection, New York Public Library.

30. *Railway Post Office*, XXX (February, 1929), p. 59.

31. Abram L. Harris, *The Negro as Capitalist: A Study of Banking and Business Among American Negroes* (Philadelphia: American Academy of Political and Social Science, 1936), pp. 48-49.

32. *Ibid.*

33. The National Negro Business League, *Proceedings of the Twenty-second Annual Meeting*, Atlanta, Georgia, 1921, pp. 62-66. The singers mentioned in this account were more or less well known. Some, like Roland Hayes and Bert Williams, were figures of major importance. After enjoying some considerable success, Black Swan Records finally succumbed to the competition of radio and dissolved in the late 1920s. Roi Ottley and William J. Weatherby, eds., *The Negro in New York, An Informal Social History* (New York: New York Public Library and Oceana Publications, Inc., 1967), pp. 232-35.

34. These figures are in the main accurate. There were 25,000 retail merchants, but in 1929 there were only 712 drug stores. U.S., Department of Commerce, Bureau of the Census, *Negroes in the United States, 1920-32*, pp. 494, 499, Table 8.

35. The reference is to Jean Baptiste Point de Saible, whose homestead at "Chickagou" about 1790 reportedly gave rise to the saying, "The first white man to settle at Chicagou was a Negro." Drake and Cayton, *Black Metropolis*, I, p. 31.

36. National Negro Business League, *Minutes of the "Silver Jubilee" and Twenty-fifth Annual Meeting*, Chicago, 1924, pp. 60-67.

37. *Ibid.*, p. 240.

38. Harris, *Negro as Capitalist*, p. 55.

39. M. S. Stuart, *An Economic Detour: A History of Insurance in the Lives of American Negroes* (New York: Wendell Malliet and Company, 1940), p. xxi.

40. Charles S. Johnson, "Black Workers and the City," *Survey*, LIII (March 1, 1925), p. 643.

41. Langston Hughes, "Brass Spittoons," *Fine Clothes to the Jew* (New York: Alfred A. Knopf, 1927), pp. 28-29. Reprinted by permission of Harold Ober Associates Incorporated. Copyright 1927 by Langston Hughes.

Chapter Four

1. See, for example, Clarence Darrow, *The Story of My Life* (New York: Charles Scribner's Sons, 1932), pp. 301-11.

2. For example, "Big Bill" Thompson, mayor of Chicago from 1915-23 and 1927-31. See St. Clair Drake and Horace R. Cayton, *Black Metropolis: A Study of Negro Life in a Northern City* (New York: Harper and Row, 1962), I, pp. 346-51.

3. See, for example, Mary White Ovington, *The Walls Came Tumbling Down* (New York: Harcourt, Brace and Company, 1947), both a popular history of the National Association for the Advancement of Colored People and a reminiscence of Miss Ovington's role in the organization.

4. See, for example, the pronouncement of the 1927 General Conference of the Society of Friends, cited in Frank S. Loescher, *The Protestant Church and the Negro* (New York: Association Press, 1948), p. 122.

5. These views may be found in the *American Standard* and in the *National Kourier*, the *Indiana Kourier*, and other Ku Klux Klan publications.

6. Although it is widely believed that anti-Catholicism was

probably the single most important ingredient in Klan growth in the 1920s (see, for example, Kenneth T. Jackson, *The Ku Klux Klan in the City, 1915-1930* [New York: Oxford University Press, 1967], p. 272 n.), at least one contemporary observer felt that "there is at present more bitterness toward the Negro in the Middle West than there has been in the South since the days of Reconstruction." Frank Bohn, "The Ku Klux Klan Interpreted," *American Journal of Sociology*, XXX (January, 1925), pp. 205-7.

7. Jackson, *Ku Klux Klan in the City*, p. 236. Jackson argues that the traditional ascription of Klan strength to small towns ignores both the probability that about half the membership resided in metropolitan areas of more than 50,000 persons and the disproprotionate influence of the urban Klansmen in both state and national organizations.

8. David W. Griffith's silent movie epic *Birth of a Nation*, 1915, gave every indication of intense fear of sexual assault by blacks. The tragedy is that the film was so well made as to affect nearly every theatergoer.

9. George Eaton Simpson, *The Negro in the Philadelphia Press* (Philadelphia: University of Pennsylvania Press, 1936), pp. 115-16.

10. George Oscar Ferguson, Jr., "The Mental Status of the American Negro," *Scientific Monthly*, XII (June, 1921), p. 543.

11. A good contemporary discussion of the question is Morris S. Viteles, "The Mental Status of the Negro," *Annals of the American Academy of Political and Social Science*, CXL (November, 1928), pp. 166-277.

12. Robert M. Yerkes, "Testing the Human Mind," *Atlantic Monthly*, CXXXI (March, 1923), pp. 359-67.

13. Carl C. Brigham, *A Study of American Intelligence* (Princeton: Princeton University Press, 1923). Copyright 1922 by Carl C. Brigham. Pp. 190, 191-92, 205, 209-10.

14. James M. Reinhardt, "The Negro: Is He a Biological Inferior?" *American Journal of Sociology*, XXXIII (September, 1927), pp. 248-49, 254-57.

15. Edward Price Bell, *Is the Ku Klux Klan Constructive or Destructive? A Debate Between Imperial Wizard Evans, Israel Zangwill and Others* (Girard, Kans.: Haldeman-Julius Company, 1924), p. 15.

16. This view of the Garvey movement is inaccurate. See Chapter 5 for a discussion of Garvey.

17. *American Standard*, September 15, 1924, p. 10.

18. Erik Barnouw, *A Tower in Babel: A History of Broadcasting in the United States*, I: *To 1933* (New York: Oxford University. Press, 1966), p. 229.

19. Charles Correll and Freeman Gosden, *All About Amos 'n' Andy and Their Creators Correll and Gosden* (New York: Rand McNally and Company, 1929), p. 51.

20. From an interview with William Branch, cited in Barnouw, *Tower in Babel*, p. 230.

21. Correll and Gosden, *All About Amos 'n' Andy*, pp. 61-69, 73-75.

22. Octavus Roy Cohen, "A Little Child," *Saturday Evening Post*, October 18, 1924, pp. 24-25.

23. Peter Noble, *The Negro in Films* (London: Skelton Robinson, n.d.), pp. 41, 43, 44, 50-54.

24. Metro-Goldwyn-Mayer Dialogue Cutting Continuities, "Hallelujah," story, direction, and production by King Vidor, 1929, reel 2, pp. 1-2, 5. Material from the screenplay *Hallelujah* supplied by courtesy of Metro-Goldwyn-Mayer Inc.© 1929 by Metro-Goldwyn-Mayer Distributing Corporation. Copyright renewed 1957 by Loew's Incorporated.

25. Wehman Bros. published countless copies of joke books with titles like *Coon Jokes* and *Darkey Jokes* throughout the 1910s and 1920s. Barnouw, *Tower in Babel*, p. 230.

26. *Dining Car Steward*, I, (January, 1927) p. 22.

27. Chicago Commission on Race Relations, *The Negro in Chicago: A Study of Race Relations and a Race Riot* (Chicago: University of Chicago Press, 1922), pp. 459, 460-62, 463-64.

28. Alexander Jackson was a Harvard-educated businessman with considerable real estate interests. He was active in the YMCA, the National Urban League, the Boy Scouts, and various other civic groups.

29. *Chicago Daily Tribune*, May 9, 1919, p. 11. Reprinted, courtesy of the *Chicago Tribune*.

30. *Chicago Daily Tribune*, editorial, August 6, 1919, p. 8. Reprinted, courtesy of the *Chicago Tribune*.

31. Robert Moats Miller, *American Protestantism and Social Issues, 1919-1929* (Chapel Hill: University of North Carolina Press, 1958), p. 297.

32. See F. Ernest Johnson, ed., *The Social Work of the Churches* (New York: Department of Research and Education of the Federal Council of the Churches of Christ in America, 1930), pp. 154-55.

33. Federal Council of the Churches of Christ in America, Commission on the Church and Race Relations, *Toward Interracial Cooperation: What Was Said and Done at the First National Interracial Conference, Cincinnati, 1925* (New York: Federal Council of the Churches of Christ in America, 1925), p. 179.

34. *Zion's Herald*, November 1, 1922, p. 1382. Permission, *The Methodist Churchman*, formerly *Zion's Herald*.

35. *American Labor Year Book, 1929* (New York: Rand School of Social Science, 1929), p. 163.

36. Eugene V. Debs, *Appeal to Negro Workers*, address delivered Tuesday, October 30, 1923, at Commonwealth Casino, 135th Street and Madison Avenue, New York City (New York: Emancipation Publishing Company, n.d.), pp. 5, 7, 9, 11, 26, 27.

37. New York *Amsterdam News*, March 27, 1929, p. 3.

Chapter Five

1. Kelly Miller, "The Causes of Segregation," *Current History*, XXV (March, 1927), p. 831.

2. Robert Russa Moton, *What the Negro Thinks* (New York: Doubleday, Doran and Co., 1929), p. 116.

3. Edmund David Cronon, *Black Moses: The Story of Marcus Garvey and the Universal Negro Improvement Association* (Madison: University of Wisconsin Press, 1968), pp. 205-6.

4. A. Clayton Powell, Sr., *Against the Tide: An Autobiography* (New York: Richard R. Smith, 1938), p. 71.

5. For a particularly clear statement of what the black churches offered in this regard, see Benjamin Elijah Mays and Joseph William Nicholson, *The Negro's Church* (New York: Institute of Social and Religious Research, 1933), pp. 282 ff.

6. See George E. Haynes, "The Church and Negro Progress," *Annals of the American Academy of Political and Social Science*, CXL (November, 1928), pp. 264-71.

7. For a sampling of such organizations see Robert R. Moton, "Organized Effort for Racial Progress," *ibid.*, pp. 257-63; Eugene Kinckle Jones, "Social Work Among Negroes," *ibid.*, pp. 287-93; James Gardner, "Negro Medical Associations," WPA Writers Program, Negroes of New York Papers, Schomburg Collection, New York Public Library.

8. Chicago Commission on Race Relations, *The Negro in Chica-*

go: A *Study of Race Relations and a Race Riot* (Chicago: University of Chicago Press, 1922), pp. 494-519.

9. For an account of Miller's leftward movement prior to the Great Migration, see August Meier, "The Racial and Educational Philosophy of Kelly Miller, 1895-1915, " *Journal of Negro Education,* XXIX (Spring, 1960), pp. 121-27.

10. "Kelly Miller Says," Baltimore *Afro-American,* August 8, 1924.

11. *Ibid.,* August 14, 1926.

12. Robert Russa Moton, *What the Negro Thinks* (Garden City, N.Y.: Doubleday, Doran and Co., 1929), pp. 55-56, 64-68.

13. Sterling D. Spero and Abraham L. Harris, *The Black Worker: The Negro and the Labor Movement* (New York: Atheneum, 1968), p. 390.

14. *Messenger,* V (November, 1923), pp. 851-914, subtitled "Negro Business Achievement Number."

15. Monroe N. Work, "Survey of Negro Business 1863-1923," *ibid.,* pp. 568-69.

16. "The Realization of a Dream, An Epic Story of Negro Business," *ibid.,* pp. 871-74.

17. Chandler Owen and A. Philip Randolph, "The Negro and the New social Order," *Messenger,* March, 1919, pp. 3, 7-10.

18. *Twentieth Annual Report of the National Association for the Advancement of Colored People,* 1929, p. 43.

19. Guinn v. United States, 238 U.S. 347.

20. Buchanan v. Warley, 245 U.S. 60.

21. Voting cases taken to the Supreme Court include Nixon v. Herndon, 273 U.S. 536 (1927) and Nixon v. Condon, 286 U.S. 73 (1932). In both of these cases, the Court struck down attempts by the State of Texas to deny blacks the right to participate in primary elections. Residential segregation cases include Corrigan v. Buckley, 271 U.S. 323 (1926), in which the Court held race restrictive covenants to be private agreements outside the scope of constitutional protection.

22. See the treatment of the Parker case in Warren D. St. James, *The National Association for the Advancement of Colored People: A Case Study in Pressure Groups* (New York: Exposition Press, 1958), chapter vi.

23. "The N.A.A.C.P. Battle Front," *Crisis,* XXXV (February, 1928), p. 50. This feature appeared monthly, keeping readers informed of that organization's activities.

24. Eugene Kinckle Jones, "The National Urban League," *Opportunity*, III (January, 1925), pp. 13-15. Reprinted with permission of the National Urban League, Inc. This address was originally given by Mr. Jones, Executive Secretary of the League, at the Annual Conference in Cleveland, December 4, 1924.

25. These figures vary from those supplied by the Census Bureau. As of 1926 there were 42,585 all-black churches with 5,203,487 members. The value of their church property was put at $205,782,628. U.S., Department of Commerce, Bureau of the Census, *Negroes in the United States, 1920-32*, pp. 530-31.

26. George E. Haynes, "The Church and the Negro Spirit," *Survey*, LIII (March 1, 1925), pp. 696-97, 708.

27. Detroit Bureau of Governmental Research, "The Negro in Detroit," Section X, "Religion." Detroit, 1926, pp. 9-12. (Mimeographed.)

28. U.N.I.A. Manifesto, Booker T. Washington Mss., Library of Congress, quoted in Edmond David Cronon, *Black Moses: The Story of Marcus Garvey and the Universal Negro Improvement Association* (Madison: University of Wisconsin Press, 1968), p. 17.

29. Marcus Garvey, *Philosophy and Opinions of Marcus Garvey*, ed. Amy Jacques-Garvey (New York: Atheneum, 1969), II, pp. 3, 23.

30. Charles Flint Kellogg, *NAACP: A History of the National Association for the Advancement of Colored People* (Baltimore: The Johns Hopkins Press, 1967), I, pp. 279-80.

31. Elliott M. Rudwick, *W. E. B. DuBois: Propagandist of the Negro Protest* (New York: Atheneum, 1968), pp. 220-27, 232-35.

32. Garvey, *Philosophy and Opinions*, I, pp. 52-53.

33. *Ibid.*, pp. 93-97.

34. E. Franklin Frazier, "The Garvey Movement," *Opportunity*, IV (November, 1926), pp. 346-47. Reprinted with permission of the National Urban League, Inc.

35. "Harlem," *Survey Graphic*, LIII (March 1, 1925), pp. 629-30.

36. James Weldon Johnson, *Black Manhattan* (New York: Alfred A. Knopf, 1930), pp. 160-63, 168-69.

37. E. Franklin Frazier, "Chicago: A Cross-Section of Negro Life," *Opportunity*, VII (March, 1929), pp. 70-73. Reprinted with permission of the National Urban League, Inc.

38. For a discussion of these developments, see August Meier, *Negro Thought in America 1880-1915: Racial Ideologies in the Age of Booker T. Washington* (Ann Arbor: University of Michigan Press, 1963) pp. 256-78.

39. Johnson, *Black Manhattan*, pp. 74 ff.

40. Alain Locke, "Enter the New Negro," *Survey Graphic*, LIII (March 1, 1925), p. 632.

41. Langston Hughes, *The Big Sea* (New York: Hill and Wang, 1963), p. 228.

42. See, for example, the moving and expressive essays in *The Souls of Black Folk* (Chicago, A. C. McClurg and Co., 1903), and the exceptional scholarship in *The Philadelphia Negro: A Social Study* (Philadelphia: Published for the University [of Pennsylvania], 1899).

43. This theme is developed in Elliott M. Rudwich, *W. E. B. DuBois: A Study in Minority Group Leadership* (Philadelphia: University of Pennsylvania Press, 1960). See especially chapter x for DuBois' relationship with the New Negro Movement.

44. Gwendolyn B. Bennett, "To a Dark Girl," *Opportunity*, V (October, 1927), p. 299. Reprinted with permission of the National Urban League, Inc.

45. Waring Cuney, "No Images," *Opportunity*, IV (June, 1926), p. 180. Reprinted with permission of the National Urban League, Inc. Cuney was awarded one-half of the first and second poetry prizes in the 1926 *Opportunity* Literature Contest.

46. Langston Hughes, *Fine Clothes to the Jew* (New York: Alfred A. Knopf, 1927), p. 77. Reprinted by permission of Harold Ober Associates Incorporated. Copyright 1927 by Langston Hughes.

47. W. E. Burghardt DuBois, *Darkwater: The Twentieth Century Completion of "Uncle Tom's Cabin"* (Washington, D.C.: Austin Jenkins Co., 1920) pp. 211-25. By permission of Shirley Graham DuBois.

48. Rudolph Fisher, *The Walls of Jericho* (New York: Alfred A. Knopf, 1928), Arno Press edition, pp. 103-14.

49. Ragen's Colts were members of a Chicago "political club" noted for rowdy and sometimes violent behavior.

50. Chicago Commission on Race Relations, *The Negro in Chicago: A Study of Race Relations and a Race Riot* (Chicago: University of Chicago Press, 1920), pp. 481-84.

51. Claude McKay, *Harlem Shadows: The Poems of Claude McKay* (New York: Harcourt, Brace and Company, 1922), p. 53. From the *Selected Poems of Claude McKay*. Copyright 1953 by Bookman Associates. By permission of Twayne Publishers, Inc.

Afterword

1. U.S., Department of Commerce, Bureau of the Census, and Department of Labor, Bureau of Labor Statistics, *The Social and Economic Status of Negroes in the United State,* 1970 (Washington, D.C.: Government Printing Office, 1971), pp. 9, 11.

2. Alphonso Pinkney, *Black Americans* (Englewood Cliffs, N.J.: Prentice-Hall, Inc., 1969), pp. 49-50.

3. U.S., Department of Commerce, Bureau of the Census, *Social and Economic Status of Negroes . . . 1970,* p. 13.

4. Pinkney, *Black Americans,* p. 50.

5. U.S., Department of Commerce, Bureau of the Census, *Social and Economic Status of Negroes . . . 1970,* p. 19.

6. Rashi Fein, "An Economic and Social Profile of the Negro American," *The Negro American,* ed. by Talcott Parsons and Kenneth B. Clark (Boston: Houghton Mifflin Company, 1966) p. 108. In Lowndes County, Alabama, the rates for Negroes and Caucasians were 9 and 96 per 100, respectively.

7. U.S., Department of Commerce, Bureau of the Census, *Social and Economic Status of Negroes . . . 1970,* p. 98.

8. Fein, "Economic and Social Profile," p. 110.

9. U.S., Bureau of the Census, *Statistical Abstract of the United States, 1966,* p. 52, cited in Pinkney, *Black Americans,* p. 43.

10. Fein, "Economic and Social Profile," pp. 114-15.

11. U.S., Department of Commerce, Bureau of the Census, *Social and Economic Status of Negroes . . . 1970,* pp. 48-49.

12. *Ibid.,* p. 32.

13. *Ibid.,* p. 35.

14. Fein, "Economic and Social Profile," p. 118.

15. U.S., Department of Commerce, Bureau of the Census, *Social and Economic Status of Negroes . . . 1970,* p. 34.

16. *Report of the National Advisory Commission on Civil Disorders* (New York: Bantam Books, 1968), p. 203.

Bibliography

This is by no means a complete bibliography of the writings available that deal with the history of black people, in the northern cities of the United States, between the Great Migration and the Great Depression. It indicates the sources that have been consulted in the preparation of this collection and it suggests the magnitude of the total quantity of literature available on the subject.

The bibliography is arranged in several categories: (1) general works; (2) the Migration; (3) living conditions in northern cities; (4) employment and business; (5) city life; (6) Negro thought and social action; (7) Caucasian opinion; (8) the arts; (9) religion; and (10) education. In some cases there is further subdivision within a category to facilitate examination by the reader. A number of the writings listed might easily fit into more than one of the above categories. In such cases listing is according to major emphasis to avoid the risk of confusion through much cross listing.

GENERAL WORKS ON THE BLACK AMERICAN

These writings are characterized by their broad coverage. Newspapers and periodicals consulted have been listed with inclusive dates, but particularly noteworthy articles are listed separately as well in the appropriate categories below.

Books and Articles

Franklin, John Hope. *From Slavery to Freedom: A History of American Negroes.* 2nd ed., rev. New York: Alfred A. Knopf, 1963.

Graham, James D. "Negro Protest in America, 1900-1955: A Bibliographical Guide." *South Atlantic Quarterly*, LXVII (Winter, 1968), 94-107.

Johnson, Charles S., ed. *Ebony and Topaz: A Collecteana.* New York: *Opportunity* and the National Urban League, 1927.

———. *The Negro in American Civilization: A Study of Negro Life and Race Relations in the Light of Social Research.* New York: Henry Holt and Company, 1930.

Logan, Rayford W. *The Betrayal of the Negro from Rutherford B. Hayes to Woodrow Wilson.* New York: Collier Books, 1965.

Mangum, Charles S., Jr. *The Legal Status of the Negro.* Chapel Hill: University of North Carolina Press, 1940.

Meier, August, and Rudwick, Elliott M. *From Plantation to Ghetto: An Interpretive History of American Negroes.* New York: Hill and Wang, 1966.

Myrdal, Gunnar. *An American Dilemma: The Negro Problem and Modern Democracy.* New York: Harper and Row, Publishers, 1944.

Pinkney, Alphonso. *Black Americans.* Englewood Cliffs, N.J.: Prentice-Hall, Inc., 1968.

Work, Monroe N., comp. *A Bibliography of the Negro in Africa and America.* New York: H. W. Wilson Company, 1928.

U.S. Department of Commerce. Bureau of the Census. *Negroes in the United States, 1920-32.* Washington, D.C.: Government Printing Office, 1935.

———. ———. *Negro Population 1790-1915.* Washington, D.C.: Government Printing Office, 1918.

———. ———; U.S. Department of Labor. Bureau of Labor Statistics. *The Social and Economic Status of Negroes in the United States. 1970.* Washington, D.C.: Government Printing Office, 1971.

Newspapers and Periodicals

American Standard, April 15, 1924-December 15, 1925.
Chicago Daily Tribune, April 1, 1917-July 15, 1921.
Chicago Defender, January 1, 1916-December 29, 1928.
Crisis, April, 1916-December, 1929.

Detroit Free Press, November 15-20, 1925.
Messenger, June, December, 1922: January-December, 1923; January, March-December, 1924; January-October/November, 1925; May/June, 1928.
Negro Year Book, Tuskegee Institute, Alabama, 1914-15, 1918-19, 1925-26.
New York Amsterdam News, November 29, 1922-December 28, 1929.
New York Times, January 1, 1915-July 15, 1923.
Opportunity, January, 1923-December, 1928.

THE BLACK MIGRATION

Baldwin, George J. "The Migration: A Southern View." *Opportunity*, II (June, 1924), 183.
Beales, LaVerne. "Negro Enumeration of 1920." *Scientific American*, XIV (April, 1922), 352-60.
Beloit, Wisconsin, *News*. Editorial, August 25, 1916.
Bontemps, Arna, and Conroy, Jack. *They Seek a City*. Garden City, N.Y.: Doubleday Doran and Company, Inc., 1945.
Davis, P. O. "The Negro Exodus and Southern Agriculture." *American Review of Reviews*, LXVIII (October, 1923), 401-7.
Florant, Lyonel C. "Negro Migration 1860-1940." Revised draft of a memorandum prepared for the Carnegie Corporation's study of the Negro in America, 1942. Schomburg Collection, New York Public Library.
Johnson, Charles S. "How Much Is the Migration a Flight from Persecution?" *Opportunity*, I (September, 1923), 272-74.
Johnston, V. D. "Negro Migration and the Census of 1920." *Opportunity*, I (June, 1923), 235-38.
Jones, Eugene Kinckle. "Negro Migration in New York State." *Opportunity*, IV (January, 1926), 7-11.
Kennedy, Louise Venable. *The Negro Peasant Turns Cityward: Effects of Recent Migrations to Northern Centers*. New York: Columbia University Press, 1930.
Kiser, Clyde Vernon. *Sea Island to City: A Study of St. Helena Islanders in Harlem and Other Urban Centers*. New York: Columbia University Press, 1932.
Lewis, Edward E. *The Mobility of the Negro: A Study in the American Labor Supply*. New York: Columbia University Press, 1931.

Memphis *Commercial Appeal*. Editorial, October 5, 1916.

Miller, Kelly. "Enumeration Errors in Negro Population." *Scientific American*, XIV (February, 1922), 168.

"Negro Migration as the South Sees It." *Survey*, XXXVIII (August 11, 1917), 428.

New York Globe. Editorial, July 31, 1916.

Palmer, Dewey H. "Moving North: Migration of Negroes During World War I." *Phylon*, XXVIII (Spring, 1967), 52-62.

Philadelphia Christian Recorder. Editorial, February 1, 1917.

Ross, Frank A., and Kennedy, Louise Venable. *A Bibliography of Negro Migration*. New York: Columbia University Press, 1934.

Scott, Emmet J., comp. "Additional Letters of Negro Migrants of 1916-1918." *Journal of Negro History*, IV (October, 1919), 412-65.

———. "Letters of Negro Migrants of 1916-1918." *Journal of Negro History*, IV (July, 1919), 290-340.

———, "Negro Migration During the War." *Preliminary Economic Studies of the War*. Edited by David Kinley. New York: Oxford University Press, 1920.

Smith, T. Lynn. "Redistribution of the Negro Population of the United States, 1910-1960." *Journal of Negro History*, LI (July, 1966), 155-73.

"The South Calling Negroes Back." *Literary Digest*, LIV (June 23, 1917), 1914.

Thornthwaite, C. Warren. *Internal Migration in the United States*. Philadelphia: University of Pennsylvania Press, 1934.

U.S. Department of Labor. Division of Negro Economics. *Negro Migration in 1916-17*. Washington, D.C.: Government Printing Office, 1919.

Woodson, Carter G. *A Century of Negro Migration*. Washington, D.C.: Association for the Study of Negro Life and History, 1918.

Woofter, Thomas Jackson, Jr. *Negro Migration: Changes in Rural Organization and Population of the Cotton Belt*. New York: W.D. Gray, 1920.

LIVING CONDITIONS IN NORTHERN CITIES

Books, Articles, and Reports

Abbott, Edith. *The Tenements of Chicago 1908-1935*. Chicago: University of Chicago Press, 1936.

Burgess, Ernest. "Residential Segregation in American Cities." *Annals of the American Academy of Political and Social Science,* CXL (November, 1928), 105-15.

Dublin, Louis I. "The Health of the Negro." *Annals of the American Academy of Political and Social Science,* CXL (November, 1928), 77-85.

Fleming, Thomas J. "The Right to Self-Defense." *Crisis,* LXXVI (January, 1969), 9-15.

Frazier, E. Franklin. "The Negro Family." *Annals of the American Academy of Political and Social Science,* CXL (Nov., 1928), 44-51.

———. *The Negro Family in Chicago.* Chicago: University of Chicago Press, 1932.

Johnson, Everett. "A Study of Negro Families in the Pinewood Avenue District of Toledo, Ohio." *Opportunity,* VII (August, 1929), 243-45.

Joint Committee on Negro Child Study in New York City. *A Study of Delinquent and Neglected Children Before the New York City Children's Court, 1925.* [New York]: Joint Committee on Negro Child Study, Department of Research of the National Urban League, and the Women's City Club of New York, 1927.

Landis, H.M.R. "Tuberculosis and the Negro." *Annals of the American Academy of Political and Social Science,* CXL (November, 1928), 86-89.

Long, Herman H., and Johnson, Charles. *People vs. Property: Race Restrictive Covenants in Housing.* Nashville, Tenn.: Fisk University Press, 1947.

McDowell, Mary E. "Hovels or Homes?" *Opportunity,* VII (March, 1929), 74-77.

Manly, A. L. "Where Negroes Live in Philadelphia." *Opportunity,* I (May, 1923), 10-15.

Mark, Mary Louise. *Negroes in Columbus.* Ohio State University Studies, Graduate School Series in Social Science No. 2. Columbus: Ohio State University Press, 1928.

Miller, Kelly. "Causes of Segregation." *Current History,* XXV (March, 1927), 827-31.

Nathan, Winfred B. *Health Conditions in North Harlem 1923-1927.* Social Research Series No. 2. New York: National Tuberculosis Association, 1932.

National Conference of Social Work. *Proceedings of the Fifty-fifth Annual Session: The Health of the Negro.* Memphis, Tenn., 1928. Chicago: University of Chicago Press, 1928.

Philadelphia Housing Association. *Housing in Philadelphia.* Annual Reports. Philadelphia, 1916-1917, 1921-1930.

President's Conference on Home Building and Home Ownership. *Negro Housing.* Washington, D.C.: President's Conference on Home Building and Home Ownership, 1932.

Reed, Ruth. *Negro Illegitimacy in New York City.* New York: n.p., 1926.

Reid, Ira deA. *The Negro Population of Denver, Colorado: A Survey of Its Economic and Social Status.* New York: National Urban League, Department of Research and Investigations, 1929.

———. "The Negro Population of Elizabeth, New Jersey: A Survey of Its Economic and Social Condition." National Urban League, Department of Research, for the Elizabeth Interracial Committee, 1930. (Mimeographed.)

———. *Social Conditions of the Negro in the Hill District of Pittsburgh.* Pittsburgh: General Committee on the Hill Survey, 1930.

———. *Twenty-four Hundred Negro Families in Harlem.* New York: New York Urban League, 1927.

Rockwood, H. L. "The Effect of Negro Migration on Community Health in Cleveland." *Proceedings of the National Conference on Social Work, 1926.* Chicago: University of Chicago Press, 1926.

Sellin, Thorsten. "The Negro Criminal: A Statistical Note." *Annals of the American Academy of Political and Social Science,* CXL (November, 1928).

Thompson, Anne J. "A Survey of Crime Among Negroes in Philadelphia." *Opportunity,* IV (July, 1926), 217-19, (August, 1926), 251-54, (September, 1926), 285-86.

Woofter, Thomas J., Jr. *Negro Housing in Philadelphia.* Philadelphia: Friends Committee on Interests of the Colored Race, 1927.

———. *Negro Problems in Cities.* Garden City. N.Y.: Doubleday, Doran and Co., Inc., 1928.

Court Cases

Buchanan v. Warley, 245 U.S. 60 (1917).

Corrigan v. Buckley, 271 U.S. 323 (1926).

Harmon v. Tyler, 273 U.S. 688 (1927).

Parmalee et al. v. Morris, 28 Mich. 625, 188 N.W. 330 (1922).

Porter v. Barrett, 233 Mich. 373, 206 N.W. 532 (1925).

EMPLOYMENT AND BUSINESS

Books, Articles and Reports

Barnett, Claude A. "We Win a Place in Industry." *Opportunity*, VII (March, 1929), 82-86.

Berry, Theodore M. "The Negro in Cincinnati Industries." *Opportunity*, VIII (December, 1930), 361-63.

Bloch, Herman D. "Discrimination Against the Negro in Employment in New York, 1920-1963." *American Journal of Economics and Sociology*, XXIV (October, 1965), 361-82.

Brazeal, Brailsford R. *The Brotherhood of Sleeping Car Porters: Its Origin and Development.* New York: Harper and Brothers, 1946.

Carpenter, Niles. *Nationality, Color, and Economic Opportunity in the City of Buffalo.* University of Buffalo Studies, Vol. V, 1926-1927. Buffalo, N.Y.: University of Buffalo Press, 1927.

Clark, John T. "The Negro in Steel." *Opportunity*, II (October, 1924), 299-301.

Dabney, Thomas L. "Negro Workers at the Crossroads." *Labor Age*, XVI (February, 1927), 8-10.

———. "Organized Labor's Attitude Toward Negro Workers." *Southern Workman*, LVII (August, 1928), 323-30.

Debs, Eugene V. *Appeal to Negro Workers.* Address delivered Tuesday, October 30, 1923, at Commonwealth Casino, New York City. New York: Emancipation Publishing Company, n.d.

Dutcher, Dean. *The Negro in Modern Industrial Society: An Analysis of Changes in the Occupations of Negro Workers, 1910-1920.* Lancaster, Pa.: n.p., 1930.

Feldman, Herman. *Racial Factors in American Industry.* New York: Harper and Brothers, Publishers, 1931.

Greene, Lorenzo J., and Woodson, Carter G. *The Negro Wage Earner.* Washington, D.C.: Association for the Study of Negro Life and History, Inc., 1930.

Harmon, J. H., Jr.; Lindsay, Arnett G.; and Woodson, Carter G. *The Negro as a Businessman.* Washington, D.C.: Association for the Study of Negro Life and History, 1929.

Harris, Abram L. *The Negro as Capitalist: A Study of Banking and Business Among American Negroes.* Philadelphia: American Academy of Political and Social Science, 1936.

————. "Negro Labor's Quarrel with White Workingmen." *Current History*, XXIV (September, 1926), 903-8.

————. "The Negro Worker." *Labor Age*, XIX (February, 1930), 5-8.

Herbst, Alma. *The Negro in the Slaughtering and Meat-Packing Industry in Chicago*. Boston: Houghton Mifflin Company, 1932.

"Industrial Problems in Cities." *Opportunity*, IV (February, 1926), 68-72; (March, 1926), 93-94.

Johnson, Charles S. "Black Workers and the City." *Survey*, LIII (March 1, 1925), 641-43, 718-21.

————. "Present Trends in the Employment of Negro Labor." *Opportunity*, VII (May, 1929), 146-48.

"Making a Living: What the Negro Faces." *World Tomorrow*, VI (May, 1923).

National Negro Business League. *Minutes of the "Silver Jubilee" and Twenty-fifth Annual Meeting*. Chicago, 1924.

————. *Proceedings of the Twenty-second Annual Meeting*. Atlanta, Georgia, 1921.

National Urban League. Department of Research and Investigations. *Negro Membership in American Labor Unions*. New York: The Alexander Press, 1930.

"Negro Business Achievement." *Messenger*, V (November, 1923), 851-914.

Northrup, Herbert R. *Organized Labor and the Negro*. New York: Harper and Brothers Publishers, 1944.

Schuyler, George S. "From Job to Job: A Personal Narrative." *World Tomorrow*, VI (May, 1923), 147-48.

Scott, Estelle Hill. "Occupational Changes Among Negroes in Chicago." Chicago, 1939. (Mimeographed.)

Snelson, Floyd G. "Major Occupations from which Negroes Are Barred." Unpublished Mss. WPA Writers Program. Negroes of New York Papers. Schomburg Collection, New York Public Library.

Spero, Sterling D., and Harris, Abram L. *The Black Worker: The Negro and the Labor Movement*. New York: Columbia University Press, 1931.

Stuart, M. S. *An Economic Detour: A History of Insurance in the Lives of American Negroes*. New York: Wendell Malliet and Company, 1940.

U. S. Congress. Senate. Committee on the Judiciary. *Limiting Scope of Injunctions in Labor Disputes. Hearings* before a subcommittee of the Committee on the Judiciary, Senate, on S. 1482, 70th Cong., 1st sess., 1928.

U.S. Department of the Interior. Office of the Advisor on Negro Affairs. *The Urban Negro Worker in the United States, 1925-1936.* 2 vols. Washington, D.C.: Government Printing Office, 1938.

U.S. Department of Labor. Division of Negro Economics. *The Negro at Work During the World War and During Reconstruction.* Washington, D.C.: Government Printing Office, 1921.

Wesley, Charles H. *Negro Labor in the United States, 1850-1925: A Study in American Economic History.* New York: Vanguard Press, 1927.

Woodson, Carter Goodwin. *The Negro Professional Man and the Community with Special Emphasis on the Physician and the Lawyer.* Washington, D.C.: Association for the Study of Negro Life and History, Inc., 1934.

Labor Union Constitutions

Brotherhood of Locomotive Firemen and Engineermen. *Constitution.* 1925.

Brotherhood of Maintenance of Way Employes. *Proceedings of the Twenty-second Regular Convention.* Detroit, 1925.

Brotherhood of Railroad Trainmen. *Constitution and General Rules.* 1928.

Brotherhood of Railway Carmen of America. *Constitution.* 1921.

Commercial Telegraphers Union of America. *Constitution.* 1928.

CITY LIFE

Bunche, Ralph J. "The Thompson-Negro Alliance." *Opportunity,* VII (March, 1929), 78-80.

Chicago Commission on Race Relations. *The Negro in Chicago; A Study of Race Relations and a Race Riot.* Chicago: University of Chicago Press, 1922.

Detroit Bureau of Governmental Research. "The Negro in Detroit." 3 vols. Detroit, 1926. (Mimeographed.)

Drake, St. Clair, and Cayton, Horace R. *Black Metropolis: A Study of Negro Life in a Northern City.* 2 vols. New York: Harper and Row, Publishers, 1962.

Frazier, E. Franklin. "Chicago: A Cross-Section of Negro Life." *Opportunity,* VII (March, 1929), 70-73.

Gosnell, Harold F. *Negro Politicians: The Rise of Negro Politics in Chicago.* Chicago: University of Chicago Press, 1935.

"Harlem: Mecca of the New Negro." *Survey Graphic,* VI, No. 6 (March, 1925).

Johnson, James Weldon. *Black Manhattan.* New York: Alfred A. Knopf, 1930.

Jones, Eugene Kinckle. "Social Work Among Negroes." *Annals of the American Academy of Political and Social Science,* CXL (November, 1928), 287-93.

McKay, Claude. *Harlem: Negro Metropolis.* New York: E.P. Dutton and Company, 1940.

Osofsky, Gilbert. *Harlem: The Making of a Ghetto; Negro New York, 1890-1930.* New York: Harper and Row, Publishers, 1966.

Ottley, Roi, and Weatherby, William J., eds. *The Negro in New York, An Informal Social History.* New York: New York Public Library and Oceana Publications, Inc., 1967.

Spear, Allan H. *Black Chicago: The Making of the Negro Ghetto, 1890-1920.* Chicago: University of Chicago Press, 1967.

Warner, Robert Austin. *New Haven Negroes: A Social History.* New Haven: Yale University Press for the Institute of Human Relations, 1940.

Waskow, Arthur I. *From Race Riot to Sit-In, 1919 and the 1960s: A Study in the Connections Between Conflict and Violence.* Garden City, N.Y.: Doubleday and Company, Inc., 1966.

NEGRO THOUGHT AND SOCIAL ACTION

Negro Thought: Essays and Commentaries

DuBois, W. E. B. *Darkwater: The Twentieth Century Completion of "Uncle Tom's Cabin."* Washington, D.C.: Austin Jenkins Co., 1920.

———. *Dusk of Dawn: An Essay Toward an Autobiography of a Race Concept.* New York: Schocken Books, 1968.

———. "Race Relations in the United States." *Annals of the American Academy of Political and Social Science,* CXL (November, 1928), 6-10.

Frazier, E. Franklin. "The Garvey Movement." *Opportunity,* IV (November, 1926), 346-48.

Garvey, Marcus. *Philosophy and Opinions of Marcus Garvey.* Edited by Amy Jacques-Garvey. 2 vols. New York: Atheneum, 1969.

Harris, Abram L. "The Negro Problem as Viewed by Negro Leaders." *Current History*, XVIII (June, 1923), 410-18.

Kerlin, Robert T. *The Voice of the Negro, 1919.* New York: E. P. Dutton and Company, 1920.

Locke, Alain. "Enter the New Negro." *Survey*, LIII (March 1, 1925), 631-34.

Meier, August. *Negro Thought in America 1880-1915; Racial Ideologies in the Age of Booker T. Washington.* Ann Arbor: University of Michigan Press, 1963.

Miller, Kelly. *The Everlasting Stain.* Washington, D.C.: The Associated Publishers, 1924.

Moton, Robert Russa. *What the Negro Thinks.* New York: Doubleday, Doran and Co., 1929.

Owen, Chandler, and Randolph, A. Philip. "The Negro and the New Social Order." *Messenger* (March, 1919), 3-12.

Social Action: Books, Articles, and Reports

Brisbane, Robert Hughes, Jr. "Some New Light on the Garvey Movement." *Journal of Negro History*, XXXVI (January, 1951), 53-62.

Bunche, Ralph J. "The Programs, Ideologies, Tactics and Achievements of Negro Betterment and Interracial Organizations." Research memorandum prepared for the Carnegie-Myrdal study *The Negro in America*, 1940. 4 vols. Schomburg Collection, New York Public Library.

————. "The Programs of Organizations Devoted to the Improvement of the Status of the American Negro." *Journal of Negro Education*, VIII (July, 1939), 539-50.

Butler, Bennie. "The Significance and Story Behind the Fight to Have 'Negro' Spelled with Capital 'N.' " Unpublished Mss. WPA Writers Program. Negroes of New York Papers. Schomburg Collection, New York Public Library.

Gardner, James. "Negro Medical Associations." Unpublished Mss. WPA Writers Program. Negroes of New York Papers. Schomburg Collection, New York Public Library.

Jack, Robert L. *History of the National Association for the Ad-*

vancement of Colored People. Boston: Meador Pub. Co., 1943.

Jones, Eugene Kinckle. "The National Urban League." *Opportunity*, III (January, 1925), 12-15.

Kellogg, Charles Flint. *NAACP: A History of the National Association for the Advancement of Colored People.* Vol. I, 1909-1920. Baltimore: The Johns Hopkins Press, 1967.

Moorland, Jesse Edward. "The Young Man's Christian Association Among Negroes." *Journal of Negro History*, IX (April, 1924), 127-38.

Moton, Robert R. "Organized Effort for Racial Progress." *Annals of the American Academy of Political and Social Science*, CXL (November, 1928), 257-63.

"The N.A.A.C.P. Battle Front." *Crisis*, XXXV (February, 1928), 50.

National Association for the Advancement of Colored People. *Annual Reports.* New York, 1917-18, 1919, 1921-1924, 1926-1930.

National Urban League. *Annual Reports.* New York, 1919, 1920, 1922. The Reports for 1922-1929 appear in the March or April issues of *Opportunity*, 1923-1930.

"Oswald Garrison Villard Issues 20th Anniversary N.A.A.C.P. Call." New York *Amsterdam News*, March 27, 1929.

Ovington, Mary White. "The National Association for the Advancement of Colored People." *Journal of Negro History*, IX (April, 1924), 107-16.

———. *The Walls Came Tumbling Down.* New York: Harcourt, Brace and Company, 1947.

Record, Wilson. *The Negro and the Communist Party.* Chapel Hill: University of North Carolina Press, 1951.

———. *Race and Radicalism: The NAACP and the Communist Party in Conflict.* Ithaca, N.Y.: Cornell University Press, 1964.

Rogers, Ben F. "William E. B. DuBois, Marcus Garvey, and Pan-Africa." *Journal of Negro History*, XL (April, 1955), 154-65.

St. James, Warren D. *The National Association for the Advancement of Colored People: A Case Study in Pressure Groups.* New York: Exposition Press, 1958.

Strickland, Arvarh E. *The History of the Chicago Urban League.* Urbana: University of Illinois Press, 1966.

Vose, Clement E. *Caucasians Only: The Supreme Court, the NAACP, and the Restrictive Covenant Cases.* Berkeley and Los Angeles: University of California Press, 1959.

Wood, L. Hollingsworth. "The Urban League Movement." *Journal of Negro History*, IX (April, 1924), 117-26.

Biographies

Broderick, Francis L. *W. E. B. DuBois: Negro Leader in a Time of Crisis.* Stanford, Cal.: Stanford University Press, 1959.

Cronon, Edmund David. *Black Moses: The Story of Marcus Garvey and the Universal Negro Improvement Association.* Madison: University of Wisconsin Press, 1962.

Hughes, William Hardin, and Patterson, Frederick D. *Robert Russa Moton of Hampton and Tuskegee.* Chapel Hill: University of North Carolina Press, 1956.

Johnson, James Weldon. *Along This Way: The Autobiography of James Weldon Johnson.* New York: Viking Press, 1961.

Ottley, Roi. *The Lonely Warrior: The Life and Times of Robert S. Abbott.* Chicago: H. Regnery Co., 1955.

Rudwick, Elliott M. *W. E. B. DuBois: Propagandist of the Negro Protest.* New York: Atheneum, 1968.

Schuyler, George S. *Black and Conservative: The Autobiography of George S. Schuyler.* New Rochelle, N.Y.: Arlington House Publishers, 1966.

CAUCASIAN OPINION

Scientific Opinion

Brigham, Carl C. *A Study of American Intelligence.* Princeton: Princeton University Press, 1923.

Davenport, Charles B. "Do Races Differ in Mental Capacity?" *Human Biology,* I (January, 1929), 31-48.

Ferguson, George Oscar, Jr. "The Mental Status of the American Negro." *Scientific Monthly,* XII (June, 1921).

Hopkins, Albert A. "Which Races Are Best?" *Scientific American,* CXXXII (February, 1925), 78-85.

Osborn, Henry Fairfield. "The Evolution of Human Races." *Natural History,* XXVI (January, 1926), 3-13.

Pettigrew, Thomas F. "Negro American Intelligence: A New Look at an Old Controversy." *Journal of Negro Education,* XXXIII (Winter, 1964), 6-25.

Reinhardt, James M. "The Negro: Is He a Biological Inferior?" *American Journal of Sociology,* XXXIII (September, 1927).

Viteles, Morris S. "The Mental Status of the Negro." *Annals of the*

262 / THE BLACK MAN COMES TO THE CITY

American Academy of Political and Social Science, CXL (November, 1928), 166-77.
Yerkes, Robert M. "Testing the Human Mind." *Atlantic Monthly,* CXXXI (March, 1923).

Racist Opinion

Bell, Edward Price. *Is the Ku Klux Klan Constructive or Destructive? A Debate Between Imperial Wizard Evans, Israel Zangwill and Others.* Girard, Kans.: Haldeman-Julius Company, 1924.
Bohn, Frank. "The Ku Klux Klan Interpreted." *American Journal of Sociology,* XXX (January, 1925), 385-407.
Chalmers, David M. *Hooded Americanism: The History of the Ku Klux Klan.* Garden City, N.Y.: Doubleday and Company, Inc. 1965.
Jackson, Kenneth T. *The Ku Klux Klan in the City, 1915-1930.* New York: Oxford University Press, 1967.
Newby, I. A. *Jim Crow's Defense: Anti-Negro Thought in America, 1900-1930.* Baton Rouge: Louisiana State University Press, 1965.
Southern Commission on the Study of Lynchings. *Lynchings and What They Mean.* Atlanta: Southern Commission on the Study of Lynchings, 1931.
Thornbrough, Emma Lou. "Segregation in Indiana During the Klan Era of the 1920's." *Mississippi Valley Historical Review,* XLVII (March, 1961).

Mainstream Racial Opinion

Baker, Ray Stannard. *Following the Color Line: American Negro Citizenship in the Progressive Era.* New York: Harper and Row. 1964.
Barnouw, Erik. *A Tower in Babel: A History of Broadcasting in the United States.* 2 vols. New York: Oxford University Press, 1966.
Cohen, Octavus Roy. "A Little Child." *Saturday Evening Post,* October 18, 1924.
————. "Assorted Chocolates," "Dark Days and Black Knights," "Black and Blue," and numerous other stories in *Saturday Evening Post,* 1921-28.
Correll, Charles, and Gosden, Freeman. *All About Amos 'n' Andy*

and Their Creators Correll and Gosden. New York: Rand Mc-Nally and Company, 1929.

Gist, Noel P. "The Negro in the Daily Press." *Social Forces*, X (March, 1932), 405-11.

Loescher, Frank S. *The Protestant Church and the Negro.* New York: Association Press, 1948.

Meier, August, and Rudwick, Elliott. "The Rise of Segregation in the Federal Bureaucracy, 1900-1930." *Phylon*, XXVIII (Summer, 1967), 178-84.

Metro-Goldwyn-Mayer Dialog Cutting Continuities. "Hallelujah." Story, direction, and production by King Vidor, 1929.

Miller, Robert Moats. *American Protestantism and Social Issues, 1919-1939.* Chapel Hill: University of North Carolina Press, 1958.

Noble, Peter. *The Negro in Films.* London: Skelton Robinson, n.d.

Simpson, George Eaton. *The Negro in the Philadelphia Press.* Philadelphia: University of Pennsylvania Press, 1936.

Smith, Helena M. "Negro Characterization in the American Novel: A Historical Survey of Work by White Authors." Unpublished Ph.D. dissertation, Pennsylvania State University, 1959.

Liberal and Radical Racial Opinion

Embree, Edwin R. *Investment in People: The Story of the Julius Rosenwald Fund.* New York: Harper and Brothers, Publishers, 1949.

Federal Council of the Churches of Christ in America. Commission on the Church and Race Relations. *Toward Interracial Cooperation: What Was Said and Done at the First National Interracial Conference, Cincinnati, 1925.* New York: Federal Council of the Churches of Christ in America, 1925.

Gilligan, Francis J. *The Morality of the Color Line: An Examination of the Right and Wrong of the Discriminations Against the Negro in the United States.* Washington, D.C.: Catholic University of America, 1928.

"New Outlook in Race Relationships." *Zion's Herald*, November 1, 1922.

"Resolutions Adopted by the Socialist Convention—Resolution on the Negro Workers." *Socialist World*, V (August, 1924), 11.

Woofter, Thomas Jackson, Jr. *The Basis of Racial Adjustment.* Boston: Ginn and Company, 1925.

"Workers' (Communist) Party National Platform, 1928—XII, Oppression of the Negroes." *American Labor Yearbook, 1929.* [New York]: Rand School of Social Science, 1929.

THE ARTS

Abramson, Doris E. *Negro Playwrights in the American Theater, 1925-1959.* New York: Columbia University Press, 1969.

Bennett, Gwendolyn B. "To a Dark Girl." *Opportunity,* V (October, 1927), 299.

Bone, Robert. *The Negro Novel in America.* Revised ed. New Haven: Yale University Press, 1965.

Bontemps, Arna, ed. *American Negro Poetry.* New York: Hill and Wang, 1963.

Bronz, Stephen H. *Roots of Negro Racial Consciousness: Three Harlem Renaissance Authors.* New York: Libra Publishers, Inc., 1964.

Brown, Sterling A.; Davis, Arthur P.; and Lee, Ulysses, eds. *The Negro Caravan.* New York: Citadel Press, 1941.

Brown, Sterling. *Negro Poetry and Drama* and *The Negro in American Fiction.* With a new Preface by Robert Bone. New York: Atheneum, 1969.

Butcher, Margaret Just. *The Negro in American Culture.* New York: New American Library, 1956.

Cooper, Wayne. "Claude McKay and the New Negro of the 1920's." *Phylon,* XXV (Fall, 1964), 297-306.

Cullen, Countee. *Color.* New York: Harper and Brothers, Publishers, 1925.

————. *One Way to Heaven.* New York: Harper and Brothers, Publishers, 1932.

Cuney, Waring. "No Images." *Opportunity,* IV (June, 1926), 180.

Fisher, Rudolph. *The Walls of Jericho.* New York: Alfred A. Knopf, 1928. (Arno Press Edition, 1969.)

Hughes, Langston. *The Big Sea.* New York: Hill and Wang, 1963.
————. *Fine Clothes to the Jew.* New York: Alfred A. Knopf, 1927.
————. *The Ways of White Folks.* New York: Alfred A. Knopf, 1933.

Johnson, James Weldon, ed. *The Book of American Negro Poetry.* New York: Harcourt, Brace, 1931.

Locke, Alain, ed. *The New Negro*. With a New Preface by Robert Hayden. New York: Atheneum, 1969.
McKay, Claude. *Harlem Shadows: The Poems of Claude McKay*. New York: Harcourt, Brace and Company, 1922.
————. *Home to Harlem*. New York: Harper and Brothers, 1929.
————. *Selected Poems of Claude McKay*. New York: Bookman Associates, 1953.
Redding, J. Saunders. *To Make a Poet Black*. Chapel Hill: University of North Carolina Press, 1939.

RELIGION

Fauset, Arthur Huff. *Black Gods of the Metropolis: Negro Religious Cults of the Urban North*. Publications of the Philadelphia Anthropological Society, Vol. III. Philadelphia: University of Pennsylvania Press, 1944.
Frazier, E. Franklin. *The Negro Church in America*. New York: Schocken Books, Inc., 1964.
Haynes, George E. "The Church and Negro Progress." *Annals of the American Academy of Political and Social Science*, CXL (November, 1928), 264-71.
————. "The Church and the Negro Spirit." *Survey*, LIII (March 1, 1925), 695-97.
Mays, Benjamin Elijah, and Nicholson, Joseph William. *The Negro's Church*. New York: Institute of Social and Religious Research, 1933.
Mays, Benjamin E. *The Negro's God as Reflected in His Literature*. New York: Atheneum, 1968.
Parker, Robert Allerton. *The Incredible Messiah: The Deification of Father Divine*. Boston: Little, Brown and Company, 1937.

EDUCATION

Bond, Horace Mann. *The Education of the Negro in the American Social Order*. New York: Prentice-Hall, Inc., 1934.
————. "Main Currents in the Educational Crisis Affecting Afro-Americans." *Freedomways*, VIII (Fall, 1968), 303-10.
Bullock, Henry Allen. *A History of Negro Education in the South: From 1619 to the Present*. New York: Praeger Publishers, 1970.

Leavell, Ullin Whitney. *Philanthropy and Negro Education*. Nashville, Tenn.: George Peabody College for Teachers, 1930.

Meier, August, and Rudwick, Elliott. "Early Boycotts of Segregated Schools: The Case of Springfield, Ohio, 1922-23." *American Quarterly*, XX (Winter, 1968), 744-58.

Miller, Kelly. "The Problem of Negro Education in Northern and Border Cities." *Elementary School Journal*, XXX (November, 1929), 192-99.

Wilkerson, Doxey A. "The Negro in American Education." Research memorandum prepared for the Carnegie-Myrdal study *The Negro in America*, 1940. 2 vols. Schomburg Collection, New York Public Library.

Woodson, Carter Goodwin. *The Mis-Education of the Negro*. Washington, D.C.: The Associated Publishers, Inc., 1933.

Index